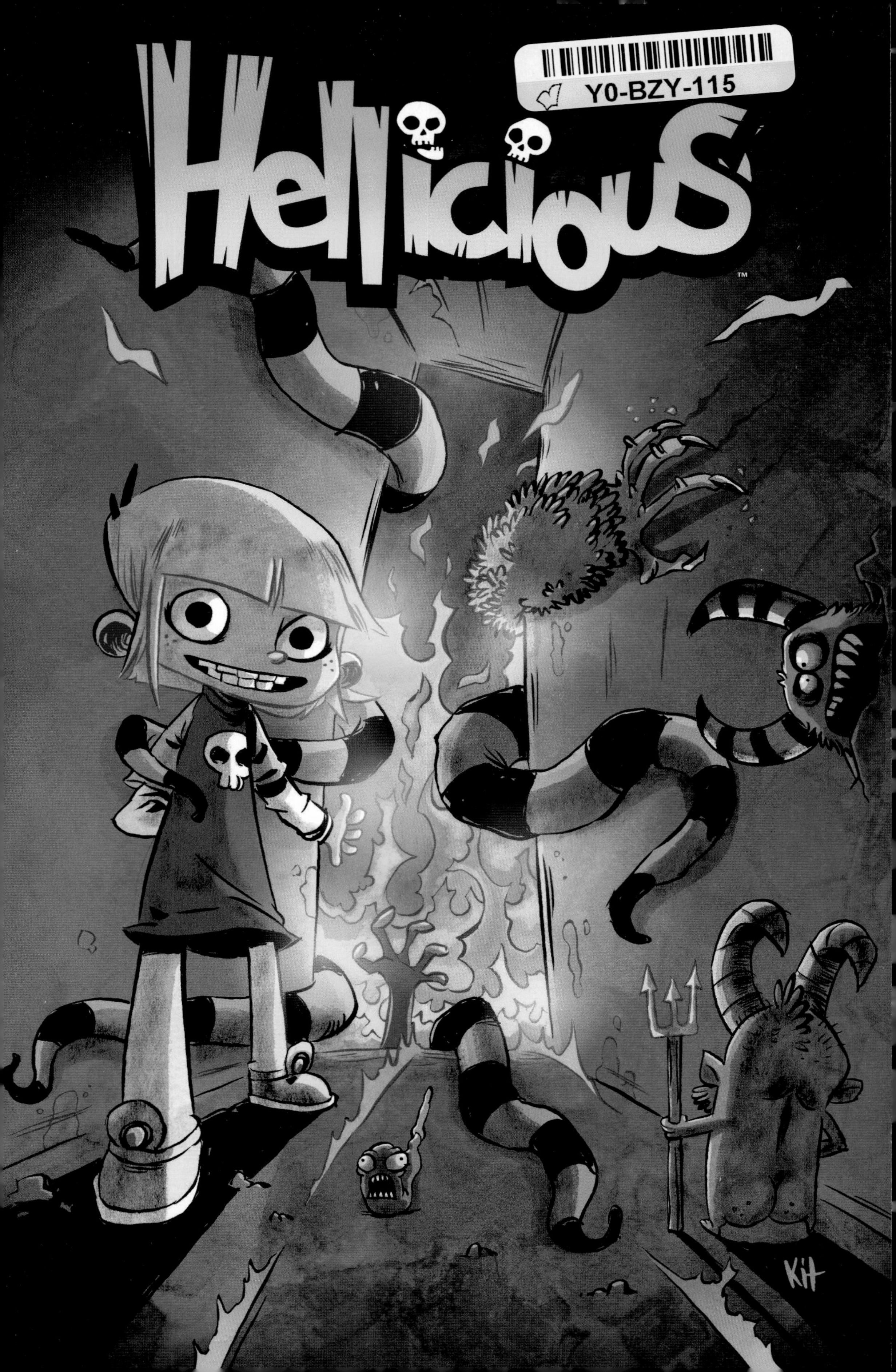
Hellicious™
Kit

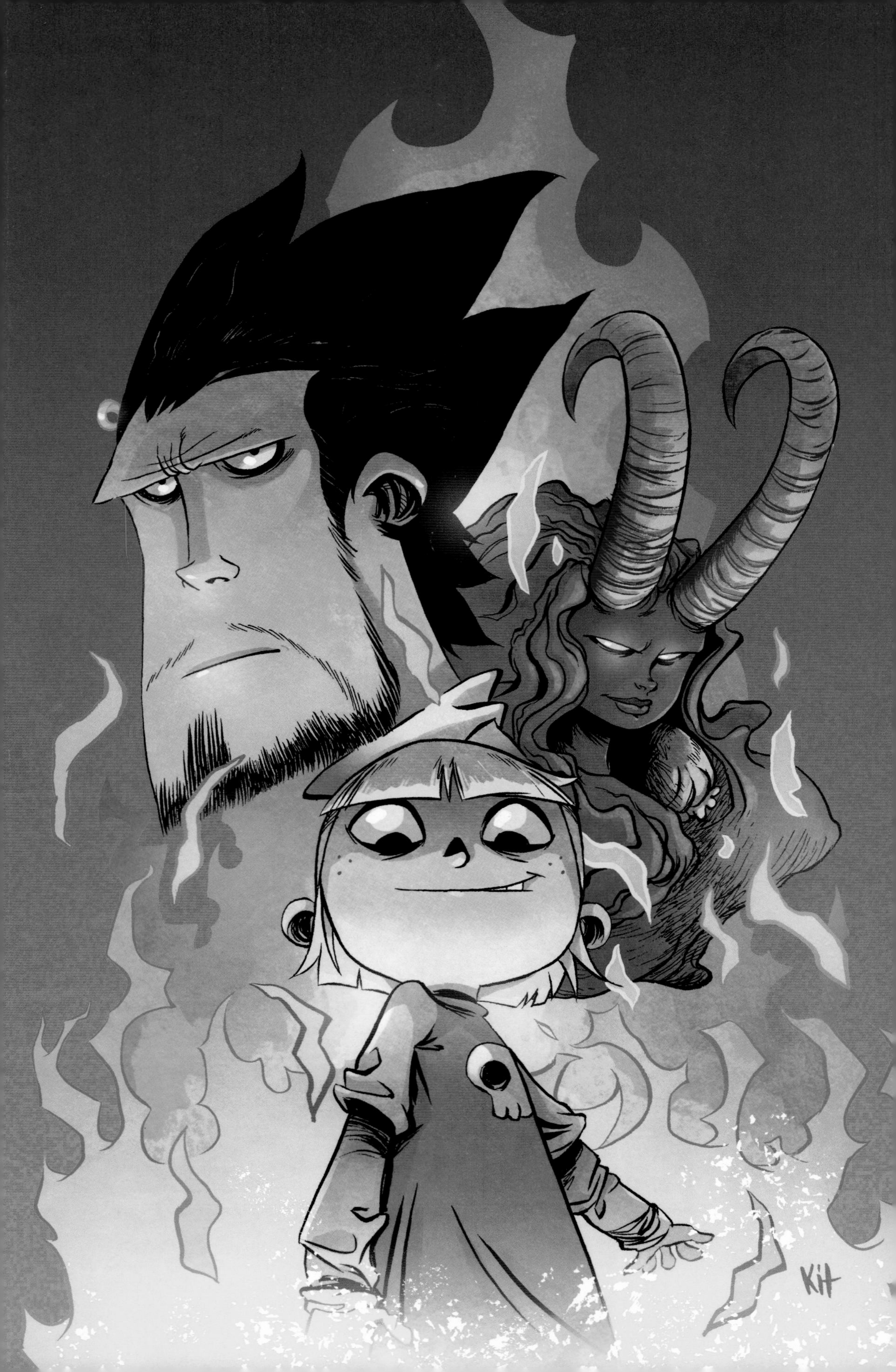
Kit

Hellicious

BOOK ONE

WELCOME TO HELL, BRIGGY BUNDY

SCRIPT
ALAN C. MEDINA & MINA ELWELL

ART
KIT WALLIS

COLOR ART
JIO BUTLER

LETTERING
MICAH MYERS

COVER ART
WALLIS & BUTLER

HELLICIOUS CREATED BY MEDINA, ELWELL, & WALLIS

SBI PRESS™

SBI PRESS

DESIGNER
JIMMY PRESLER

PRODUCTION
CONLEY PRESLER

SERIES EDITORS
TREVOR RICHARDSON & SIMON ORÉ

COLLECTION EDITOR
BRENDAN WRIGHT

SBI PRESS
CEO/PRESIDENT Simon Oré • CFO Leslie Hewitt • VP - EXECUTIVE EDITOR Brendan Wright
VP - ACQUISITIONS Trevor Richardson • VP - ANALOGUE MEDIA Casey Rup
PRODUCTION ASSISTANT Ross Clark • PR AND MARKETING Cassandra Church

Published by SBI Press
A division of Starburns Industries, Inc.
1700 W. Burbank Blvd.
Burbank, CA 91506

starburnsindustries.com | facebook.com/SBIPress | @SBI_Press

To find a comics shop in your area, visit comicshoplocator.com.

First edition: October 2018
ISBN 978-0-9889363-6-2

1 3 5 7 9 10 8 6 4 2

Printed in the United States of America

HELLICIOUS™ BOOK ONE: WELCOME TO HELL, BRIGGY BUNDY

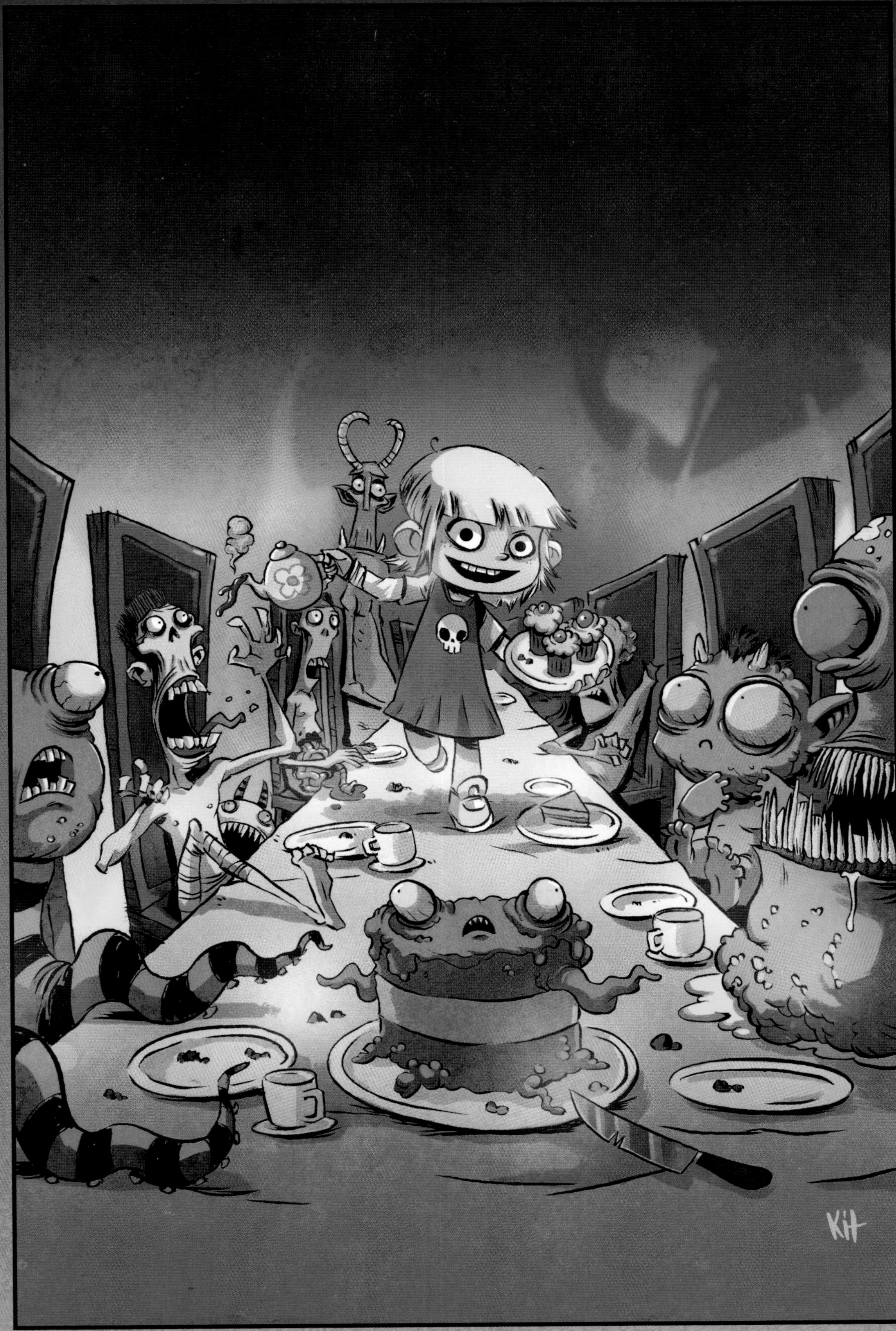
Kit

CHAPTER
ONE

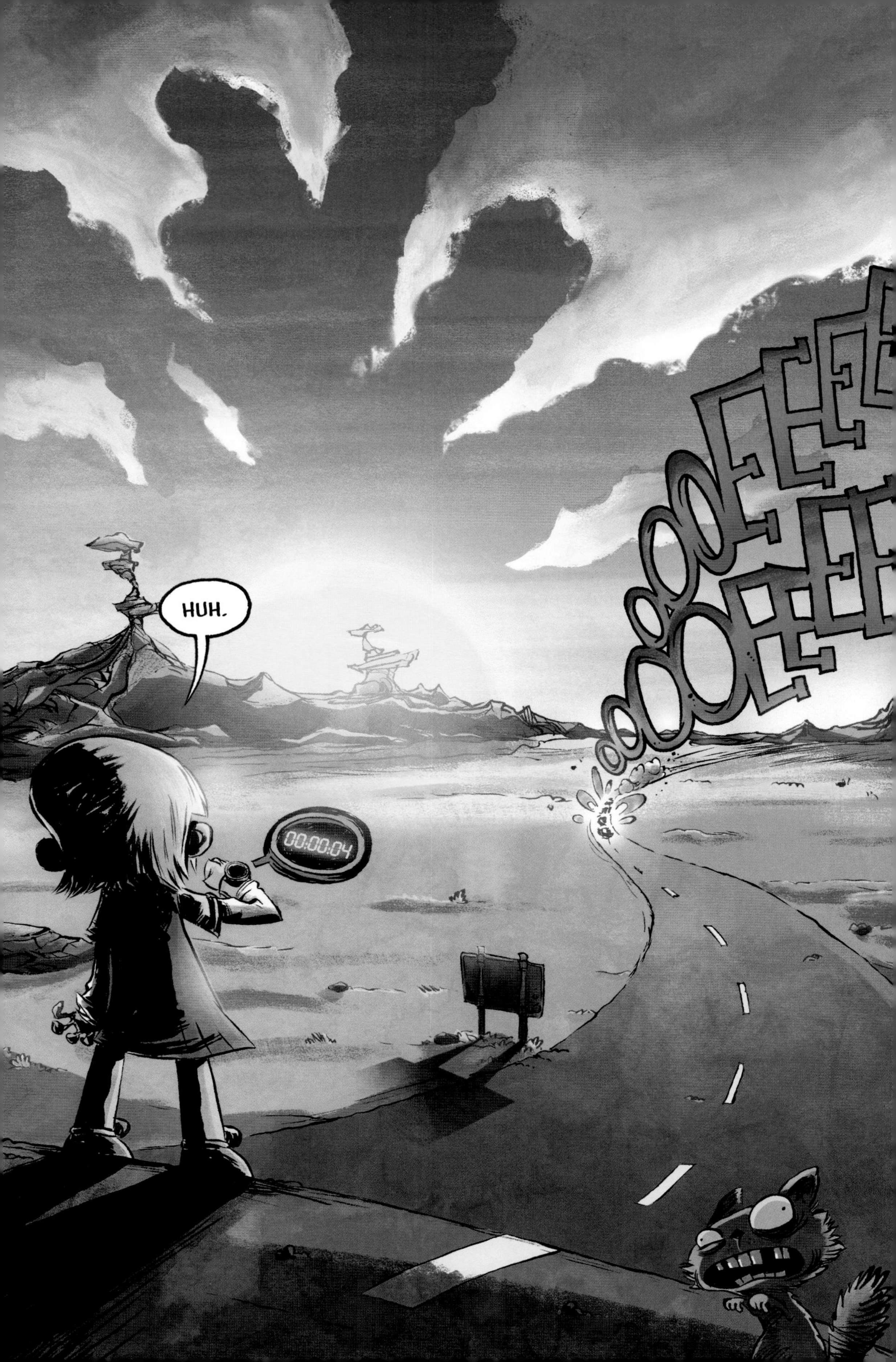
HUH.
00:00:04
OOOOOOEEEEEEEE
OOOEEEEEE

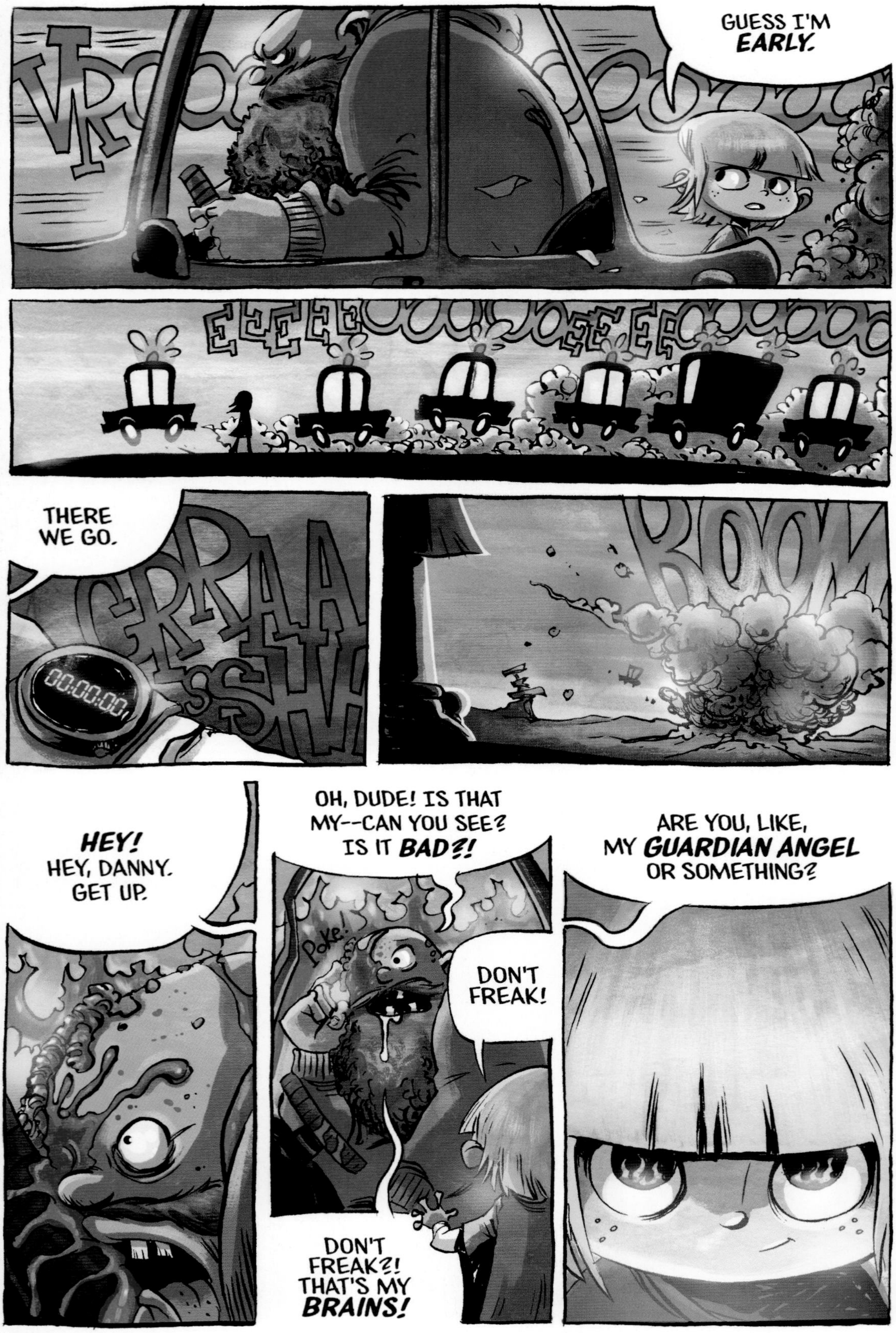
VROOOOOOOOOO
GUESS I'M *EARLY.*
EEEOOOOOOEEEEOOOOOO
THERE WE GO.
GRRAASSHH
00:00:00
BOOM
HEY! HEY, DANNY. GET UP.
OH, DUDE! IS THAT MY--CAN YOU SEE? IS IT *BAD?!*
Poke!
DON'T FREAK!
DON'T FREAK?! THAT'S MY *BRAINS!*
ARE YOU, LIKE, MY *GUARDIAN ANGEL* OR SOMETHING?

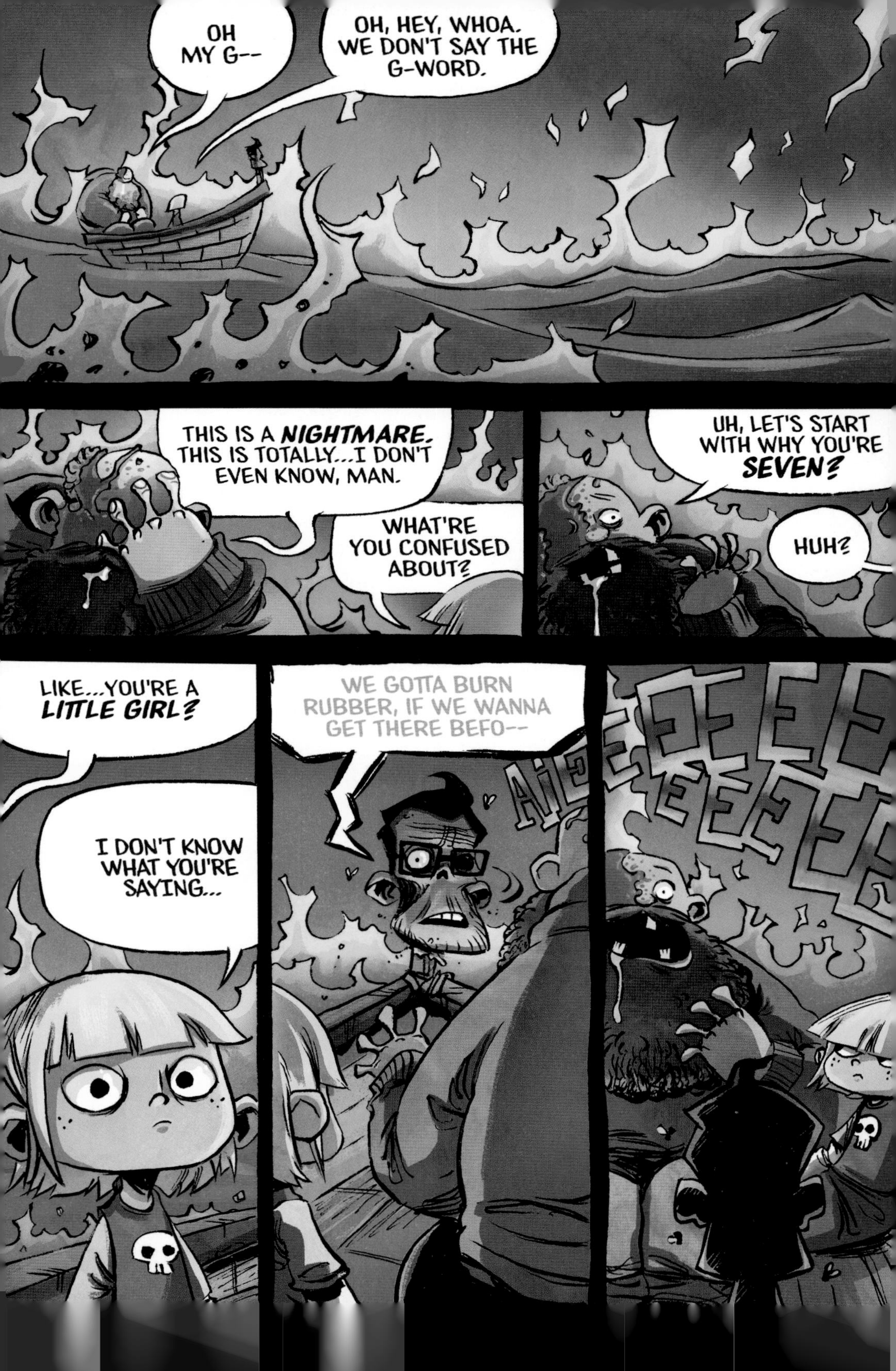
OH MY G--
OH, HEY, WHOA. WE DON'T SAY THE G-WORD.
THIS IS A NIGHTMARE. THIS IS TOTALLY...I DON'T EVEN KNOW, MAN.
WHAT'RE YOU CONFUSED ABOUT?
UH, LET'S START WITH WHY YOU'RE SEVEN?
HUH?
LIKE...YOU'RE A LITTLE GIRL?
I DON'T KNOW WHAT YOU'RE SAYING...
WE GOTTA BURN RUBBER, IF WE WANNA GET THERE BEFO--
AIEEEEEEEEEEEEEE

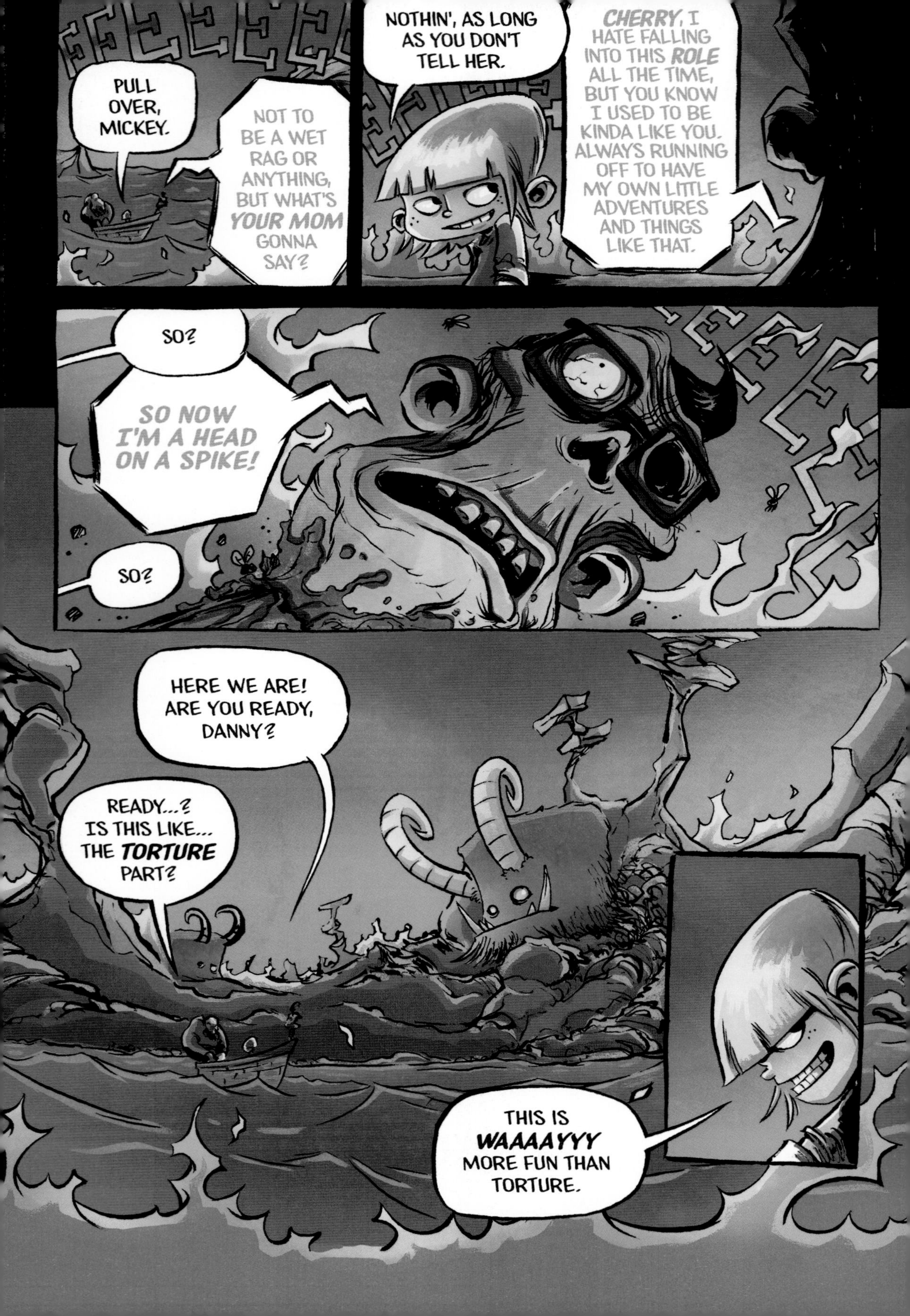

PULL OVER, MICKEY.
NOT TO BE A WET RAG OR ANYTHING, BUT WHAT'S YOUR MOM GONNA SAY?
NOTHIN', AS LONG AS YOU DON'T TELL HER.
CHERRY, I HATE FALLING INTO THIS ROLE ALL THE TIME, BUT YOU KNOW I USED TO BE KINDA LIKE YOU. ALWAYS RUNNING OFF TO HAVE MY OWN LITTLE ADVENTURES AND THINGS LIKE THAT.
SO?
SO NOW I'M A HEAD ON A SPIKE!
SO?
HERE WE ARE! ARE YOU READY, DANNY?
READY...? IS THIS LIKE... THE TORTURE PART?
THIS IS WAAAAYYY MORE FUN THAN TORTURE.

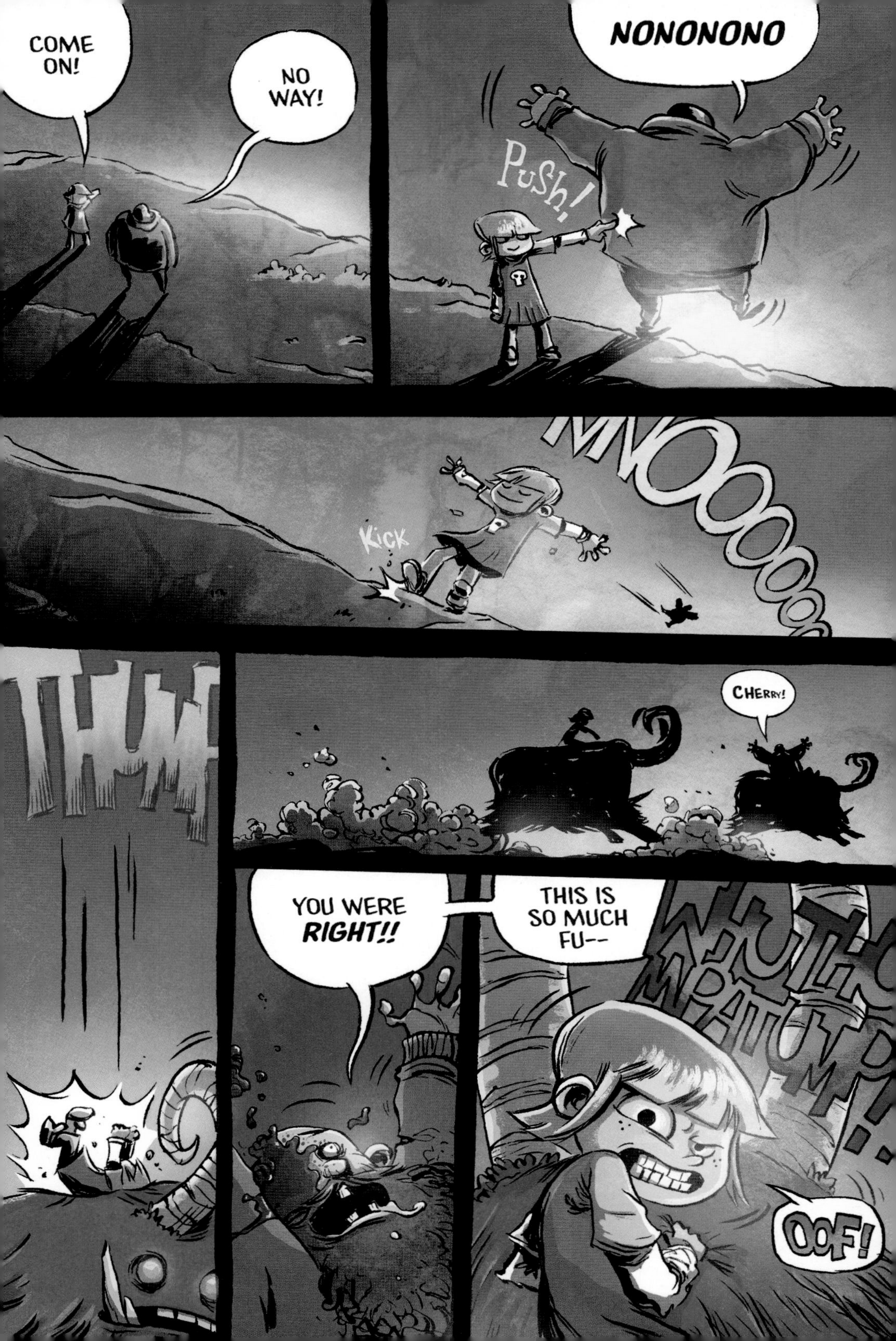
COME ON!
NO WAY!
NONONONO
PUSH!
KICK
CHERRY!
YOU WERE RIGHT!!
THIS IS SO MUCH FU--
OOF!

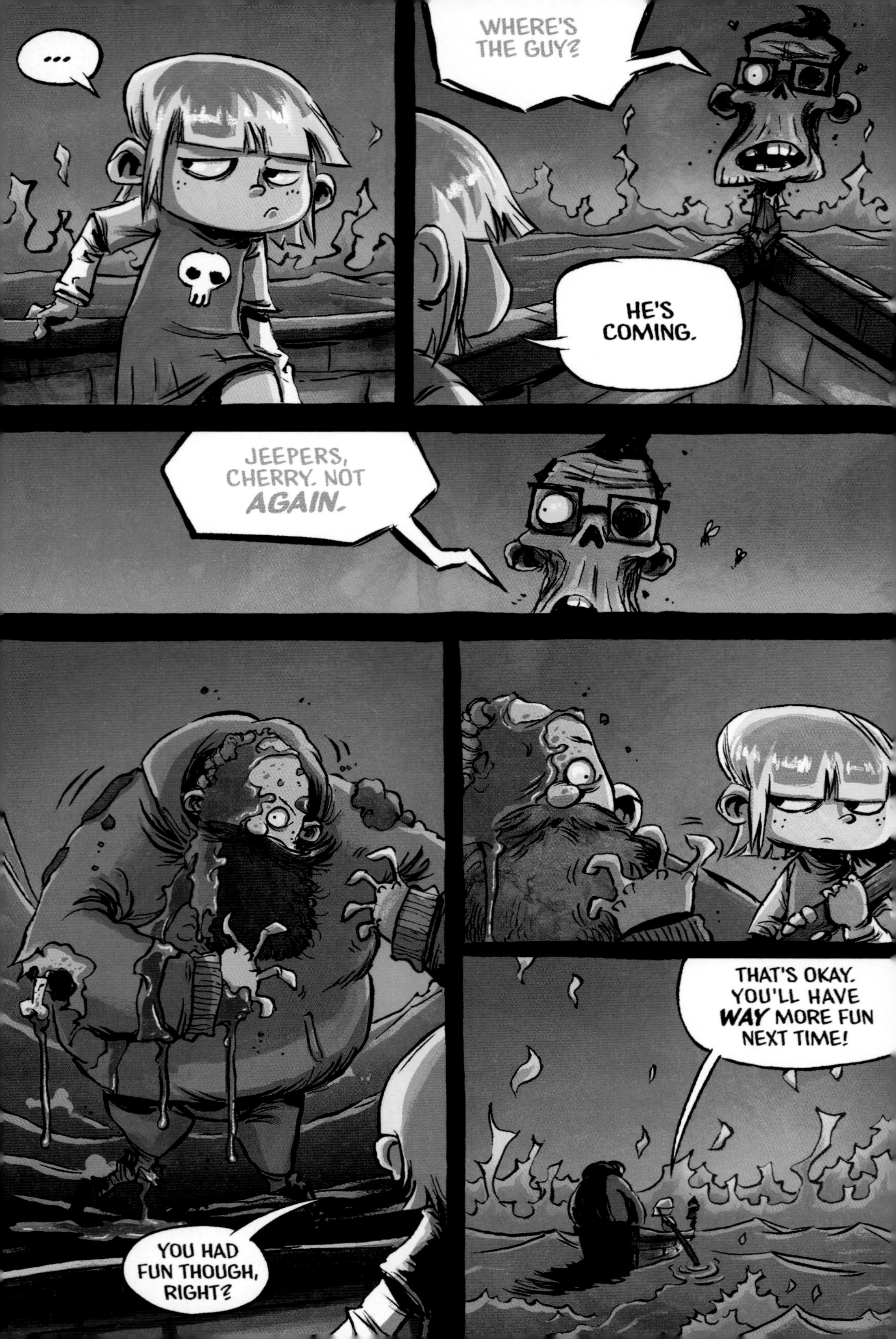
...
WHERE'S THE GUY?
HE'S COMING.
JEEPERS, CHERRY. NOT AGAIN.
YOU HAD FUN THOUGH, RIGHT?
THAT'S OKAY. YOU'LL HAVE WAY MORE FUN NEXT TIME!

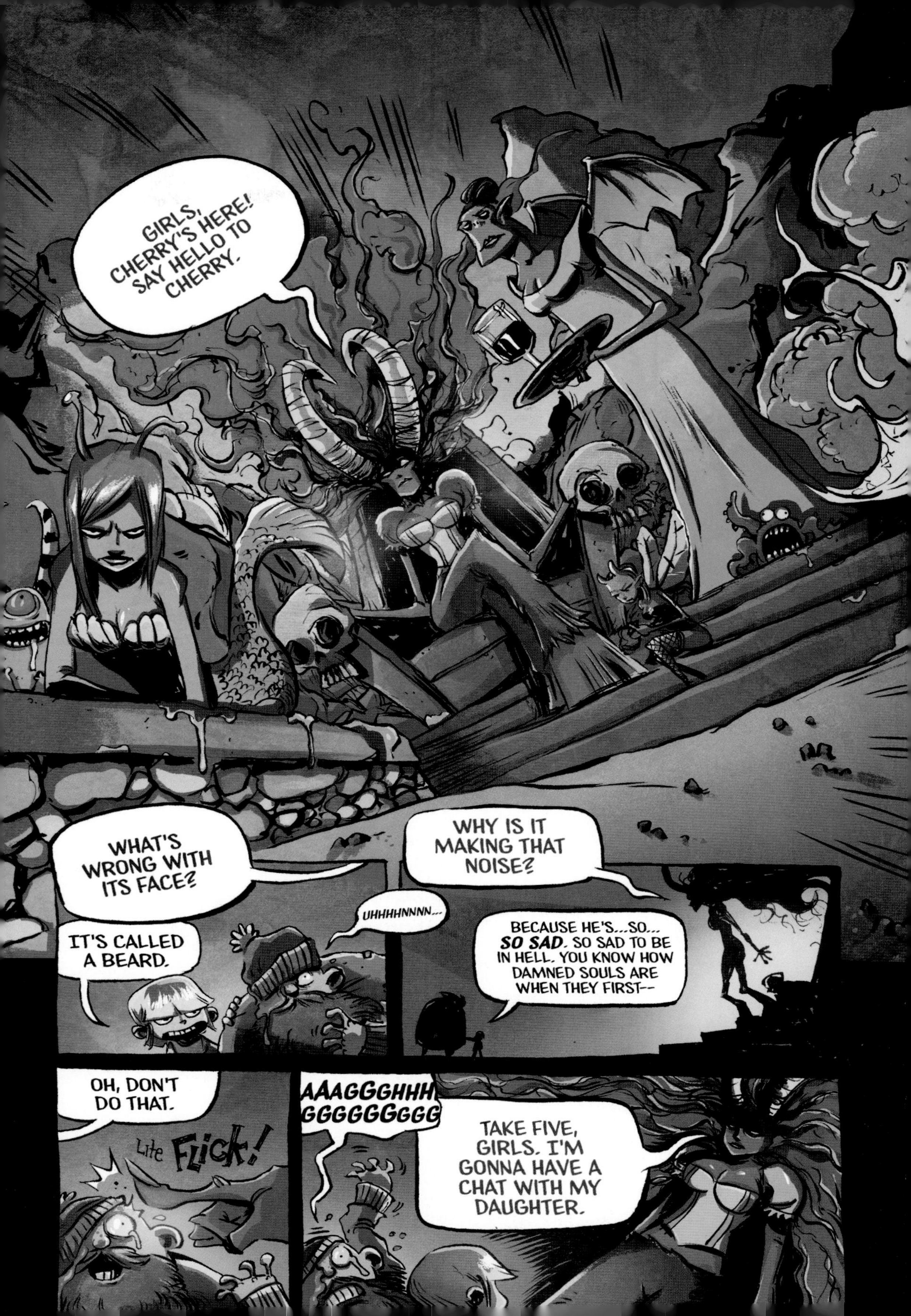
GIRLS, CHERRY'S HERE! SAY HELLO TO CHERRY.
WHAT'S WRONG WITH ITS FACE?
IT'S CALLED A BEARD.
UHHHHNNNN...
WHY IS IT MAKING THAT NOISE?
BECAUSE HE'S...SO... SO SAD. SO SAD TO BE IN HELL. YOU KNOW HOW DAMNED SOULS ARE WHEN THEY FIRST--
OH, DON'T DO THAT.
Lite FLICK!
AAAGGGHHHH GGGGGGGGG
TAKE FIVE, GIRLS. I'M GONNA HAVE A CHAT WITH MY DAUGHTER.

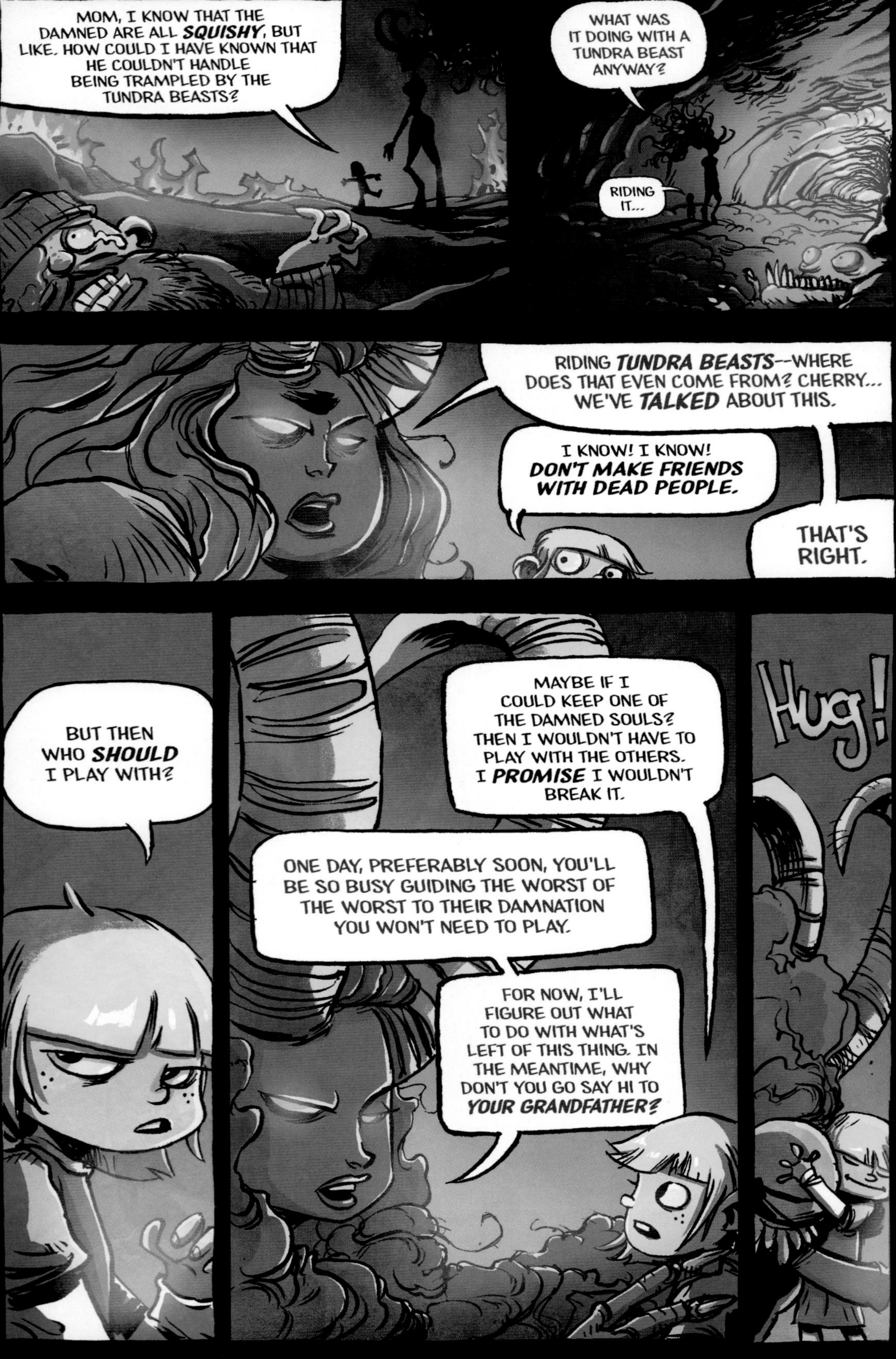
MOM, I KNOW THAT THE DAMNED ARE ALL *SQUISHY*, BUT LIKE. HOW COULD I HAVE KNOWN THAT HE COULDN'T HANDLE BEING TRAMPLED BY THE TUNDRA BEASTS?
WHAT WAS IT DOING WITH A TUNDRA BEAST ANYWAY?
RIDING IT...
RIDING *TUNDRA BEASTS*--WHERE DOES THAT EVEN COME FROM? CHERRY... WE'VE *TALKED* ABOUT THIS.
I KNOW! I KNOW! ***DON'T MAKE FRIENDS WITH DEAD PEOPLE.***
THAT'S RIGHT.
BUT THEN WHO *SHOULD* I PLAY WITH?
MAYBE IF I COULD KEEP ONE OF THE DAMNED SOULS? THEN I WOULDN'T HAVE TO PLAY WITH THE OTHERS. I *PROMISE* I WOULDN'T BREAK IT.
ONE DAY, PREFERABLY SOON, YOU'LL BE SO BUSY GUIDING THE WORST OF THE WORST TO THEIR DAMNATION YOU WON'T NEED TO PLAY.
FOR NOW, I'LL FIGURE OUT WHAT TO DO WITH WHAT'S LEFT OF THIS THING. IN THE MEANTIME, WHY DON'T YOU GO SAY HI TO *YOUR GRANDFATHER?*
Hug!

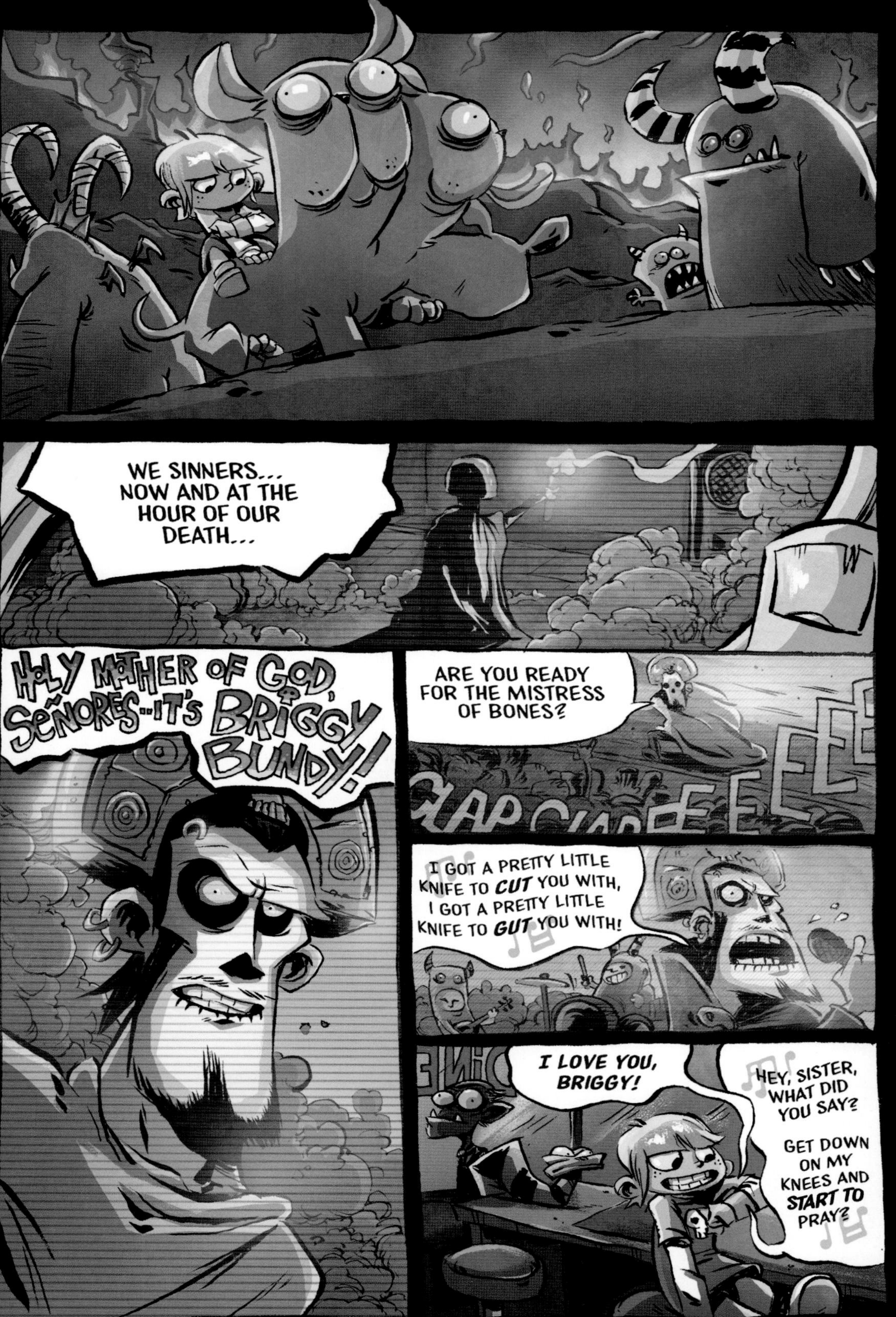
WE SINNERS... NOW AND AT THE HOUR OF OUR DEATH...
HOLY MOTHER OF GOD, SEÑORES--IT'S BRIGGY BUNDY!
ARE YOU READY FOR THE MISTRESS OF BONES?
CLAP CLAP EEEEE
I GOT A PRETTY LITTLE KNIFE TO *CUT* YOU WITH, I GOT A PRETTY LITTLE KNIFE TO *GUT* YOU WITH!
I LOVE YOU, BRIGGY!
HEY, SISTER, WHAT DID YOU SAY?
GET DOWN ON MY KNEES AND *START TO* PRAY?

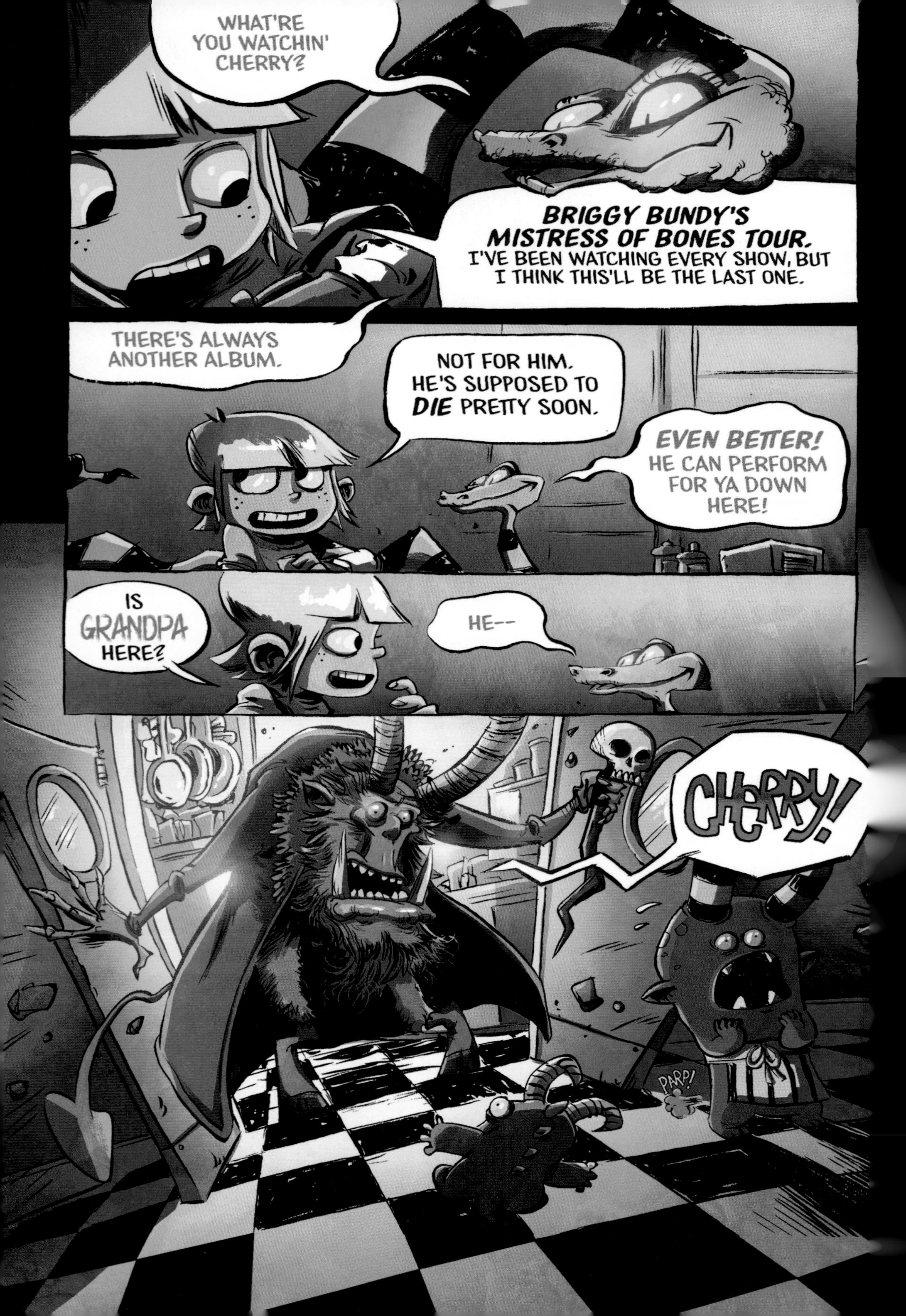
WHAT'RE YOU WATCHIN' CHERRY?
BRIGGY BUNDY'S MISTRESS OF BONES TOUR. I'VE BEEN WATCHING EVERY SHOW, BUT I THINK THIS'LL BE THE LAST ONE.
THERE'S ALWAYS ANOTHER ALBUM.
NOT FOR HIM. HE'S SUPPOSED TO DIE PRETTY SOON.
EVEN BETTER! HE CAN PERFORM FOR YA DOWN HERE!
IS GRANDPA HERE?
HE--
CHERRY!
PARP!

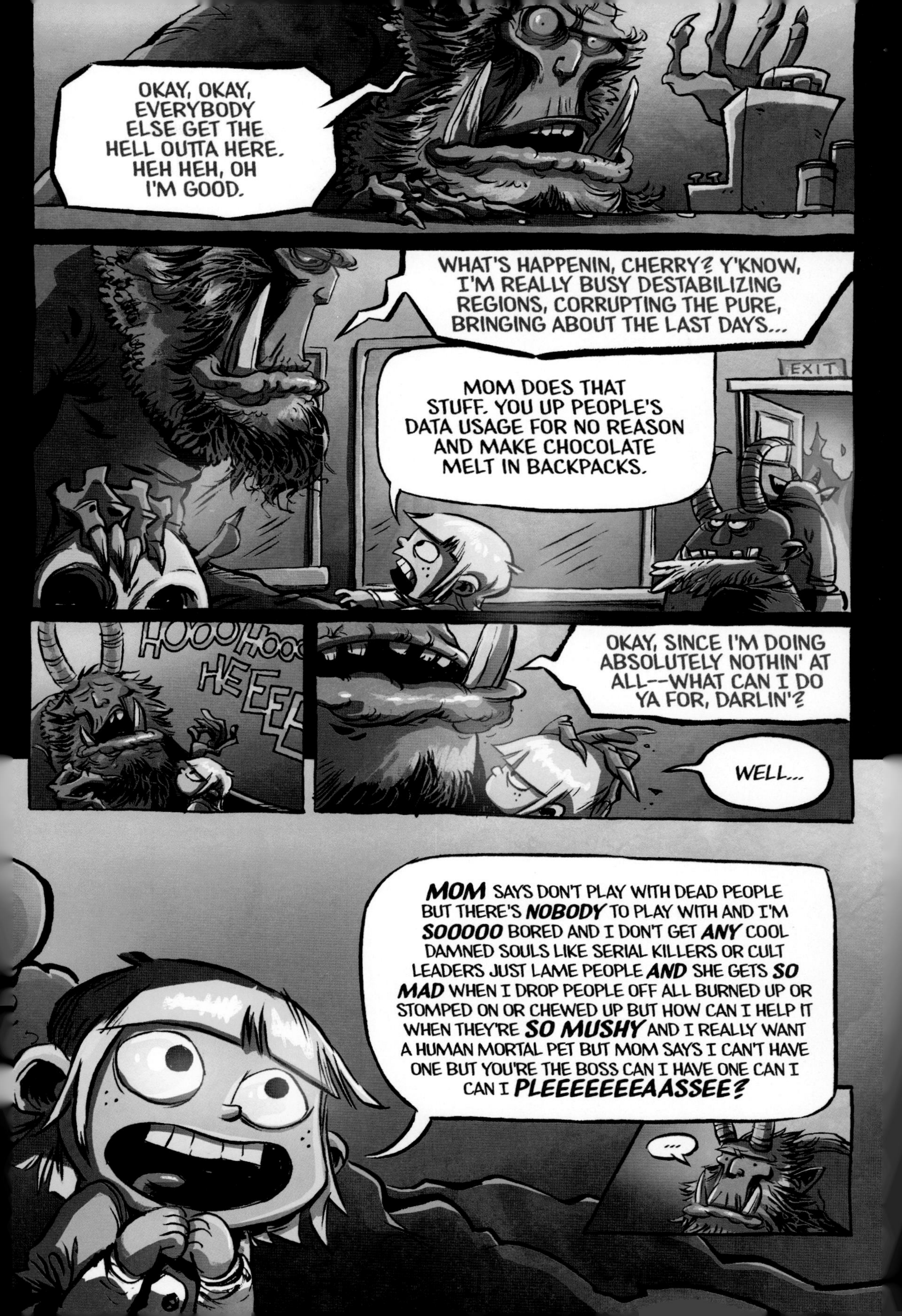
OKAY, OKAY, EVERYBODY ELSE GET THE HELL OUTTA HERE. HEH HEH, OH I'M GOOD.
WHAT'S HAPPENIN, CHERRY? Y'KNOW, I'M REALLY BUSY DESTABILIZING REGIONS, CORRUPTING THE PURE, BRINGING ABOUT THE LAST DAYS...
MOM DOES THAT STUFF. YOU UP PEOPLE'S DATA USAGE FOR NO REASON AND MAKE CHOCOLATE MELT IN BACKPACKS.
EXIT
HOOOHOO HEEEE
OKAY, SINCE I'M DOING ABSOLUTELY NOTHIN' AT ALL--WHAT CAN I DO YA FOR, DARLIN'?
WELL...
MOM SAYS DON'T PLAY WITH DEAD PEOPLE BUT THERE'S NOBODY TO PLAY WITH AND I'M SOOOOO BORED AND I DON'T GET ANY COOL DAMNED SOULS LIKE SERIAL KILLERS OR CULT LEADERS JUST LAME PEOPLE AND SHE GETS SO MAD WHEN I DROP PEOPLE OFF ALL BURNED UP OR STOMPED ON OR CHEWED UP BUT HOW CAN I HELP IT WHEN THEY'RE SO MUSHY AND I REALLY WANT A HUMAN MORTAL PET BUT MOM SAYS I CAN'T HAVE ONE BUT YOU'RE THE BOSS CAN I HAVE ONE CAN I CAN I PLEEEEEEEAASSEE?
...

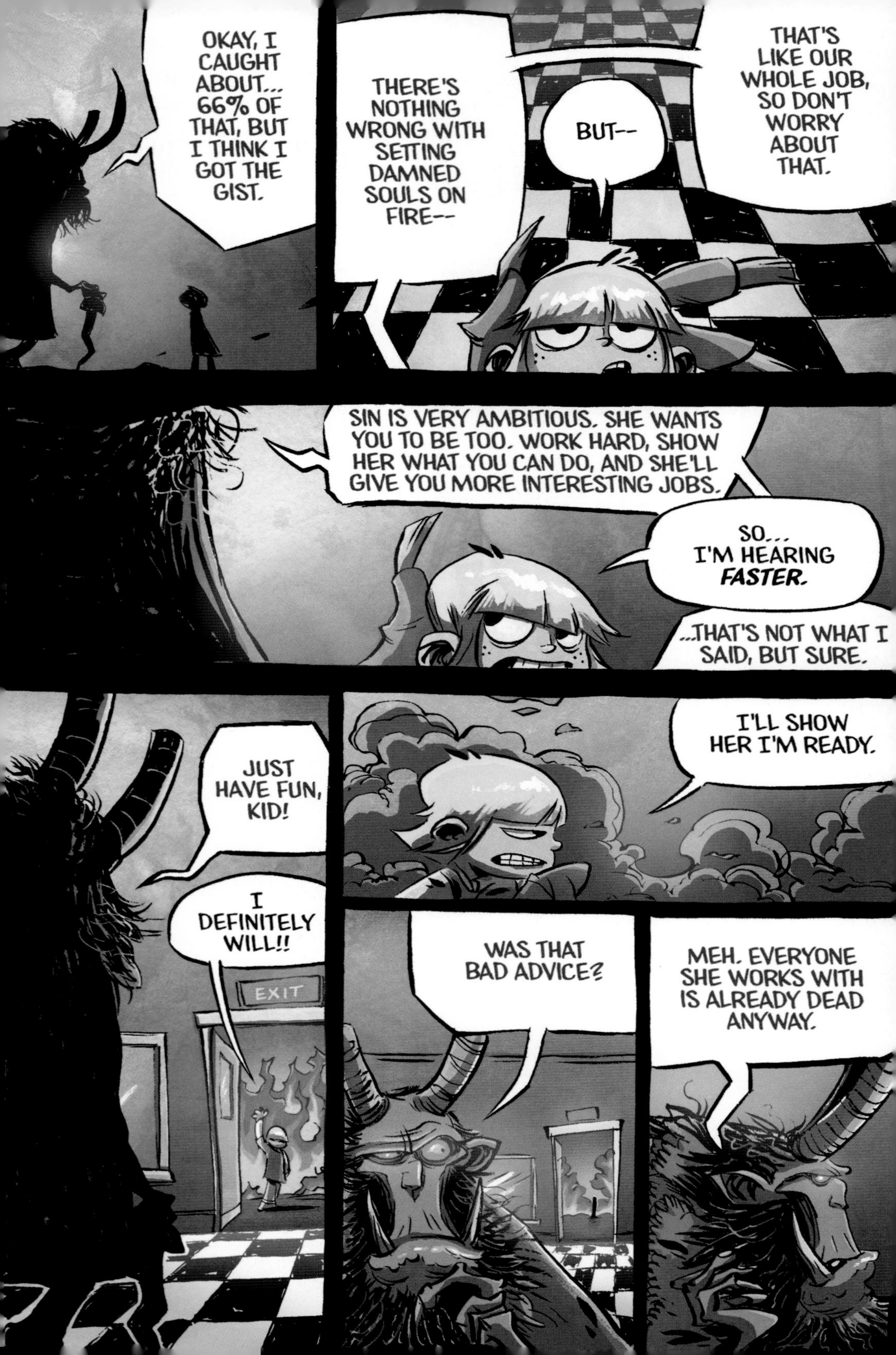
OKAY, I CAUGHT ABOUT... 66% OF THAT, BUT I THINK I GOT THE GIST.
THERE'S NOTHING WRONG WITH SETTING DAMNED SOULS ON FIRE--
BUT--
THAT'S LIKE OUR WHOLE JOB, SO DON'T WORRY ABOUT THAT.
SIN IS VERY AMBITIOUS. SHE WANTS YOU TO BE TOO. WORK HARD, SHOW HER WHAT YOU CAN DO, AND SHE'LL GIVE YOU MORE INTERESTING JOBS.
SO... I'M HEARING *FASTER.*
...THAT'S NOT WHAT I SAID, BUT SURE.
JUST HAVE FUN, KID!
I'LL SHOW HER I'M READY.
I DEFINITELY WILL!!
EXIT
WAS THAT BAD ADVICE?
MEH. EVERYONE SHE WORKS WITH IS ALREADY DEAD ANYWAY.

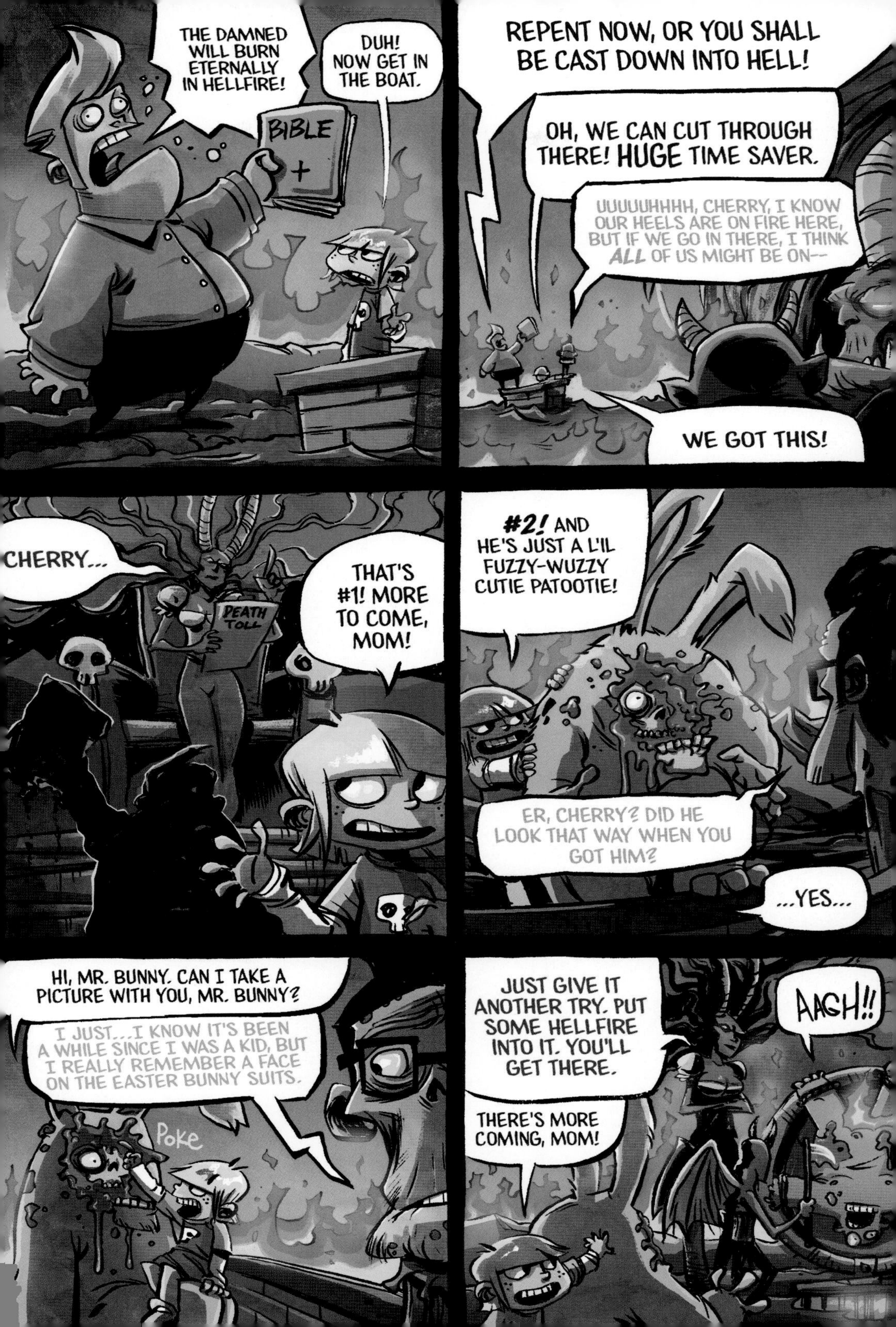
THE DAMNED WILL BURN ETERNALLY IN HELLFIRE!
BIBLE
DUH! NOW GET IN THE BOAT.
REPENT NOW, OR YOU SHALL BE CAST DOWN INTO HELL!
OH, WE CAN CUT THROUGH THERE! HUGE TIME SAVER.
UUUUUHHHH, CHERRY, I KNOW OUR HEELS ARE ON FIRE HERE, BUT IF WE GO IN THERE, I THINK ALL OF US MIGHT BE ON--
WE GOT THIS!
CHERRY...
DEATH TOLL
THAT'S #1! MORE TO COME, MOM!
#2! AND HE'S JUST A L'IL FUZZY-WUZZY CUTIE PATOOTIE!
ER, CHERRY? DID HE LOOK THAT WAY WHEN YOU GOT HIM?
...YES...
HI, MR. BUNNY. CAN I TAKE A PICTURE WITH YOU, MR. BUNNY?
I JUST... I KNOW IT'S BEEN A WHILE SINCE I WAS A KID, BUT I REALLY REMEMBER A FACE ON THE EASTER BUNNY SUITS.
POKE
JUST GIVE IT ANOTHER TRY. PUT SOME HELLFIRE INTO IT. YOU'LL GET THERE.
AAGH!!
THERE'S MORE COMING, MOM!

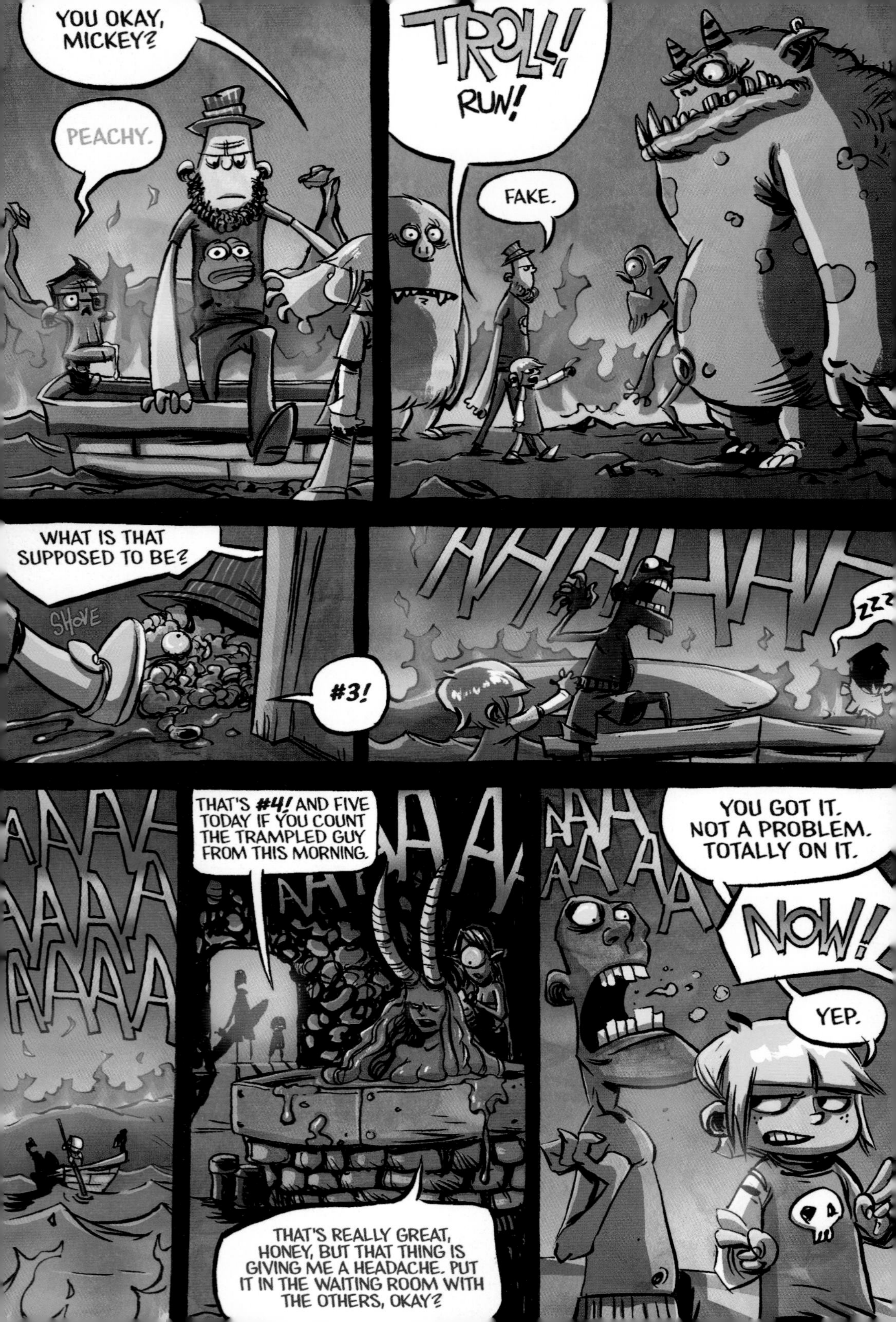
YOU OKAY, MICKEY?
PEACHY.
TROLL! RUN!
FAKE.
WHAT IS THAT SUPPOSED TO BE?
SHOVE
#3!
ZZZ
THAT'S #4! AND FIVE TODAY IF YOU COUNT THE TRAMPLED GUY FROM THIS MORNING.
THAT'S REALLY GREAT, HONEY, BUT THAT THING IS GIVING ME A HEADACHE. PUT IT IN THE WAITING ROOM WITH THE OTHERS, OKAY?
YOU GOT IT. NOT A PROBLEM. TOTALLY ON IT.
NOW!
YEP.

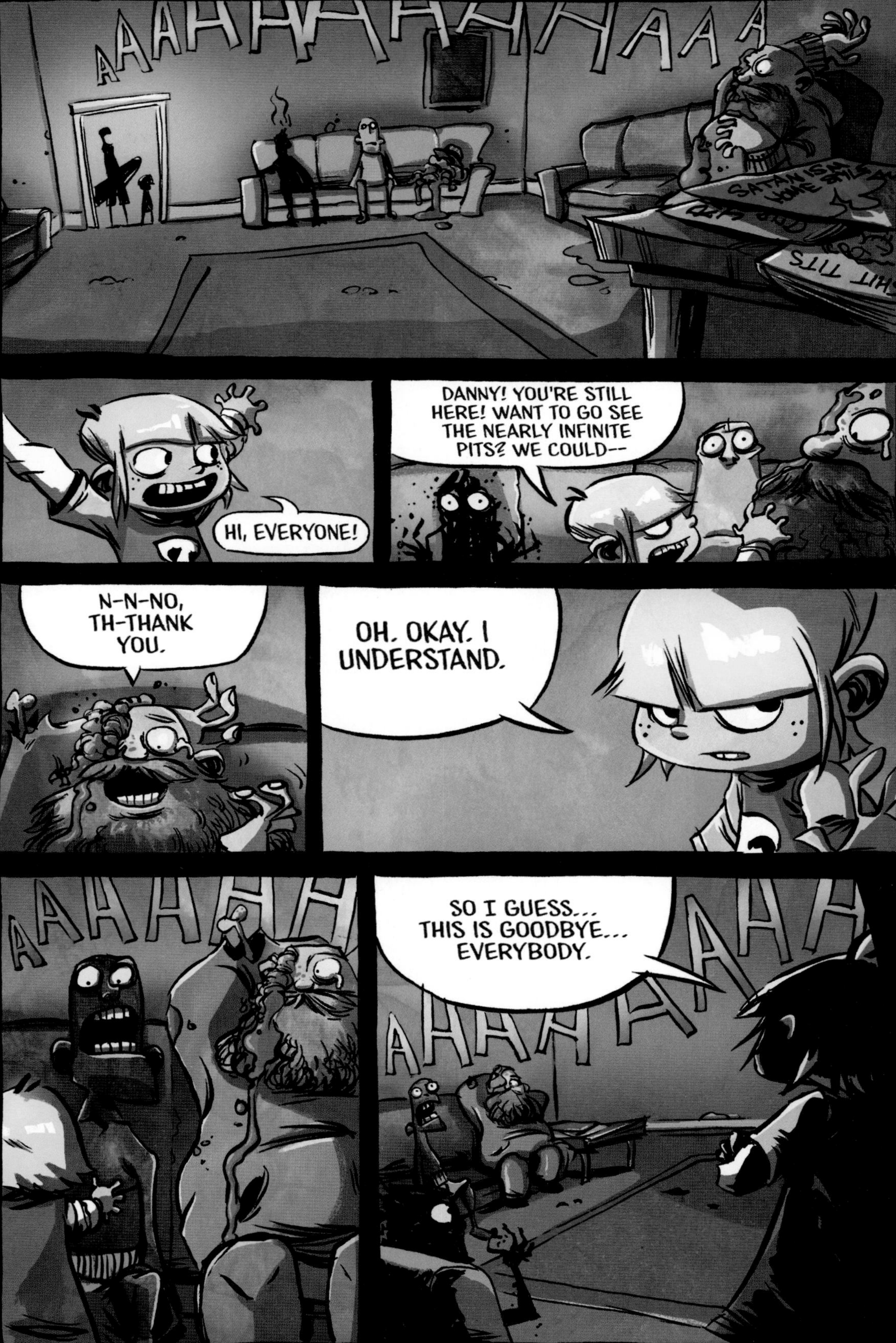
HI, EVERYONE!
DANNY! YOU'RE STILL HERE! WANT TO GO SEE THE NEARLY INFINITE PITS? WE COULD--
N-N-NO, TH-THANK YOU.
OH. OKAY. I UNDERSTAND.
SO I GUESS... THIS IS GOODBYE... EVERYBODY.

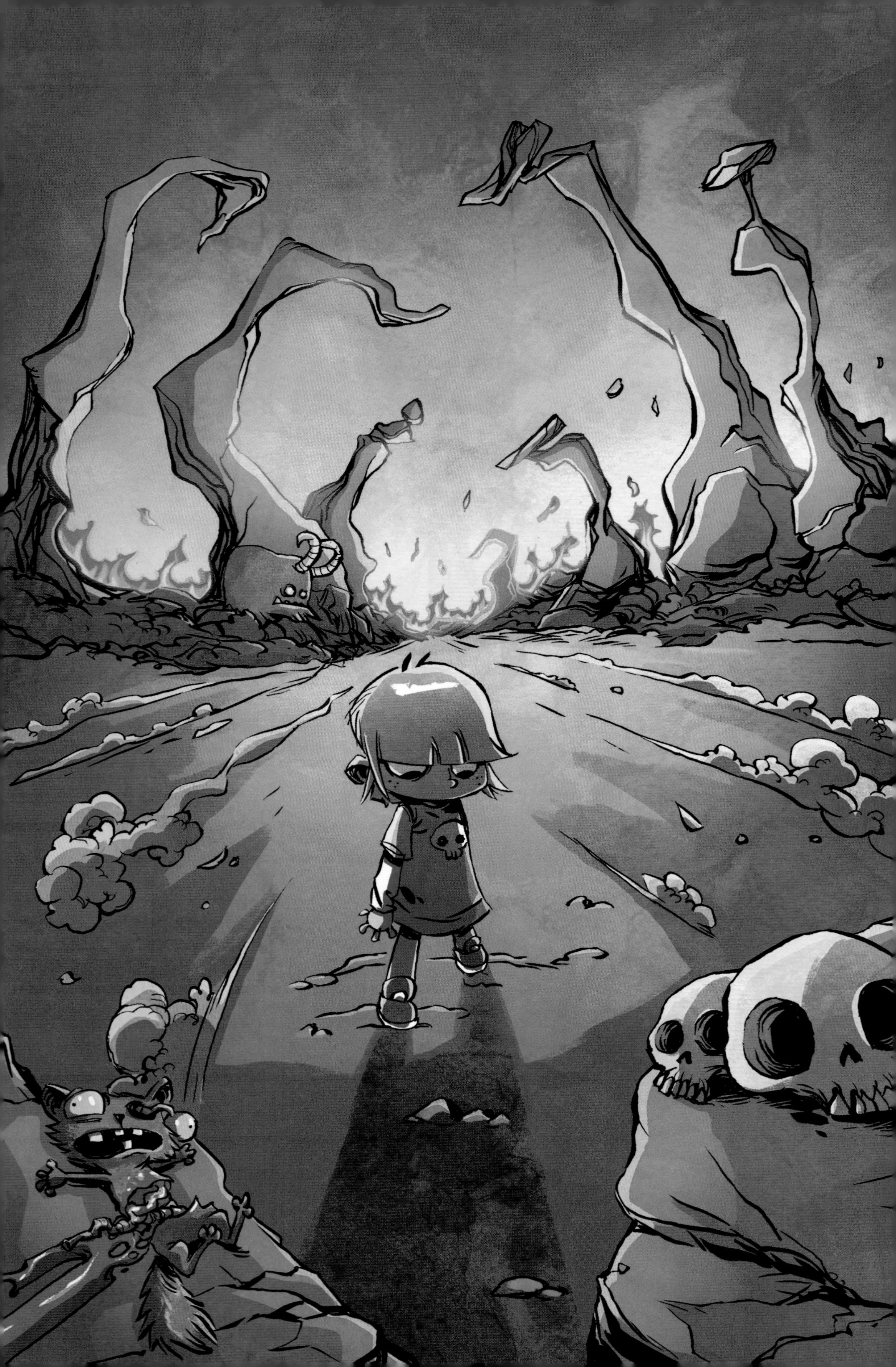

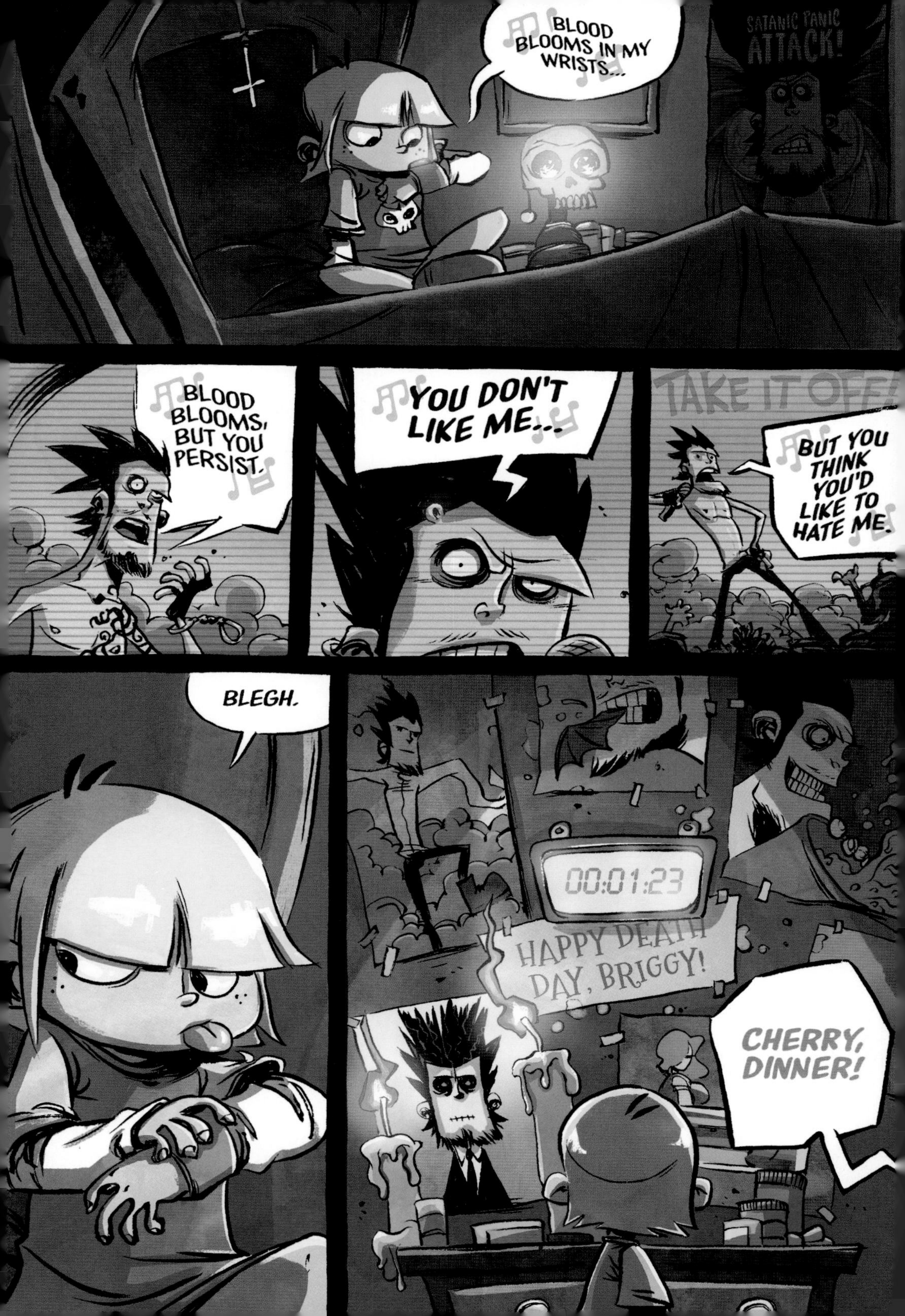

BLOOD BLOOMS IN MY WRISTS...
SATANIC PANIC ATTACK!
BLOOD BLOOMS, BUT YOU PERSIST.
YOU DON'T LIKE ME...
TAKE IT OFF!
BUT YOU THINK YOU'D LIKE TO HATE ME.
BLEGH.
00:01:23
HAPPY DEATH DAY, BRIGGY!
CHERRY, DINNER!

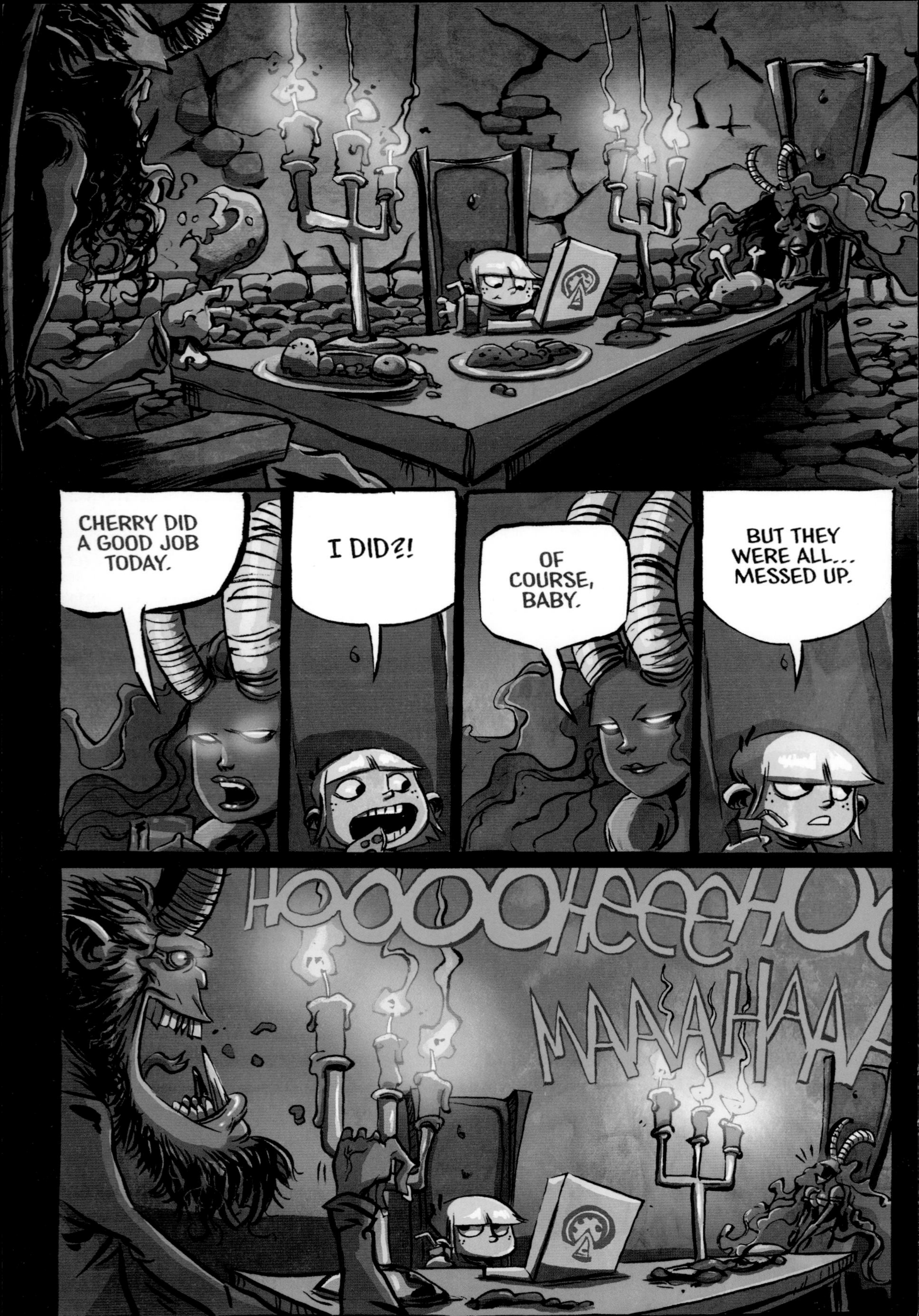
CHERRY DID A GOOD JOB TODAY.
I DID?!
OF COURSE, BABY.
BUT THEY WERE ALL... MESSED UP.
HOOOOHEEEHOO
MAAAHAAA

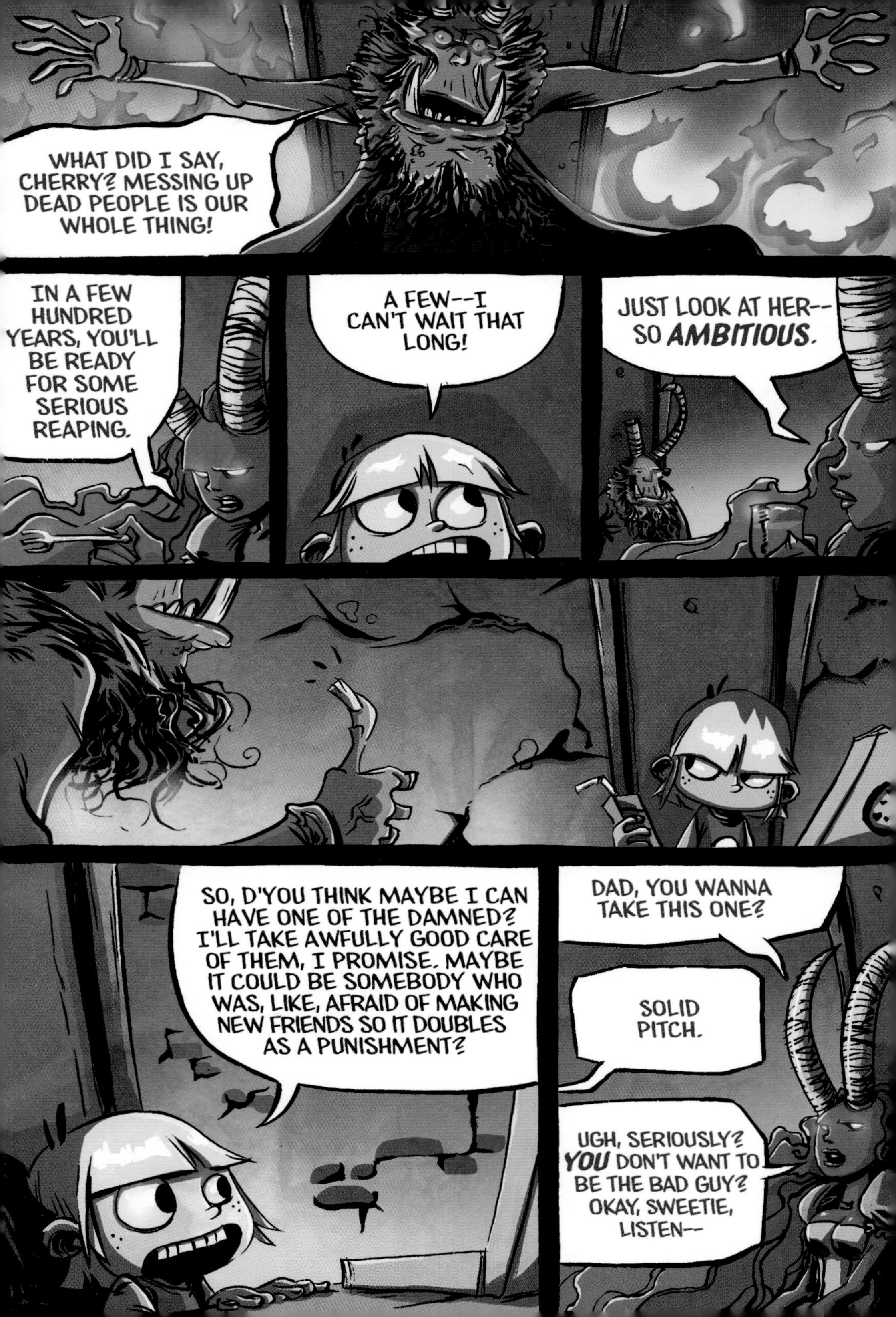
WHAT DID I SAY, CHERRY? MESSING UP DEAD PEOPLE IS OUR WHOLE THING!
IN A FEW HUNDRED YEARS, YOU'LL BE READY FOR SOME SERIOUS REAPING.
A FEW--I CAN'T WAIT THAT LONG!
JUST LOOK AT HER--SO *AMBITIOUS.*
SO, D'YOU THINK MAYBE I CAN HAVE ONE OF THE DAMNED? I'LL TAKE AWFULLY GOOD CARE OF THEM, I PROMISE. MAYBE IT COULD BE SOMEBODY WHO WAS, LIKE, AFRAID OF MAKING NEW FRIENDS SO IT DOUBLES AS A PUNISHMENT?
DAD, YOU WANNA TAKE THIS ONE?
SOLID PITCH.
UGH, SERIOUSLY? ***YOU*** DON'T WANT TO BE THE BAD GUY? OKAY, SWEETIE, LISTEN--

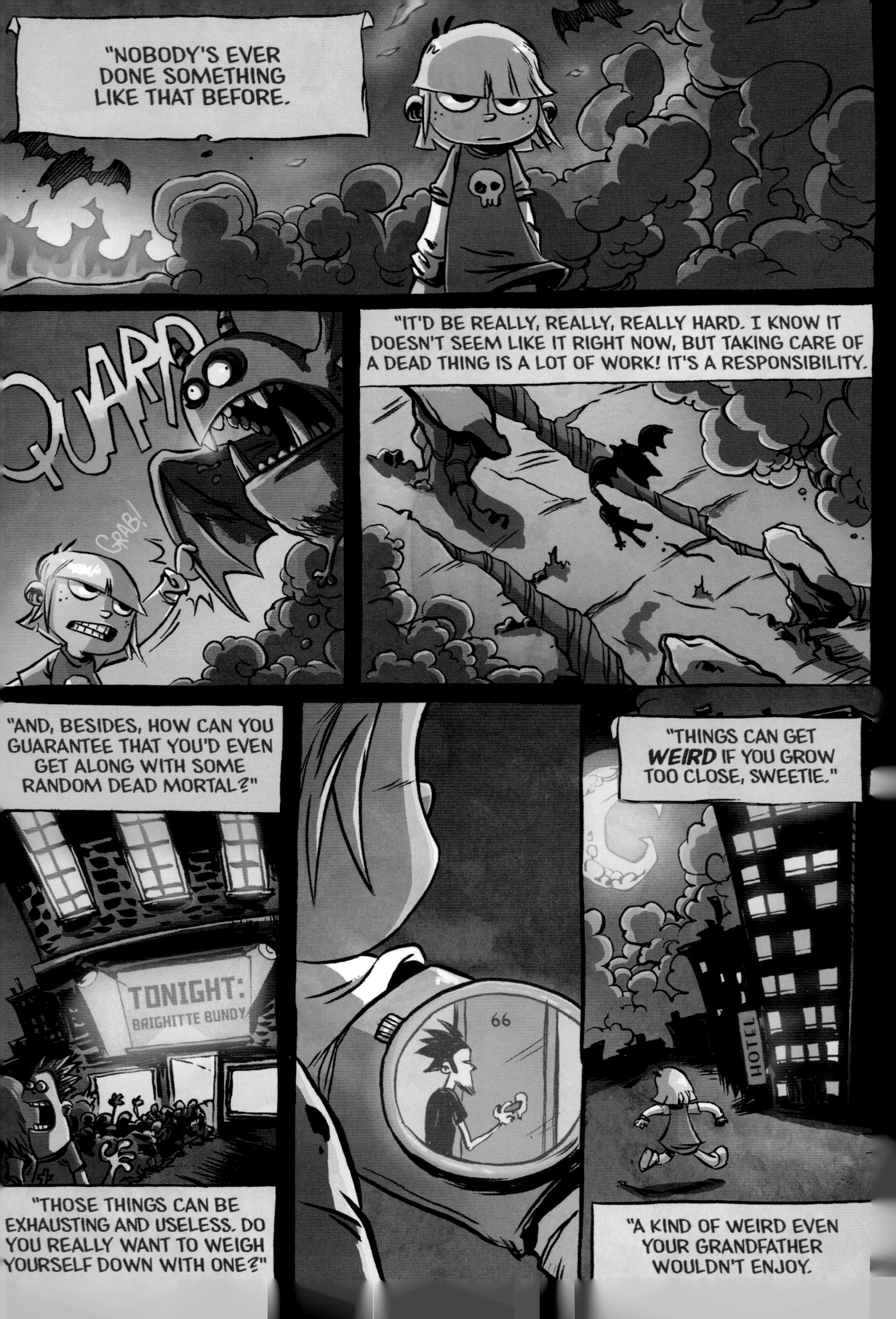
"NOBODY'S EVER DONE SOMETHING LIKE THAT BEFORE.
QUARP
GRAB!
"IT'D BE REALLY, REALLY, REALLY HARD. I KNOW IT DOESN'T SEEM LIKE IT RIGHT NOW, BUT TAKING CARE OF A DEAD THING IS A LOT OF WORK! IT'S A RESPONSIBILITY.
"AND, BESIDES, HOW CAN YOU GUARANTEE THAT YOU'D EVEN GET ALONG WITH SOME RANDOM DEAD MORTAL?"
TONIGHT:
BRIGHITTE BUNDY
"THOSE THINGS CAN BE EXHAUSTING AND USELESS. DO YOU REALLY WANT TO WEIGH YOURSELF DOWN WITH ONE?"
66
"THINGS CAN GET *WEIRD* IF YOU GROW TOO CLOSE, SWEETIE."
HOTEL
"A KIND OF WEIRD EVEN YOUR GRANDFATHER WOULDN'T ENJOY.

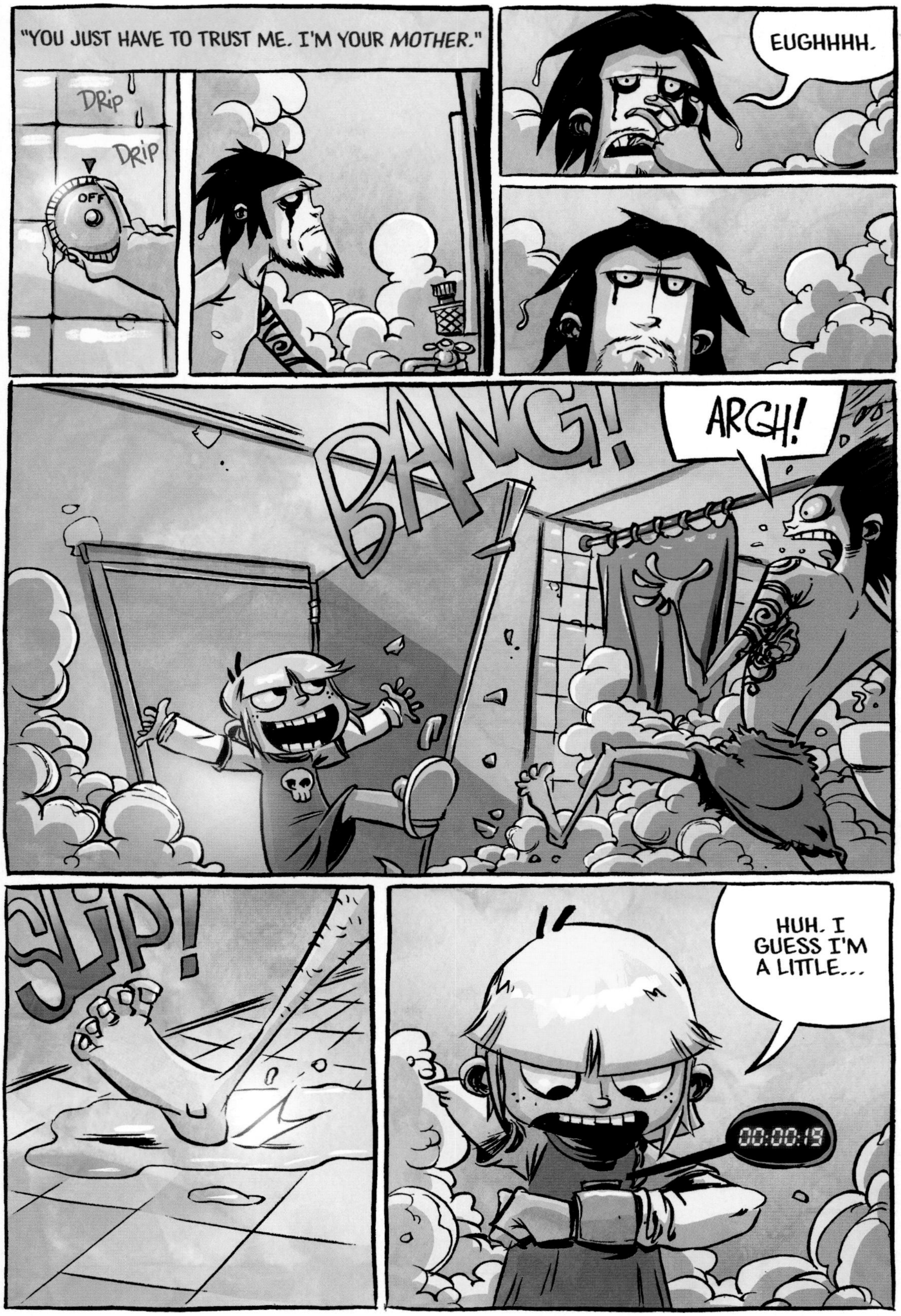
"YOU JUST HAVE TO TRUST ME. I'M YOUR *MOTHER*."
DRIP
DRIP
OFF
EUGHHHH.
BANG!
ARGH!
SLIP!
HUH. I GUESS I'M A LITTLE...
00:00:19

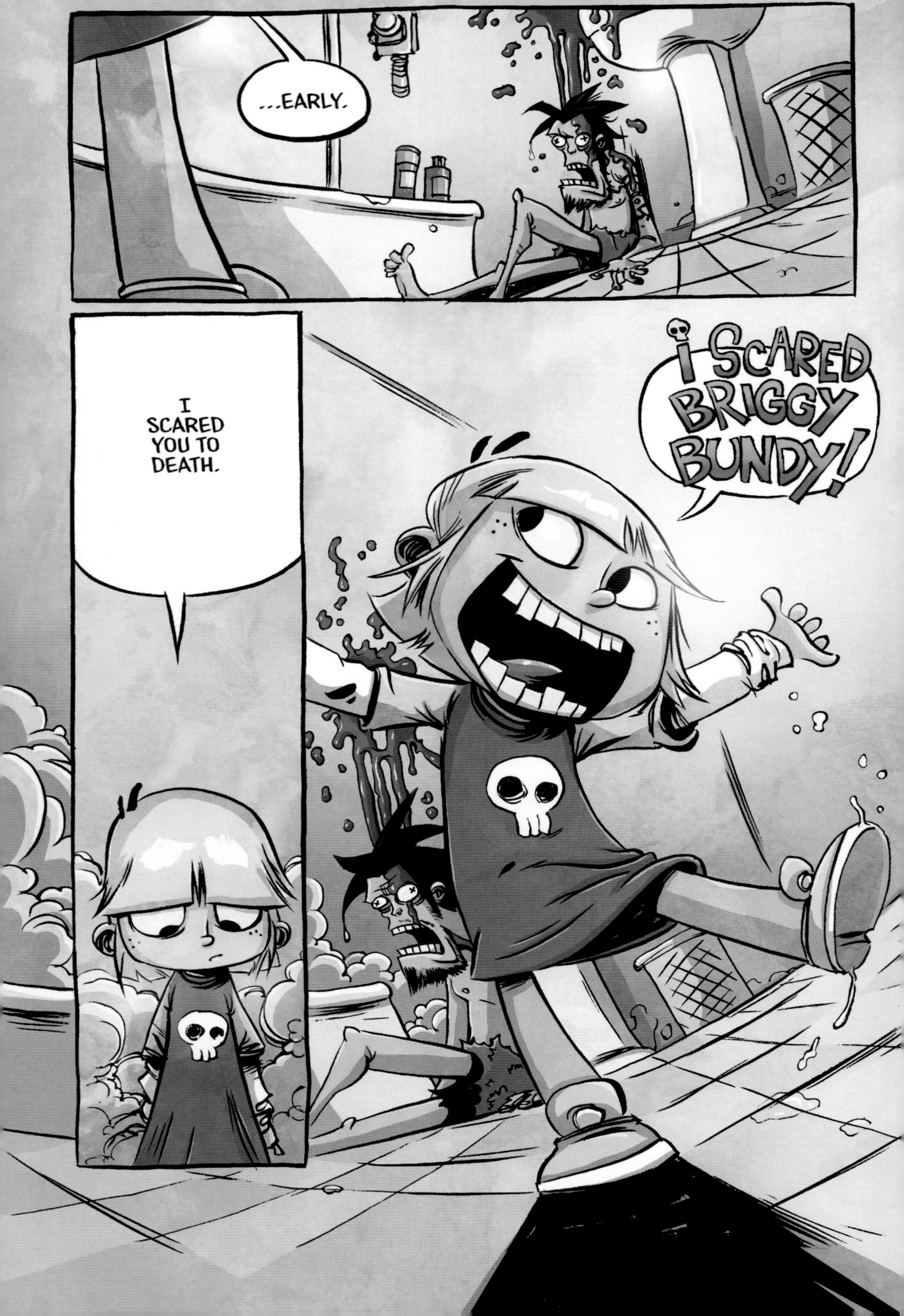
...EARLY.
I SCARED YOU TO DEATH.
I SCARED BRIGGY BUNDY!

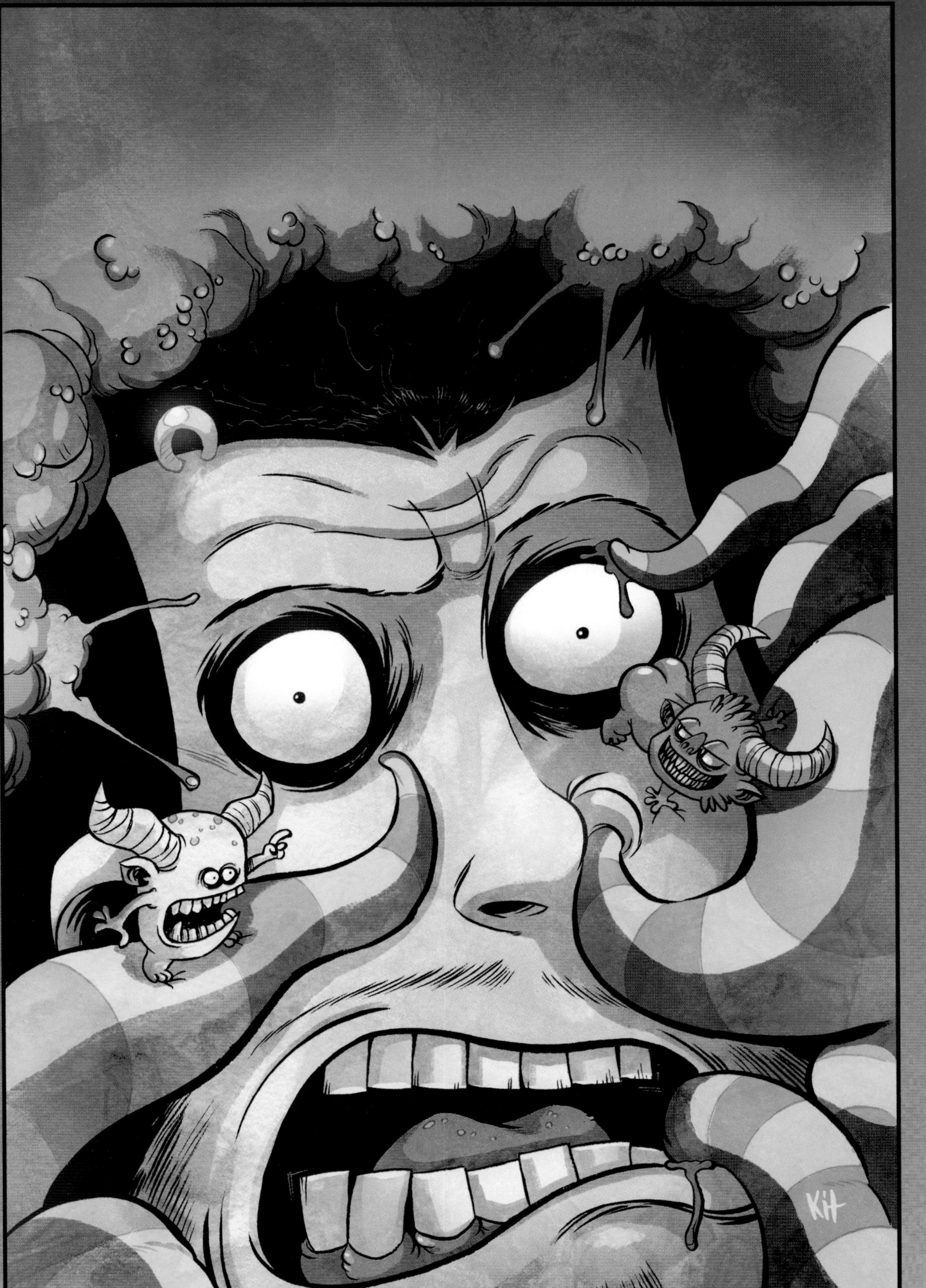

CHAPTER
TWO

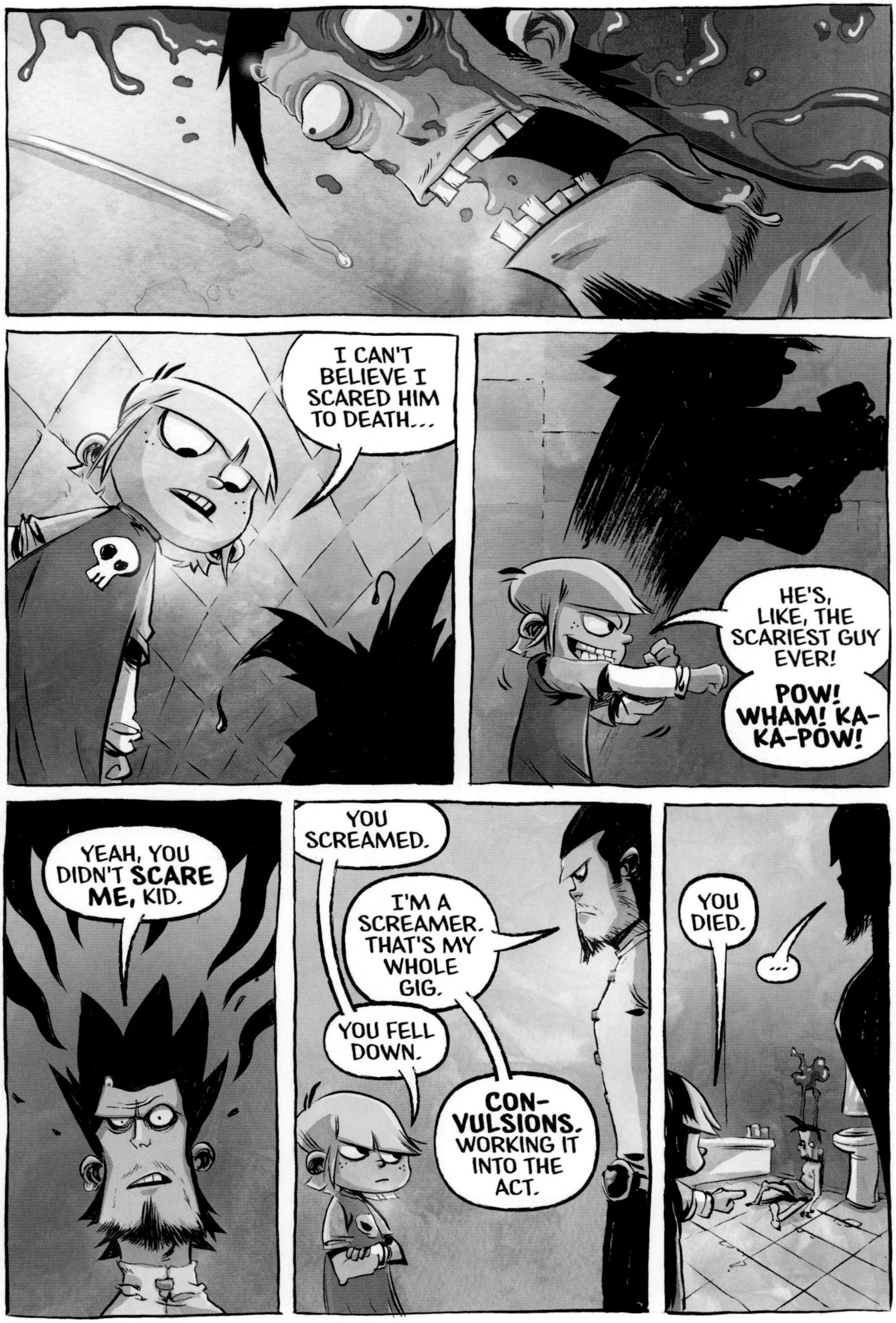
I CAN'T BELIEVE I SCARED HIM TO DEATH...
HE'S, LIKE, THE SCARIEST GUY EVER!
POW! WHAM! KA-KA-POW!
YEAH, YOU DIDN'T SCARE ME, KID.
YOU SCREAMED.
I'M A SCREAMER. THAT'S MY WHOLE GIG.
YOU FELL DOWN.
CON-VULSIONS. WORKING IT INTO THE ACT.
YOU DIED.
...

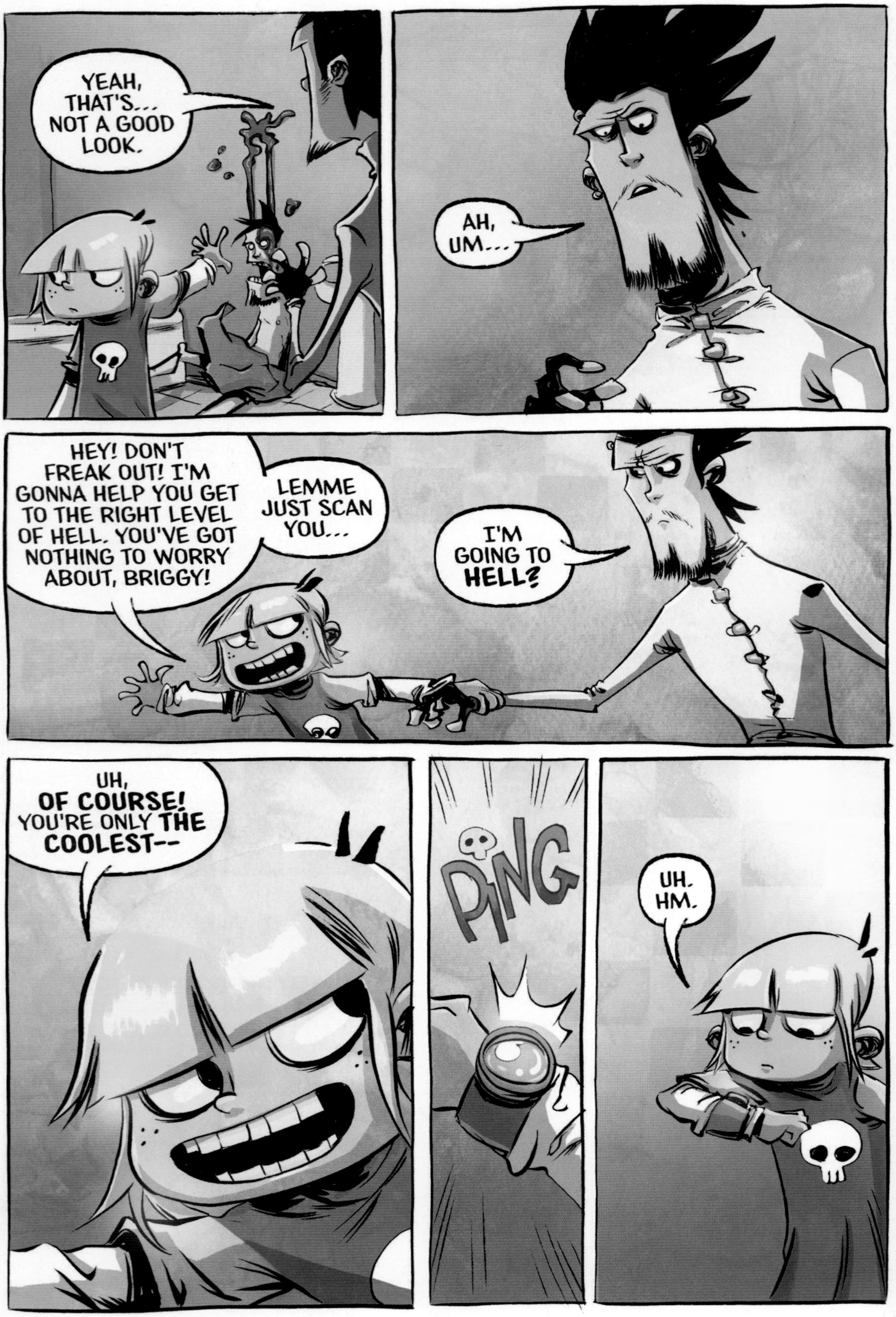
YEAH, THAT'S... NOT A GOOD LOOK.
AH, UM...
HEY! DON'T FREAK OUT! I'M GONNA HELP YOU GET TO THE RIGHT LEVEL OF HELL. YOU'VE GOT NOTHING TO WORRY ABOUT, BRIGGY!
LEMME JUST SCAN YOU...
I'M GOING TO HELL?
UH, OF COURSE! YOU'RE ONLY THE COOLEST--
PING
UH. HM.

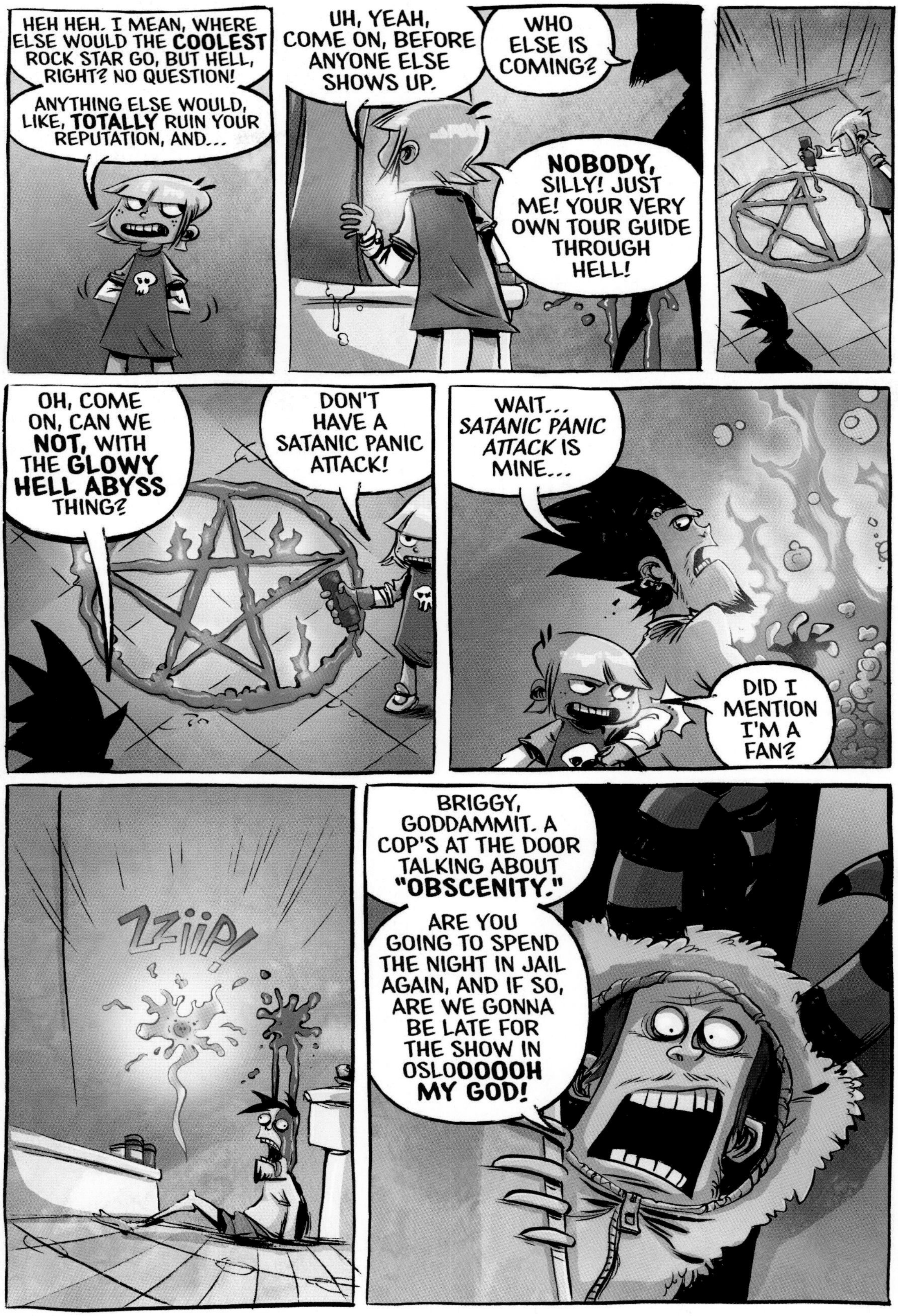
HEH HEH. I MEAN, WHERE ELSE WOULD THE **COOLEST** ROCK STAR GO, BUT HELL, RIGHT? NO QUESTION!
ANYTHING ELSE WOULD, LIKE, **TOTALLY** RUIN YOUR REPUTATION, AND...
UH, YEAH, COME ON, BEFORE ANYONE ELSE SHOWS UP.
WHO ELSE IS COMING?
NOBODY, SILLY! JUST ME! YOUR VERY OWN TOUR GUIDE THROUGH HELL!
OH, COME ON, CAN WE **NOT,** WITH THE **GLOWY HELL ABYSS** THING?
DON'T HAVE A SATANIC PANIC ATTACK!
WAIT... *SATANIC PANIC ATTACK* IS MINE...
DID I MENTION I'M A FAN?
ZZIIP!
BRIGGY, GODDAMMIT. A COP'S AT THE DOOR TALKING ABOUT **"OBSCENITY."**
ARE YOU GOING TO SPEND THE NIGHT IN JAIL AGAIN, AND IF SO, ARE WE GONNA BE LATE FOR THE SHOW IN OSLO**OOOOH MY GOD!**

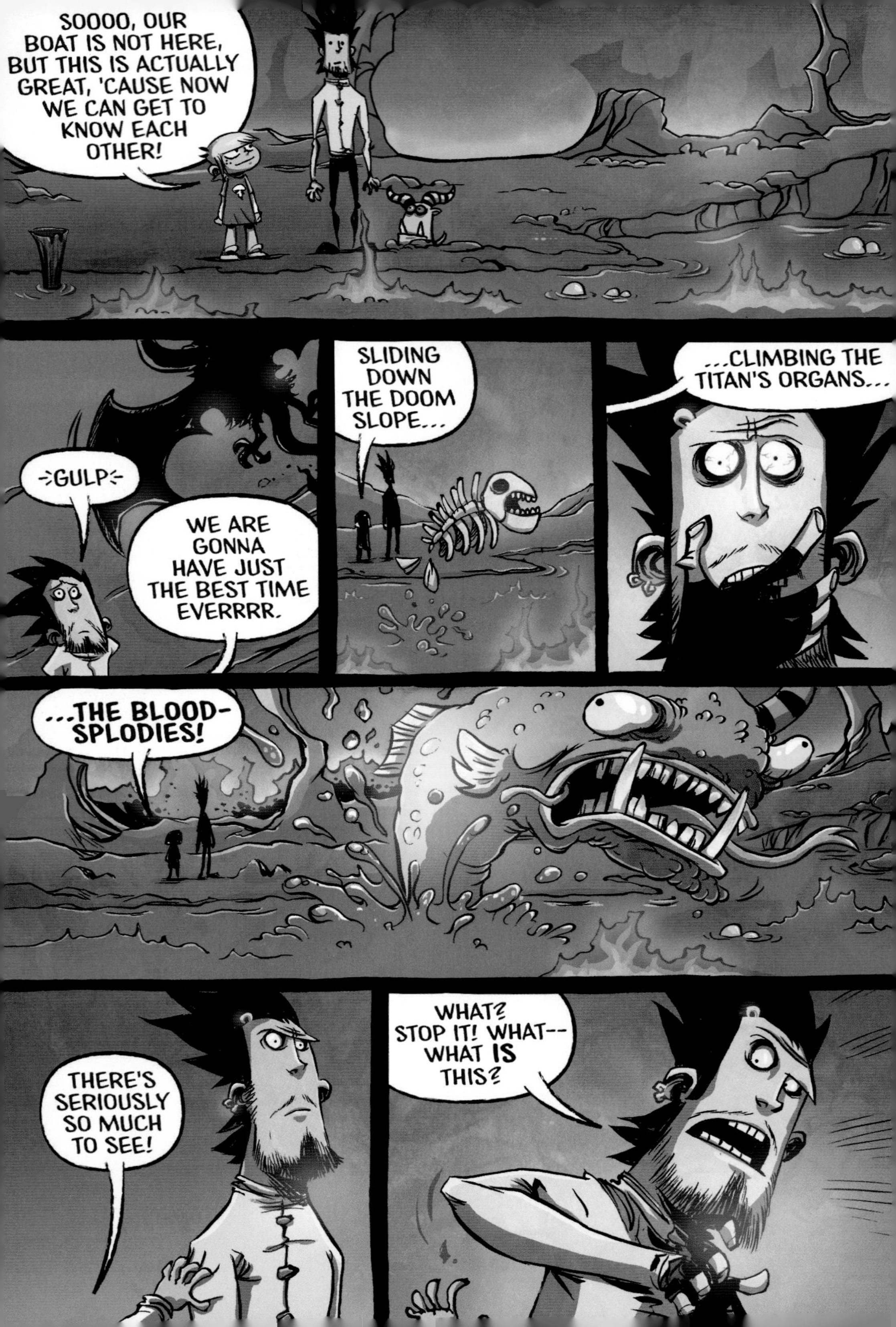
SOOOO, OUR BOAT IS NOT HERE, BUT THIS IS ACTUALLY GREAT, 'CAUSE NOW WE CAN GET TO KNOW EACH OTHER!
-GULP-
WE ARE GONNA HAVE JUST THE BEST TIME EVERRRR.
SLIDING DOWN THE DOOM SLOPE...
...CLIMBING THE TITAN'S ORGANS...
...THE BLOOD-SPLODIES!
THERE'S SERIOUSLY SO MUCH TO SEE!
WHAT? STOP IT! WHAT-- WHAT IS THIS?

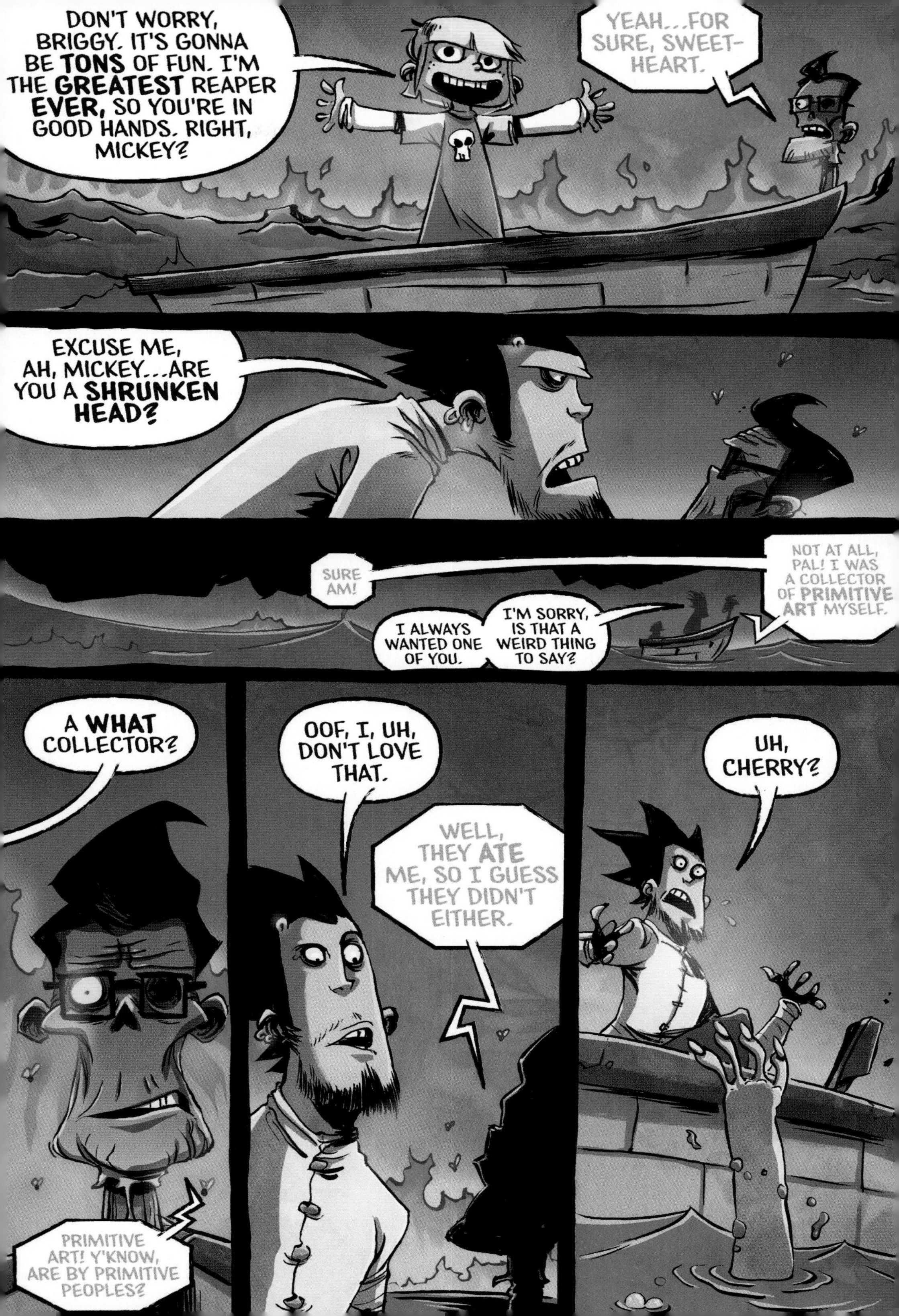
DON'T WORRY, BRIGGY. IT'S GONNA BE TONS OF FUN. I'M THE GREATEST REAPER EVER, SO YOU'RE IN GOOD HANDS. RIGHT, MICKEY?
YEAH...FOR SURE, SWEET-HEART.
EXCUSE ME, AH, MICKEY...ARE YOU A SHRUNKEN HEAD?
SURE AM!
I ALWAYS WANTED ONE OF YOU.
I'M SORRY, IS THAT A WEIRD THING TO SAY?
NOT AT ALL, PAL! I WAS A COLLECTOR OF PRIMITIVE ART MYSELF.
A WHAT COLLECTOR?
PRIMITIVE ART! Y'KNOW, ARE BY PRIMITIVE PEOPLES?
OOF, I, UH, DON'T LOVE THAT.
WELL, THEY ATE ME, SO I GUESS THEY DIDN'T EITHER.
UH, CHERRY?

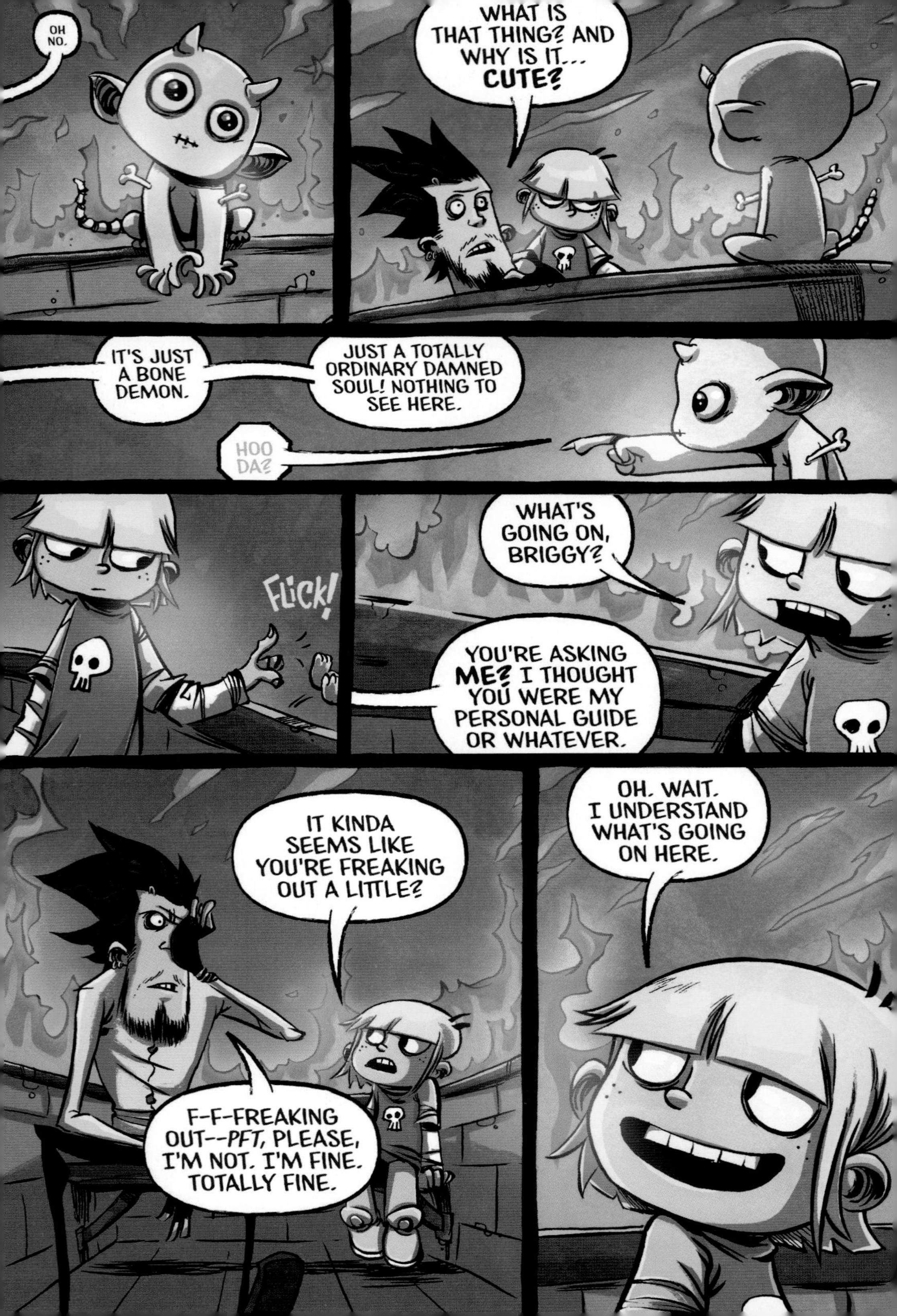
OH NO.
WHAT IS THAT THING? AND WHY IS IT... CUTE?
IT'S JUST A BONE DEMON.
JUST A TOTALLY ORDINARY DAMNED SOUL! NOTHING TO SEE HERE.
HOO DA?
FLICK!
WHAT'S GOING ON, BRIGGY?
YOU'RE ASKING ME? I THOUGHT YOU WERE MY PERSONAL GUIDE OR WHATEVER.
IT KINDA SEEMS LIKE YOU'RE FREAKING OUT A LITTLE?
F-F-FREAKING OUT--PFT, PLEASE, I'M NOT. I'M FINE. TOTALLY FINE.
OH. WAIT. I UNDERSTAND WHAT'S GOING ON HERE.

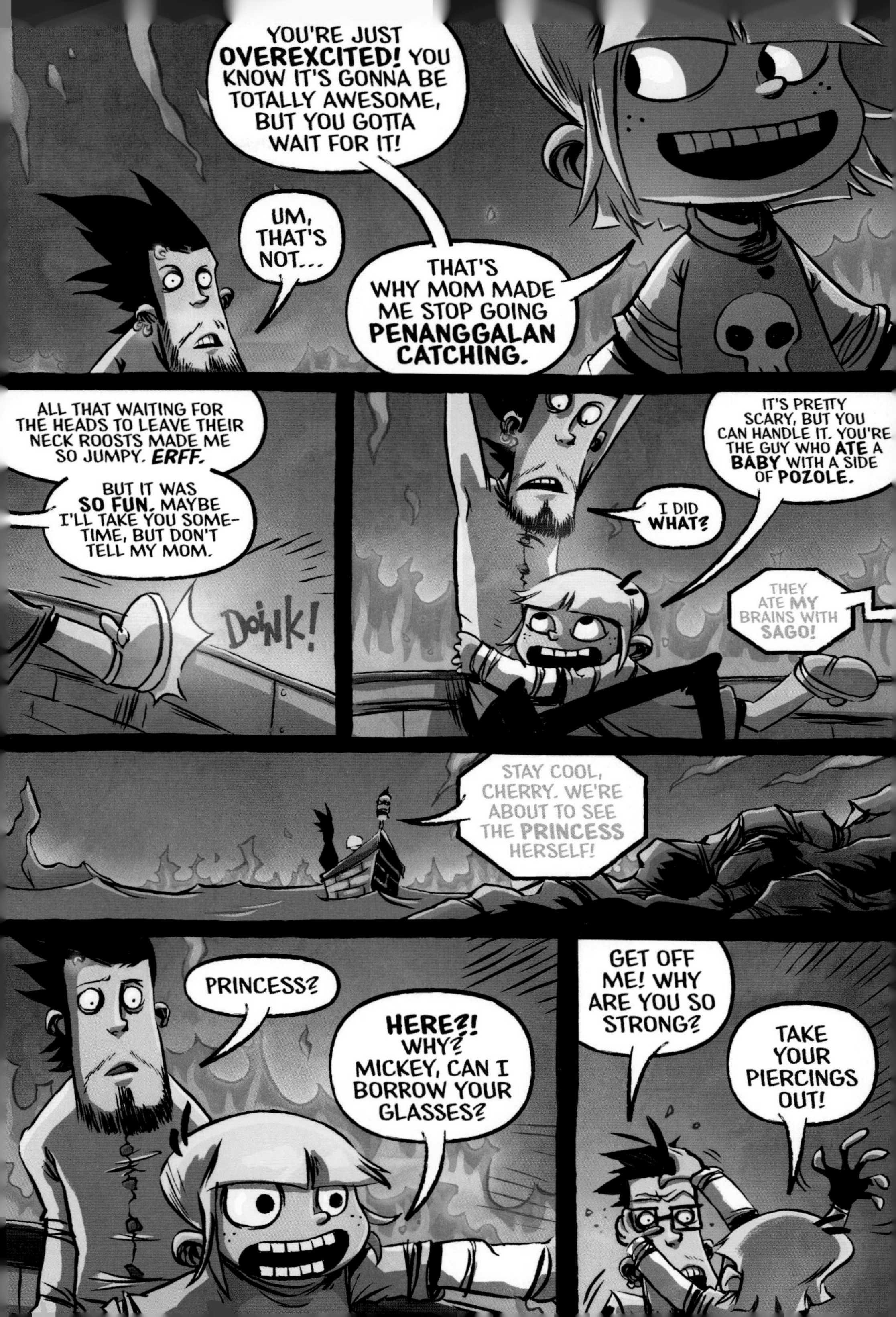
YOU'RE JUST OVEREXCITED! YOU KNOW IT'S GONNA BE TOTALLY AWESOME, BUT YOU GOTTA WAIT FOR IT!
UM, THAT'S NOT...
THAT'S WHY MOM MADE ME STOP GOING PENANGGALAN CATCHING.
ALL THAT WAITING FOR THE HEADS TO LEAVE THEIR NECK ROOSTS MADE ME SO JUMPY. ERFF.
BUT IT WAS SO FUN. MAYBE I'LL TAKE YOU SOMETIME, BUT DON'T TELL MY MOM.
DOINK!
IT'S PRETTY SCARY, BUT YOU CAN HANDLE IT. YOU'RE THE GUY WHO ATE A BABY WITH A SIDE OF POZOLE.
I DID WHAT?
THEY ATE MY BRAINS WITH SAGO!
STAY COOL, CHERRY. WE'RE ABOUT TO SEE THE PRINCESS HERSELF!
PRINCESS?
HERE?! WHY? MICKEY, CAN I BORROW YOUR GLASSES?
GET OFF ME! WHY ARE YOU SO STRONG?
TAKE YOUR PIERCINGS OUT!

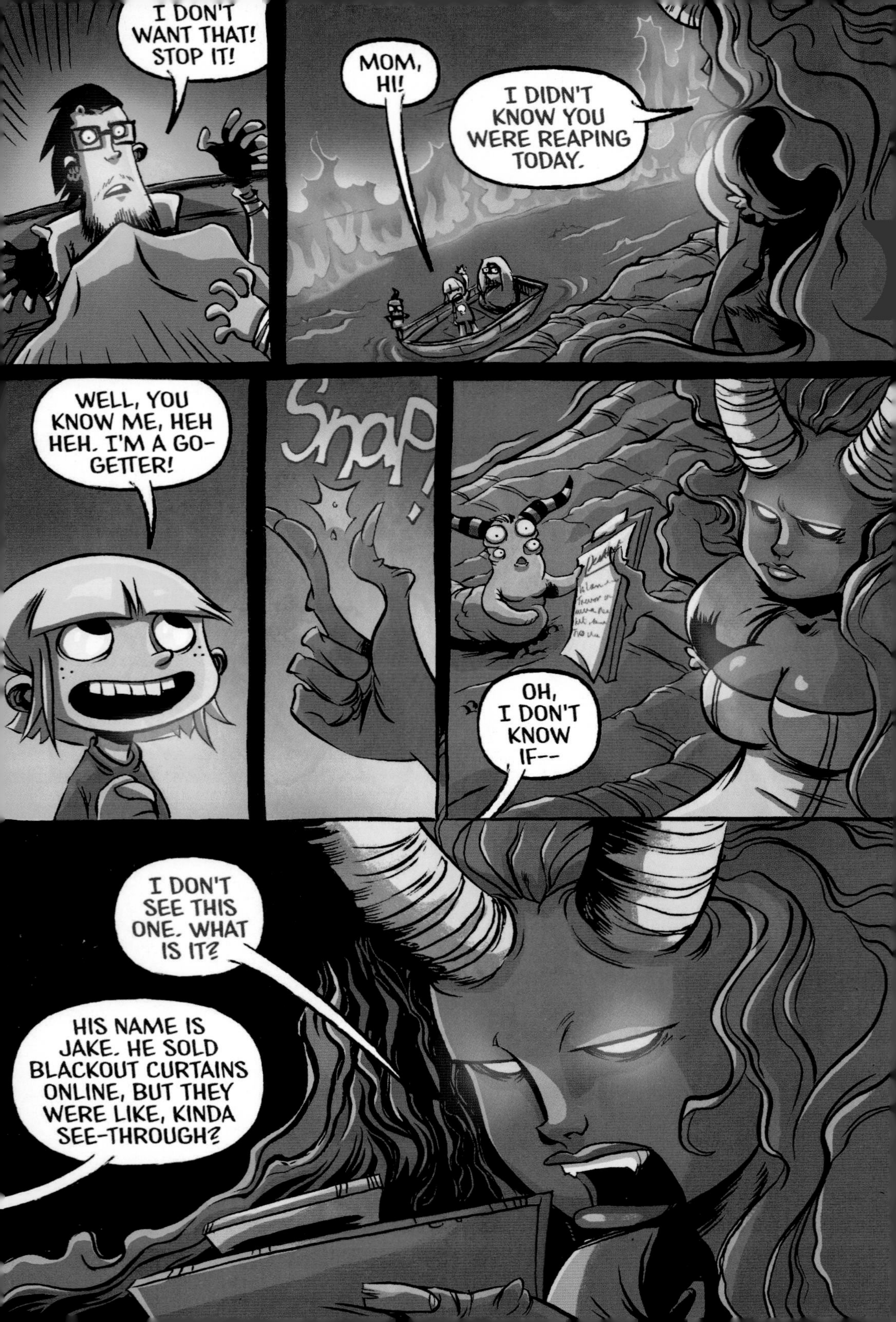
I DON'T WANT THAT! STOP IT!
MOM, HI!
I DIDN'T KNOW YOU WERE REAPING TODAY.
WELL, YOU KNOW ME, HEH HEH. I'M A GO-GETTER!
Snap!
OH, I DON'T KNOW IF--
I DON'T SEE THIS ONE. WHAT IS IT?
HIS NAME IS JAKE. HE SOLD BLACKOUT CURTAINS ONLINE, BUT THEY WERE LIKE, KINDA SEE-THROUGH?

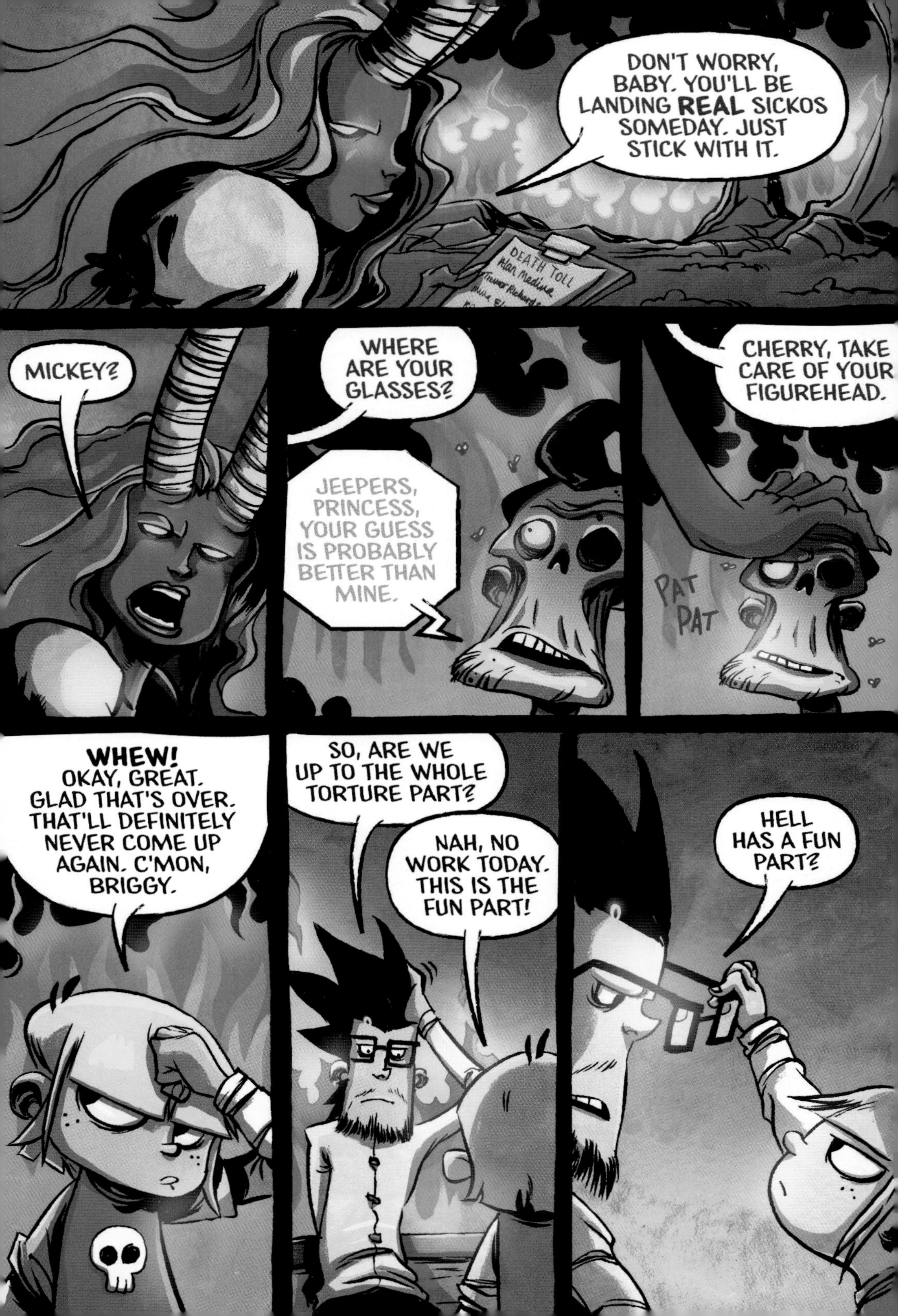

DON'T WORRY, BABY. YOU'LL BE LANDING **REAL** SICKOS SOMEDAY. JUST STICK WITH IT.
DEATH TOLL
Alan Medina
MICKEY?
WHERE ARE YOUR GLASSES?
JEEPERS, PRINCESS, YOUR GUESS IS PROBABLY BETTER THAN MINE.
CHERRY, TAKE CARE OF YOUR FIGUREHEAD.
PAT PAT
WHEW! OKAY, GREAT. GLAD THAT'S OVER. THAT'LL DEFINITELY NEVER COME UP AGAIN. C'MON, BRIGGY.
SO, ARE WE UP TO THE WHOLE TORTURE PART?
NAH, NO WORK TODAY. THIS IS THE FUN PART!
HELL HAS A FUN PART?

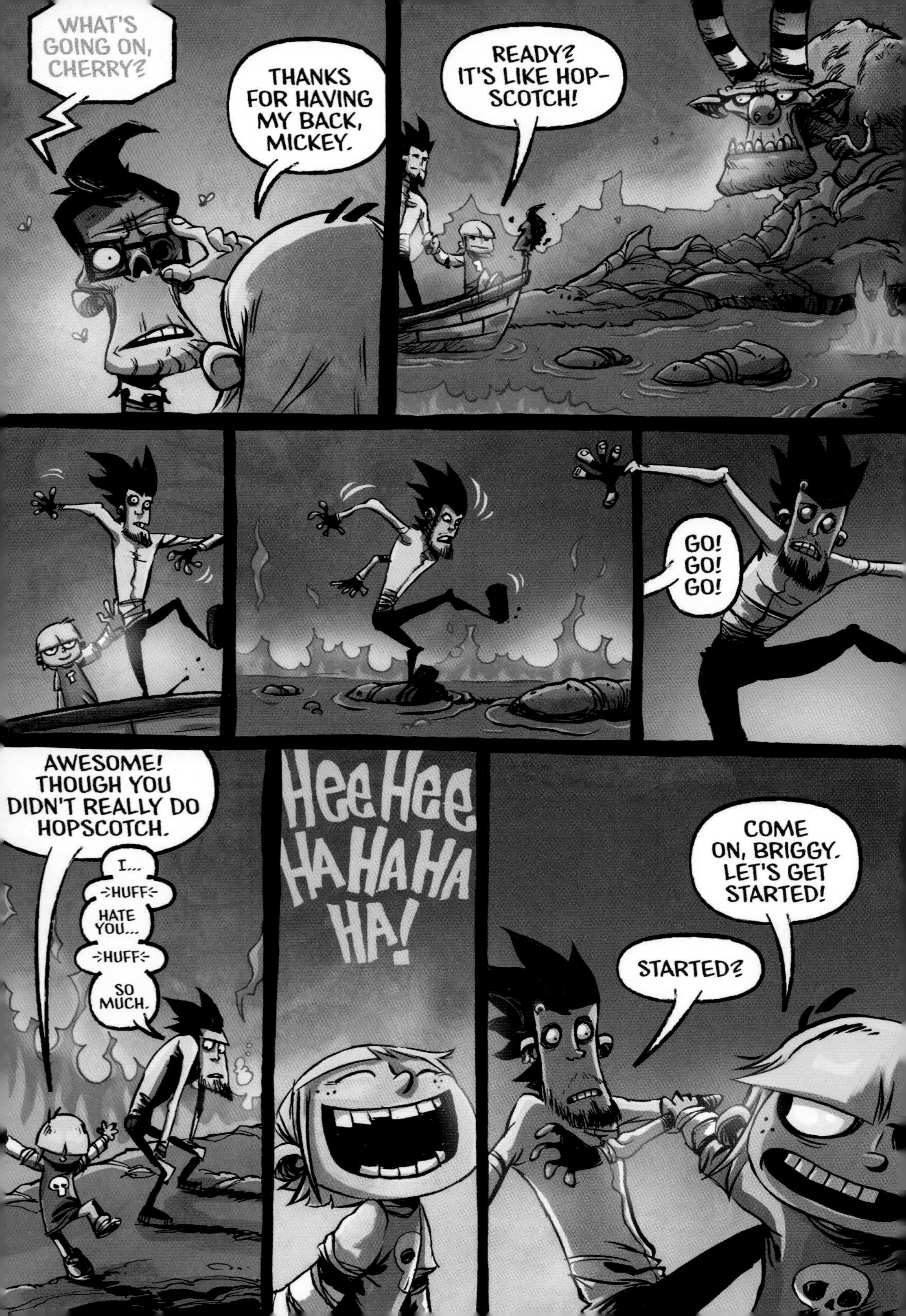
WHAT'S GOING ON, CHERRY?
THANKS FOR HAVING MY BACK, MICKEY.
READY? IT'S LIKE HOP-SCOTCH!
GO! GO! GO!
AWESOME! THOUGH YOU DIDN'T REALLY DO HOPSCOTCH.
I...
HUFF
HATE YOU...
HUFF
SO MUCH.
Hee Hee HA HA HA HA!
COME ON, BRIGGY. LET'S GET STARTED!
STARTED?

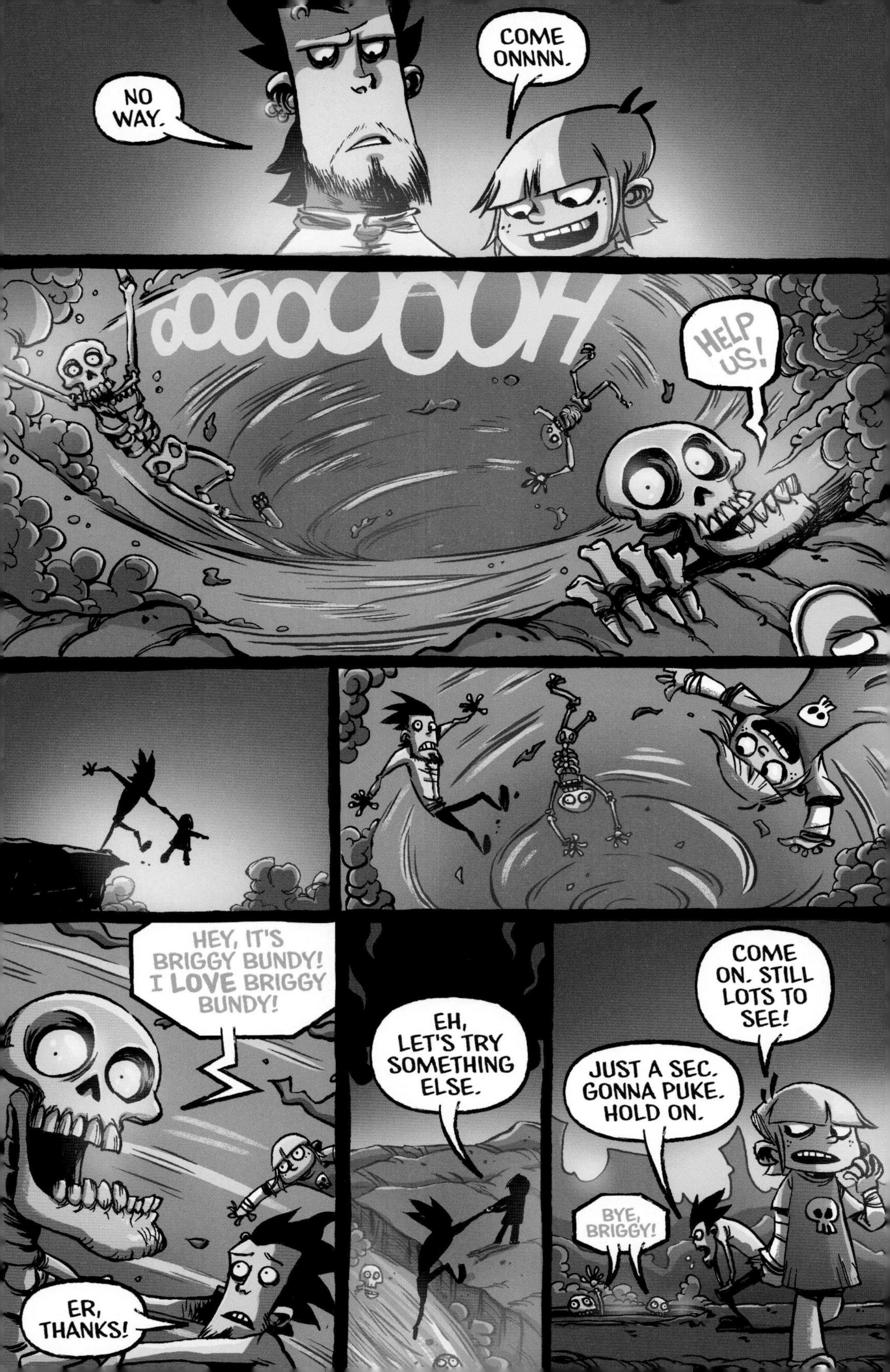
NO WAY.
COME ONNNN.
OOOOOOOH
HELP US!
HEY, IT'S BRIGGY BUNDY! I LOVE BRIGGY BUNDY!
ER, THANKS!
EH, LET'S TRY SOMETHING ELSE.
COME ON. STILL LOTS TO SEE!
JUST A SEC. GONNA PUKE. HOLD ON.
BYE, BRIGGY!

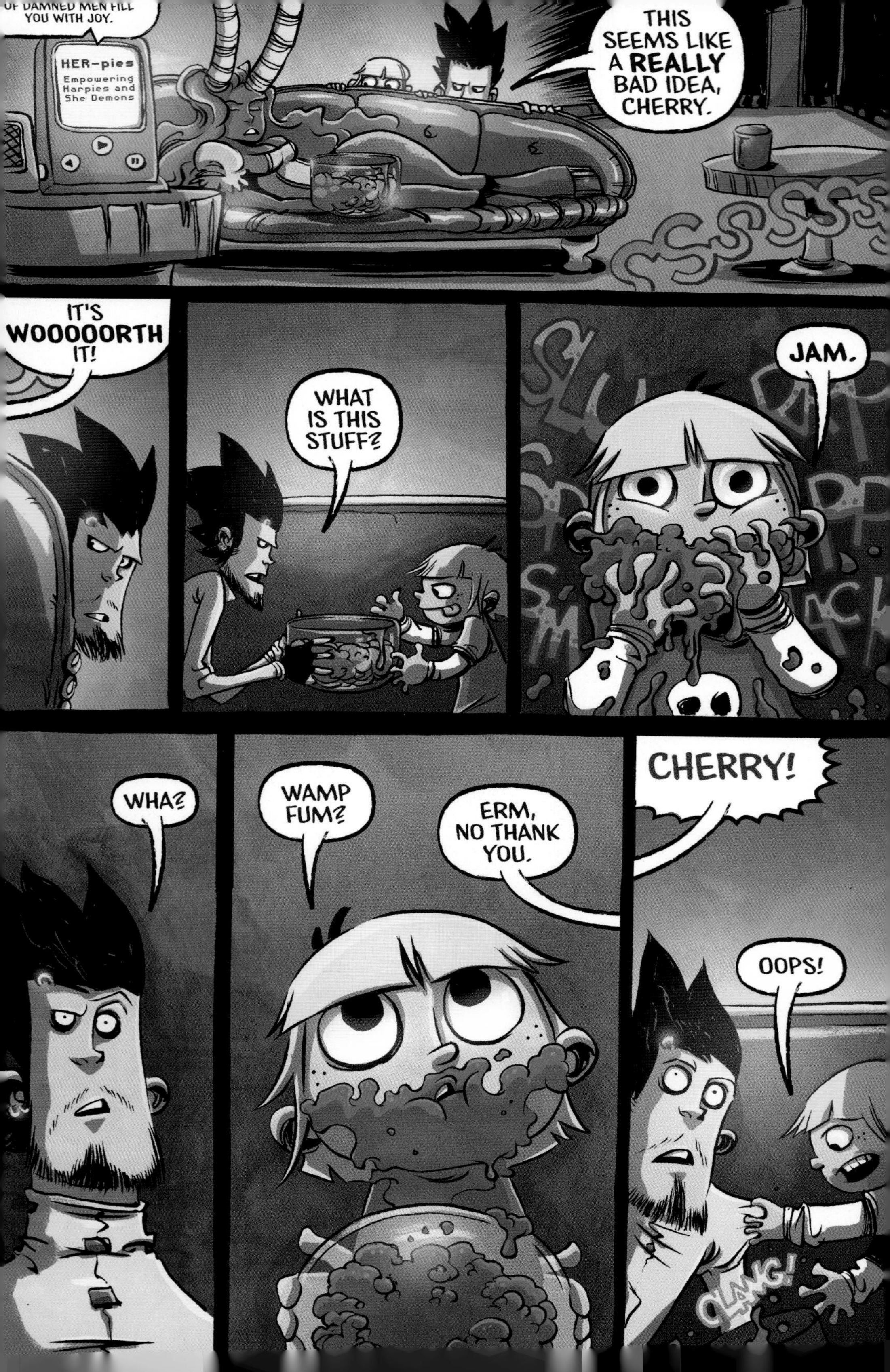
OF DAMNED MEN FILL YOU WITH JOY.
HER-pies
Empowering Harpies and She Demons
THIS SEEMS LIKE A **REALLY** BAD IDEA, CHERRY.
IT'S WOOOOORTH IT!
WHAT IS THIS STUFF?
JAM.
WHA?
WAMP FUM?
ERM, NO THANK YOU.
CHERRY!
OOPS!
CLANG!

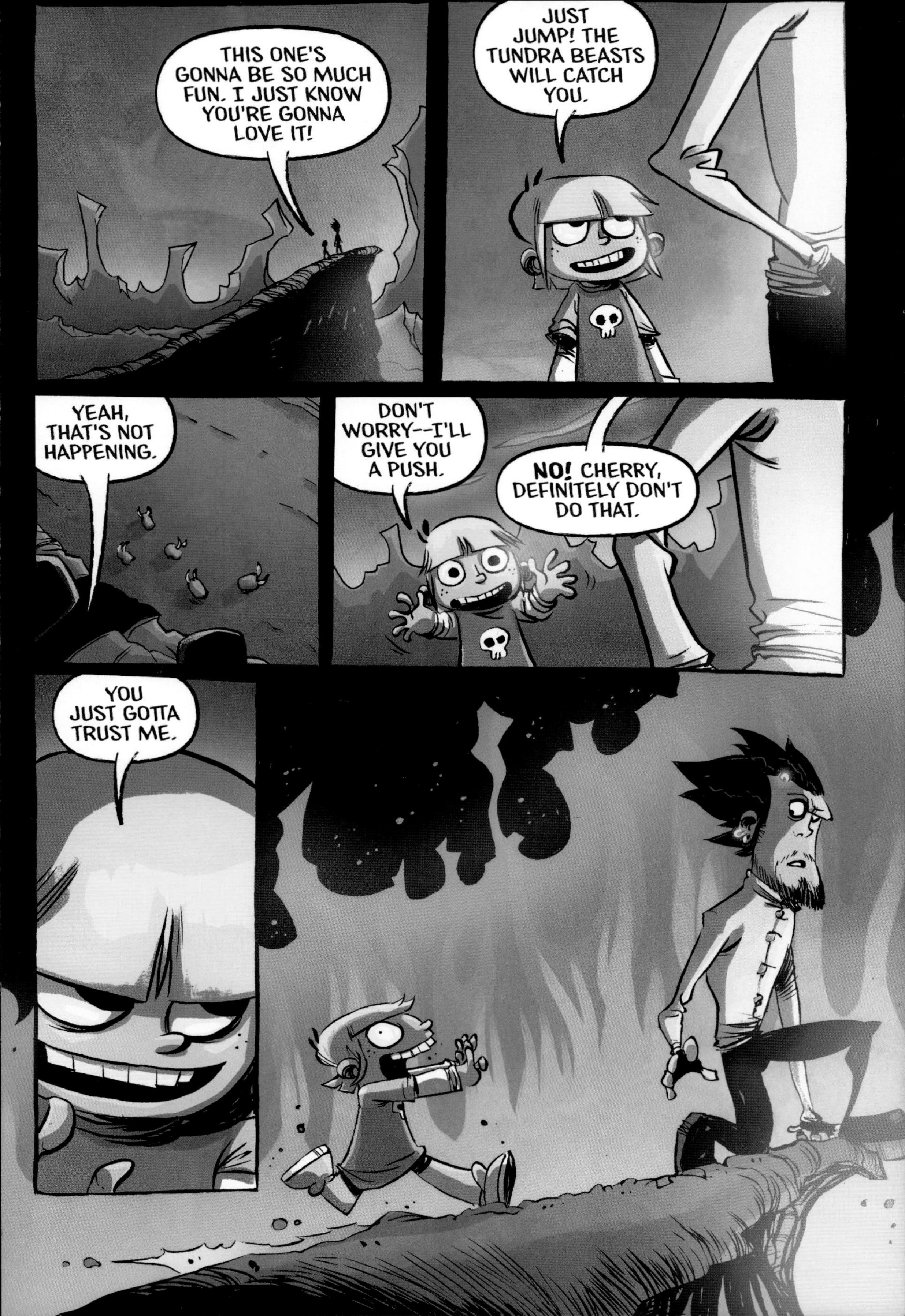
THIS ONE'S GONNA BE SO MUCH FUN. I JUST KNOW YOU'RE GONNA LOVE IT!
JUST JUMP! THE TUNDRA BEASTS WILL CATCH YOU.
YEAH, THAT'S NOT HAPPENING.
DON'T WORRY--I'LL GIVE YOU A PUSH.
NO! CHERRY, DEFINITELY DON'T DO THAT.
YOU JUST GOTTA TRUST ME.

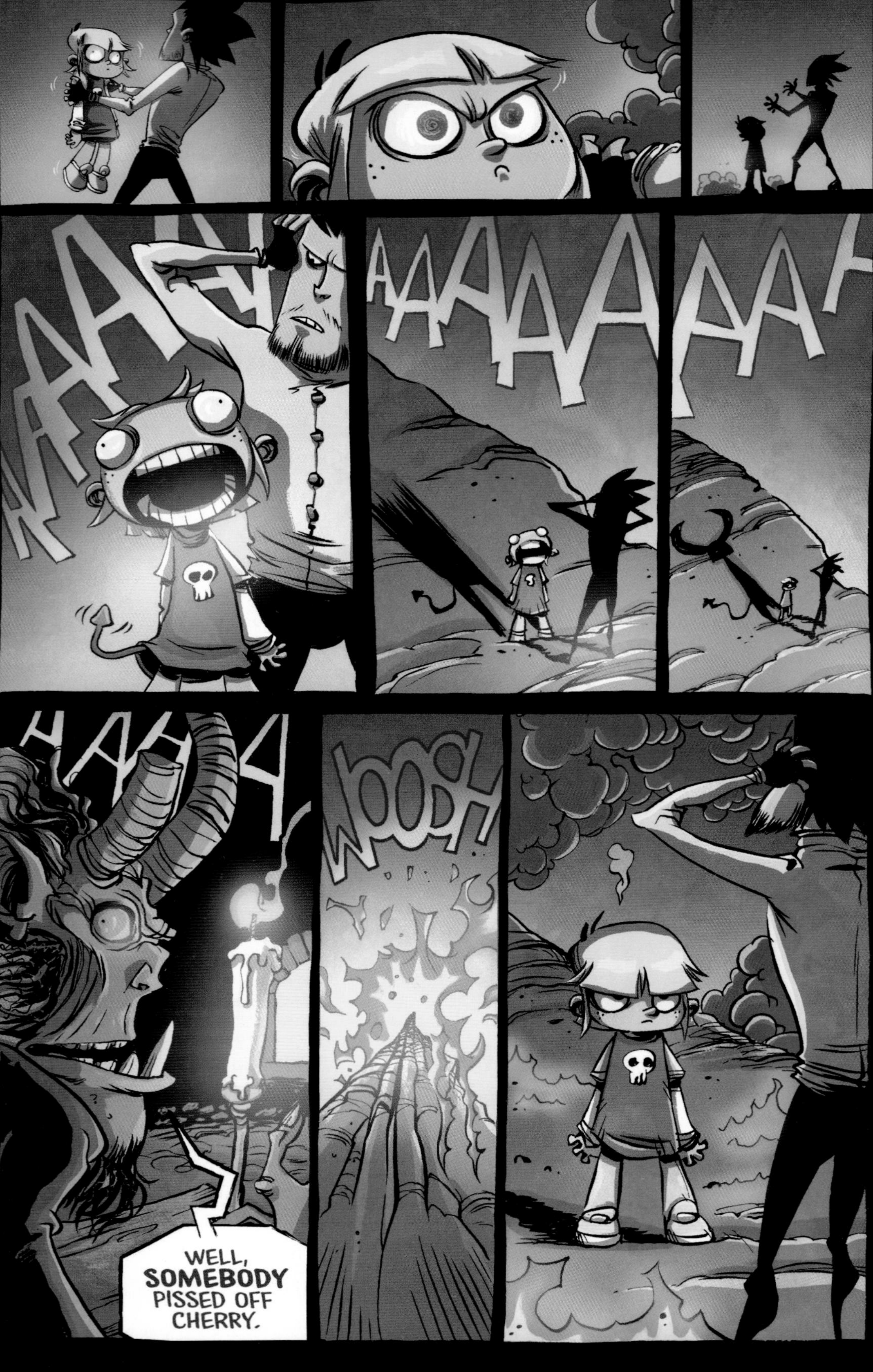
WOOSH
WELL, **SOMEBODY** PISSED OFF CHERRY.

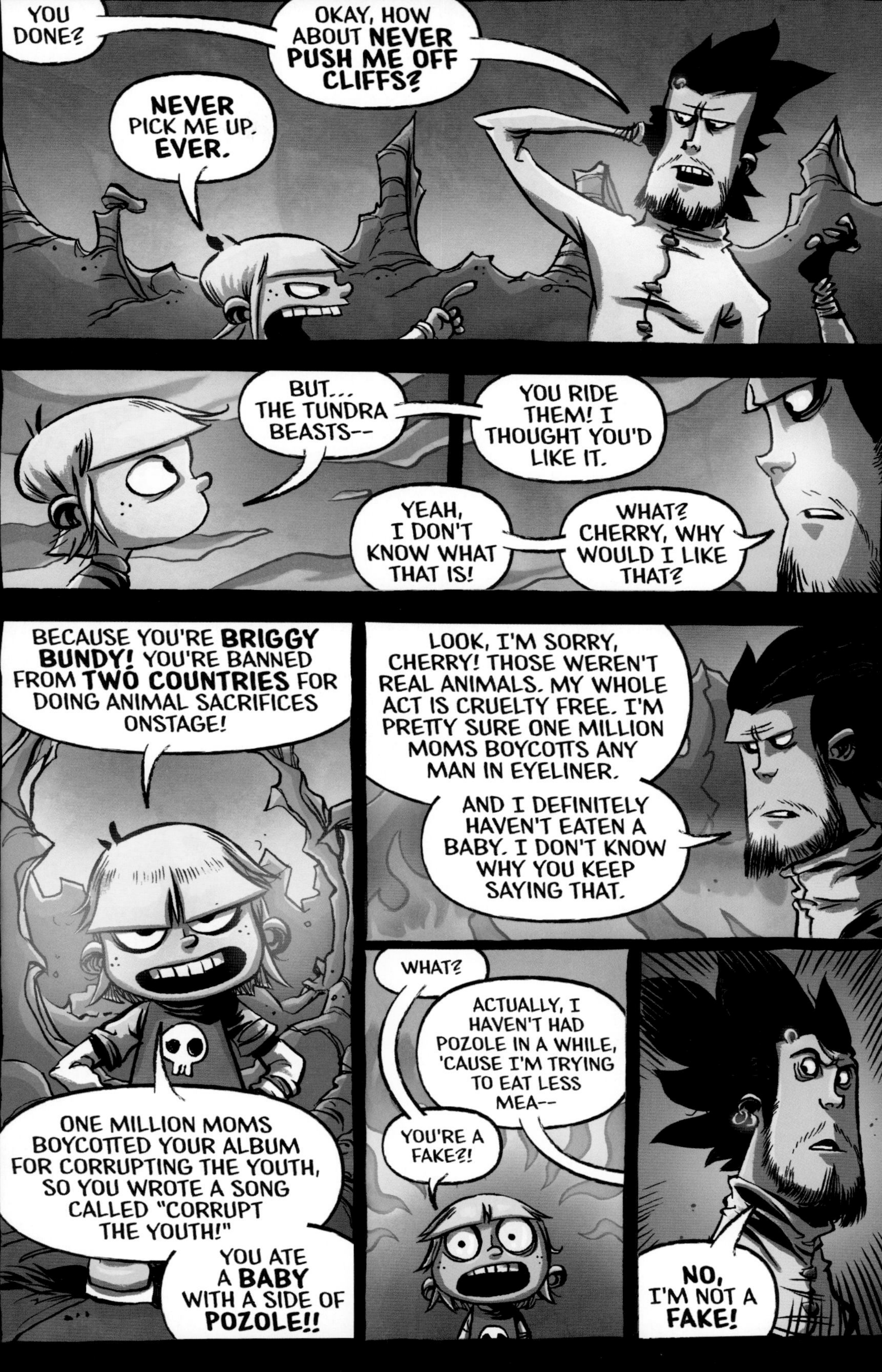
YOU DONE?
OKAY, HOW ABOUT NEVER PUSH ME OFF CLIFFS?
NEVER PICK ME UP. EVER.
BUT... THE TUNDRA BEASTS--
YOU RIDE THEM! I THOUGHT YOU'D LIKE IT.
YEAH, I DON'T KNOW WHAT THAT IS!
WHAT? CHERRY, WHY WOULD I LIKE THAT?
BECAUSE YOU'RE BRIGGY BUNDY! YOU'RE BANNED FROM TWO COUNTRIES FOR DOING ANIMAL SACRIFICES ONSTAGE!
ONE MILLION MOMS BOYCOTTED YOUR ALBUM FOR CORRUPTING THE YOUTH, SO YOU WROTE A SONG CALLED "CORRUPT THE YOUTH!"
YOU ATE A BABY WITH A SIDE OF POZOLE!!
LOOK, I'M SORRY, CHERRY! THOSE WEREN'T REAL ANIMALS. MY WHOLE ACT IS CRUELTY FREE. I'M PRETTY SURE ONE MILLION MOMS BOYCOTTS ANY MAN IN EYELINER.
AND I DEFINITELY HAVEN'T EATEN A BABY. I DON'T KNOW WHY YOU KEEP SAYING THAT.
WHAT?
ACTUALLY, I HAVEN'T HAD POZOLE IN A WHILE, 'CAUSE I'M TRYING TO EAT LESS MEA--
YOU'RE A FAKE?!
NO, I'M NOT A FAKE!

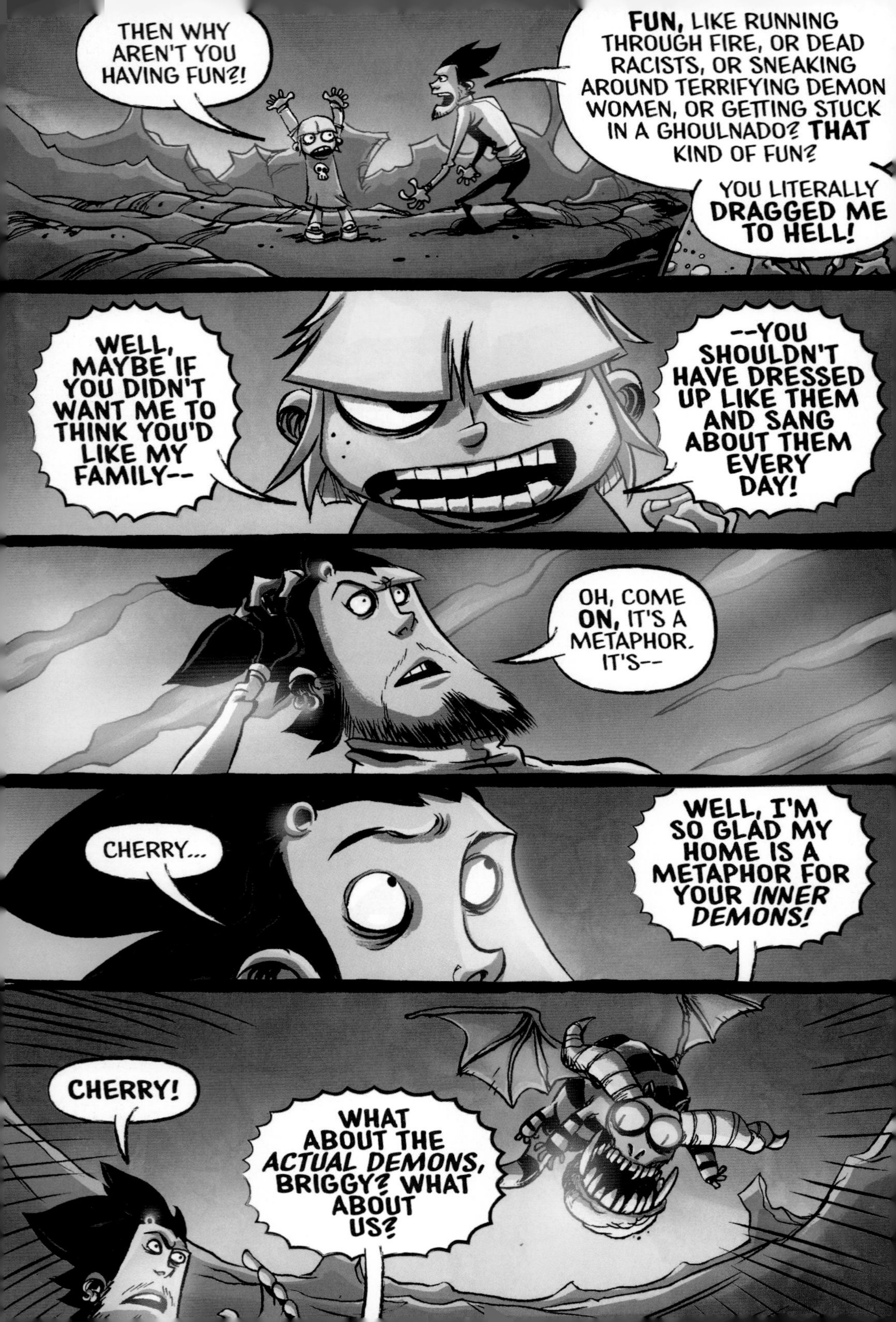
THEN WHY AREN'T YOU HAVING FUN?!
FUN, LIKE RUNNING THROUGH FIRE, OR DEAD RACISTS, OR SNEAKING AROUND TERRIFYING DEMON WOMEN, OR GETTING STUCK IN A GHOULNADO? THAT KIND OF FUN?
YOU LITERALLY DRAGGED ME TO HELL!
WELL, MAYBE IF YOU DIDN'T WANT ME TO THINK YOU'D LIKE MY FAMILY--
--YOU SHOULDN'T HAVE DRESSED UP LIKE THEM AND SANG ABOUT THEM EVERY DAY!
OH, COME ON, IT'S A METAPHOR. IT'S--
CHERRY...
WELL, I'M SO GLAD MY HOME IS A METAPHOR FOR YOUR INNER DEMONS!
CHERRY!
WHAT ABOUT THE ACTUAL DEMONS, BRIGGY? WHAT ABOUT US?

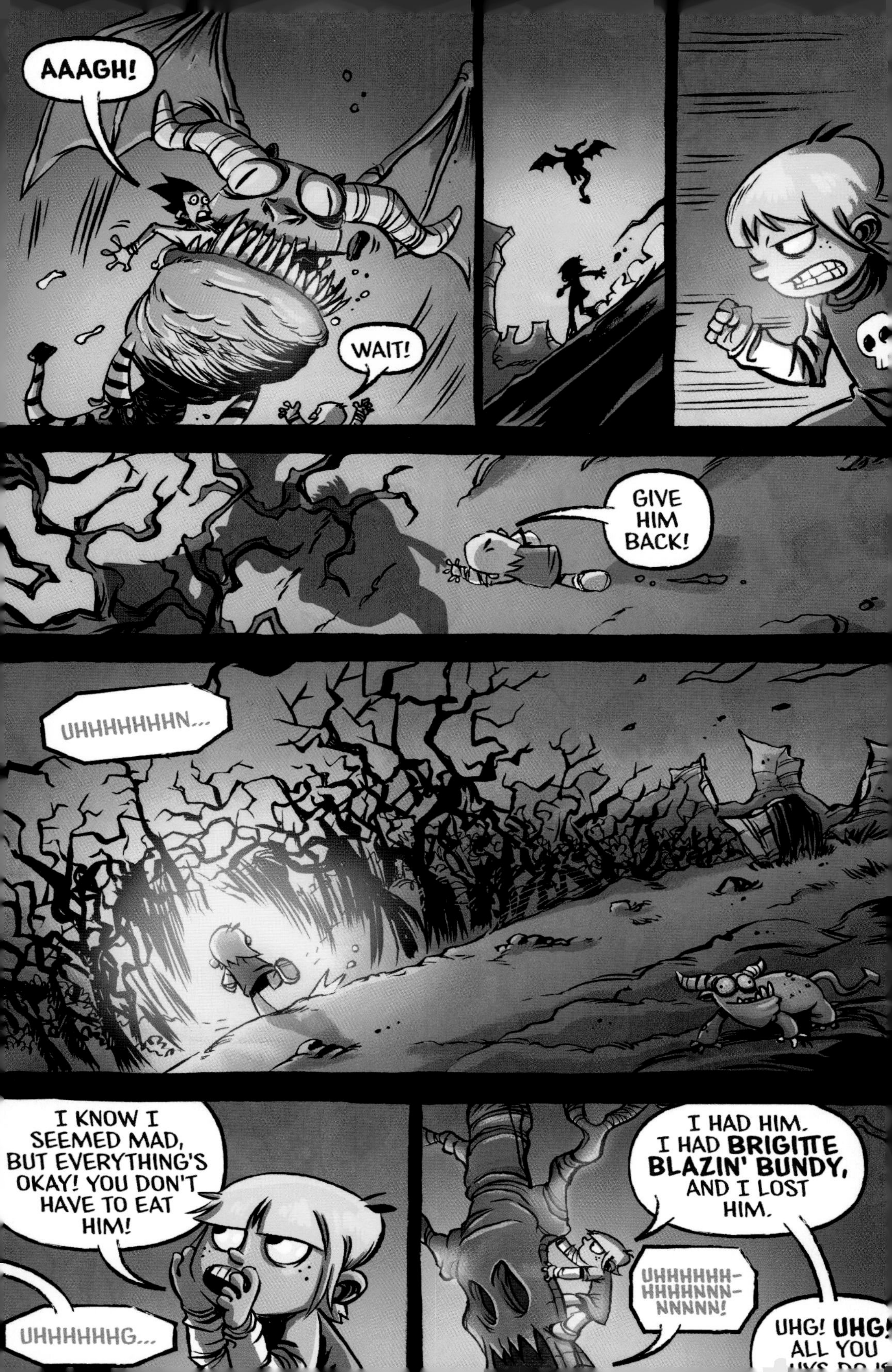
AAAGH!
WAIT!
GIVE HIM BACK!
UHHHHHHHN...
I KNOW I SEEMED MAD, BUT EVERYTHING'S OKAY! YOU DON'T HAVE TO EAT HIM!
UHHHHHHG...
I HAD HIM. I HAD BRIGITTE BLAZIN' BUNDY, AND I LOST HIM.
UHHHHHH-HHHHNNN-NNNNN!
UHG! UHG! ALL YOU

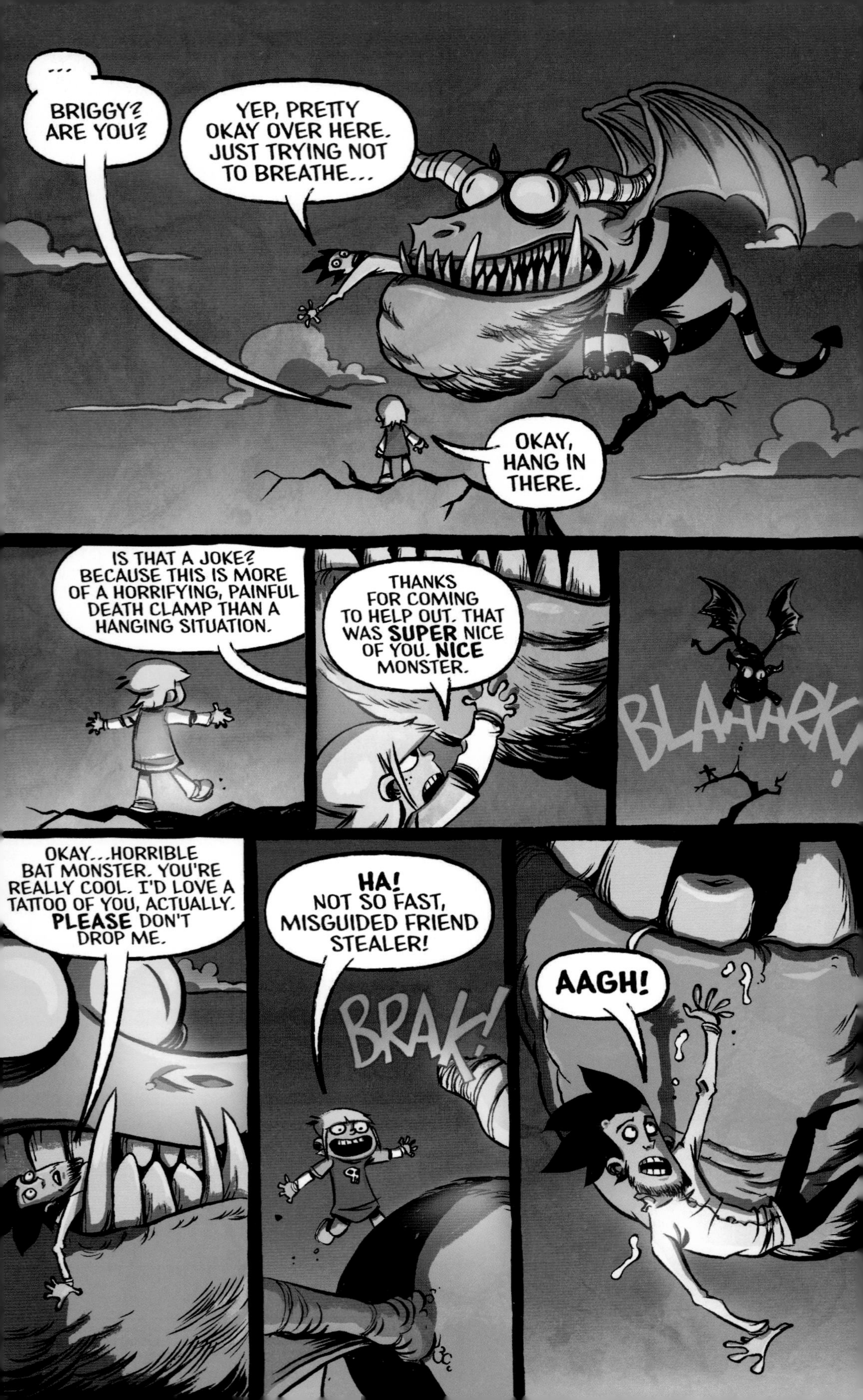
...
BRIGGY? ARE YOU?
YEP, PRETTY OKAY OVER HERE. JUST TRYING NOT TO BREATHE...
OKAY, HANG IN THERE.
IS THAT A JOKE? BECAUSE THIS IS MORE OF A HORRIFYING, PAINFUL DEATH CLAMP THAN A HANGING SITUATION.
THANKS FOR COMING TO HELP OUT. THAT WAS SUPER NICE OF YOU. NICE MONSTER.
BLAHARK!
OKAY...HORRIBLE BAT MONSTER. YOU'RE REALLY COOL. I'D LOVE A TATTOO OF YOU, ACTUALLY. PLEASE DON'T DROP ME.
HA! NOT SO FAST, MISGUIDED FRIEND STEALER!
BRAK!
AAGH!

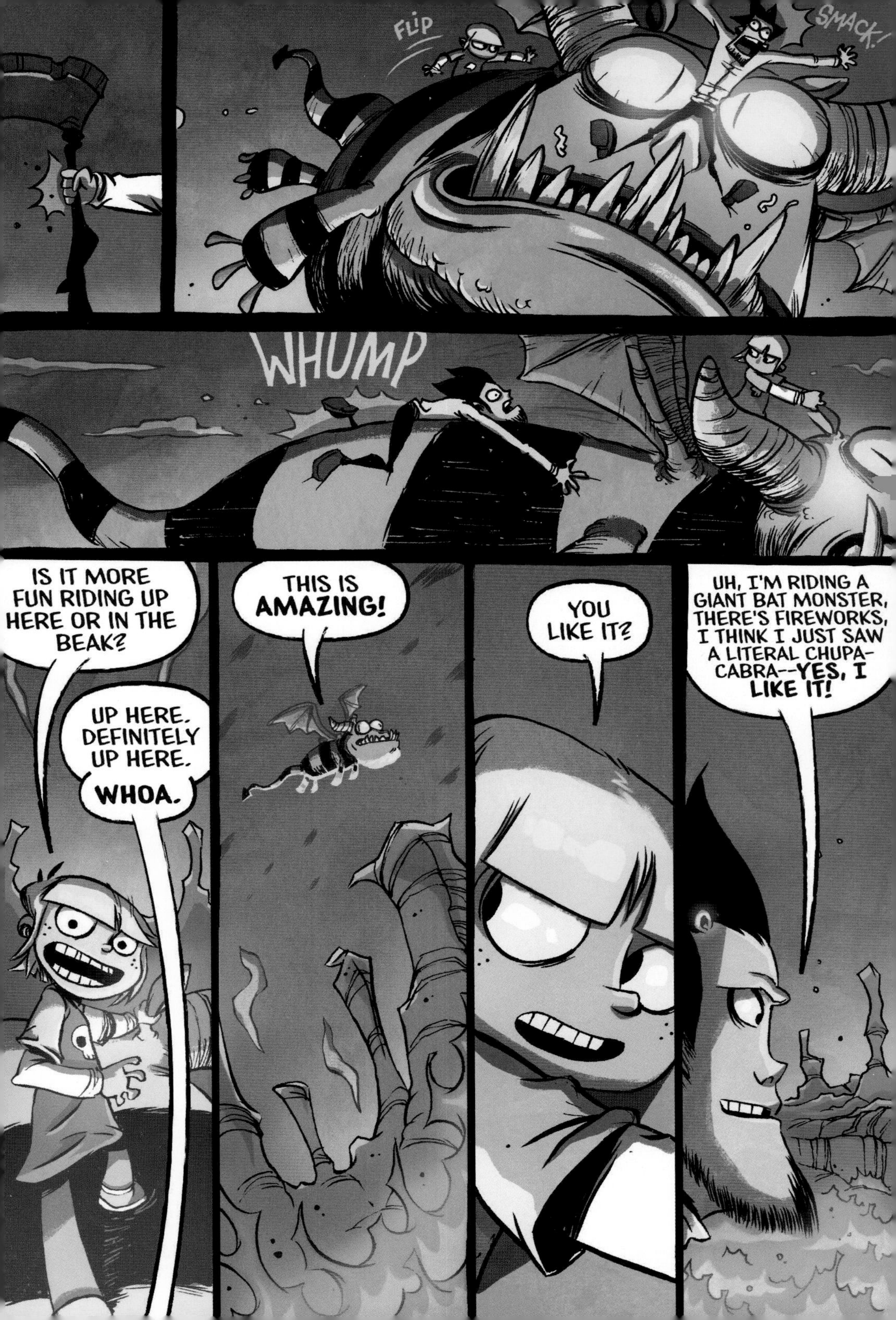

FLIP
SMACK!
WHUMP
IS IT MORE FUN RIDING UP HERE OR IN THE BEAK?
UP HERE. DEFINITELY UP HERE.
WHOA.
THIS IS AMAZING!
YOU LIKE IT?
UH, I'M RIDING A GIANT BAT MONSTER, THERE'S FIREWORKS, I THINK I JUST SAW A LITERAL CHUPA-CABRA--YES, I LIKE IT!

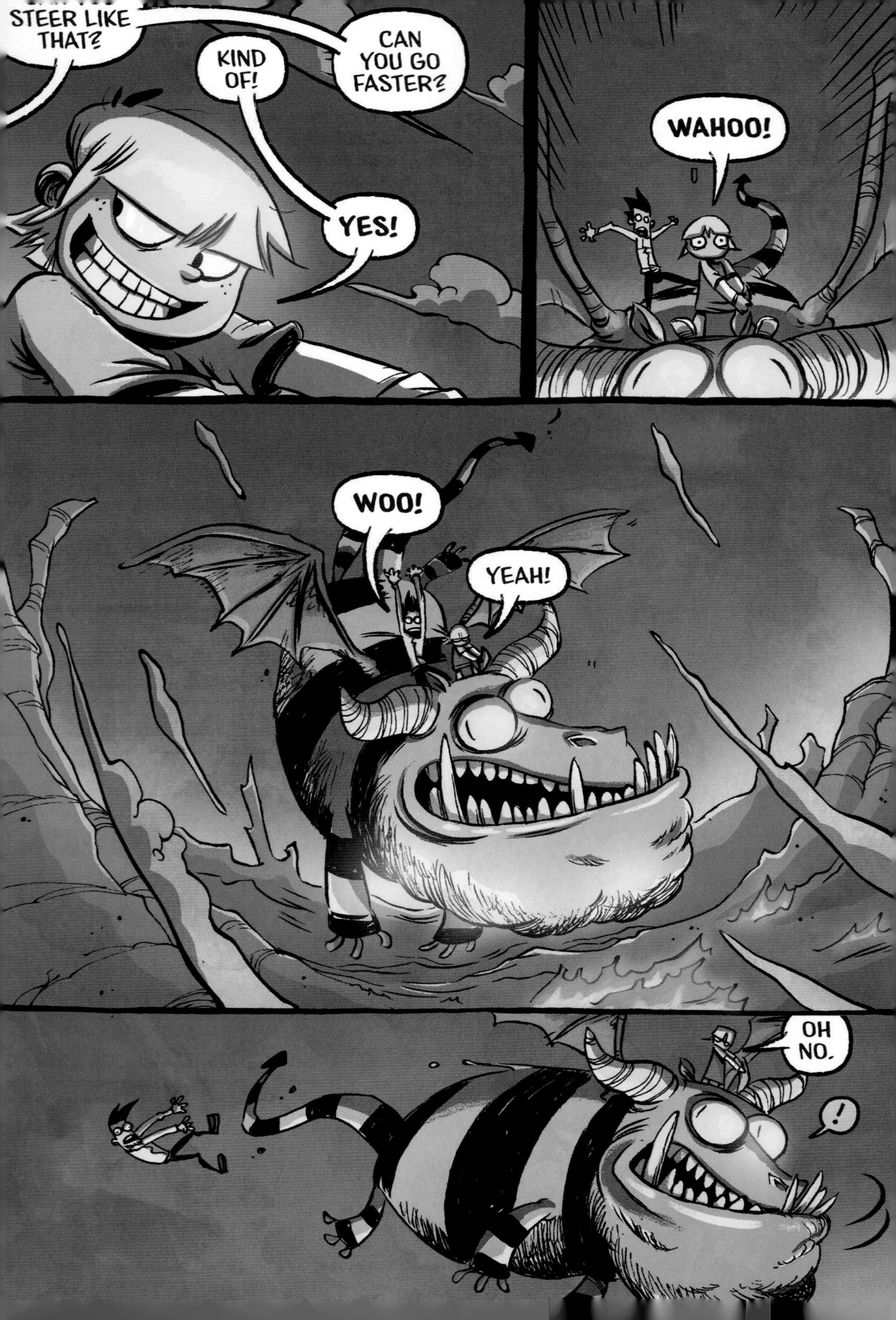
STEER LIKE THAT?
KIND OF!
CAN YOU GO FASTER?
YES!
WAHOO!
WOO!
YEAH!
OH NO.
!

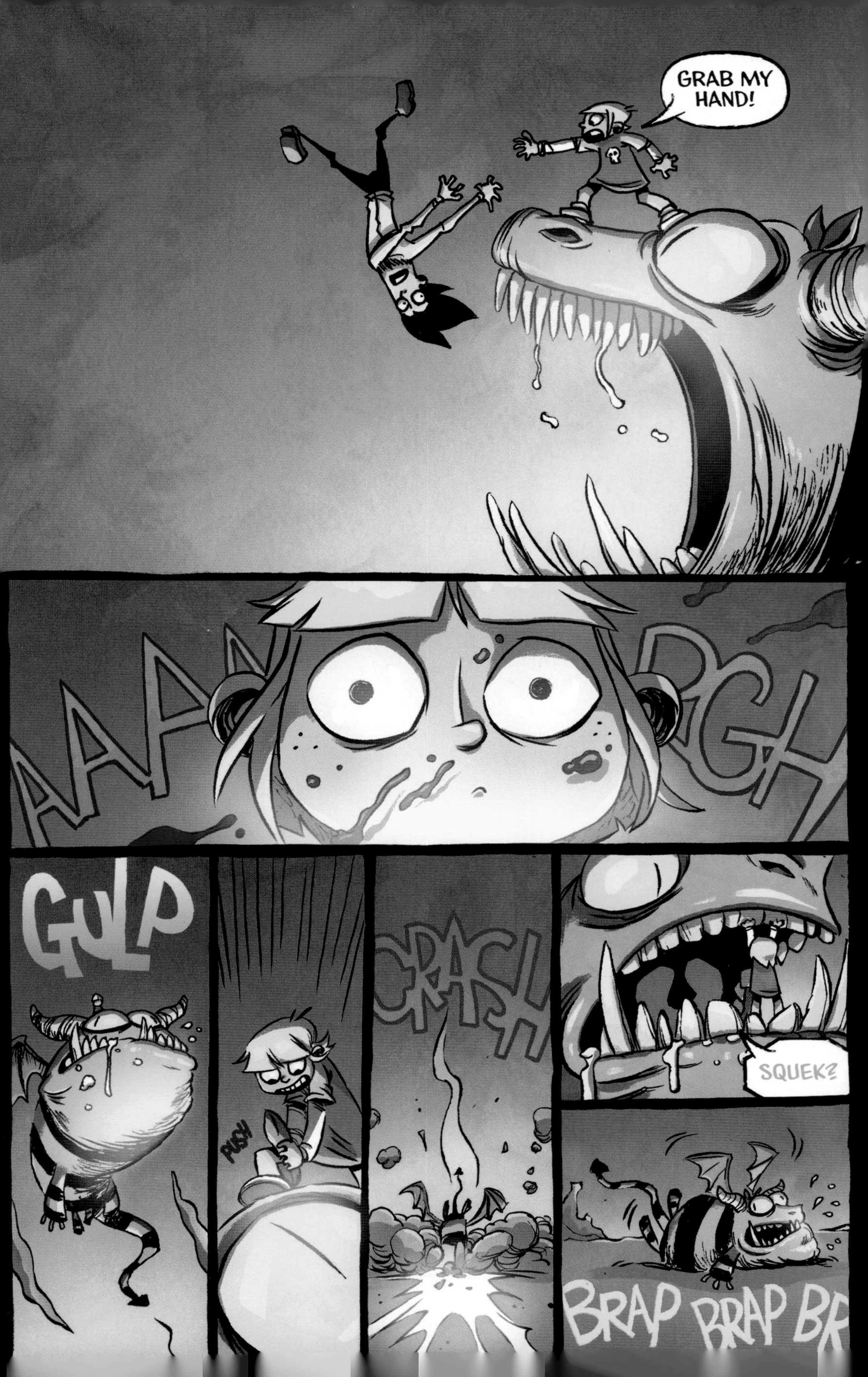
GRAB MY HAND!
AAAARGH
GULP
PUSH
CRASH
SQUEK?
BRAP BRAP BR

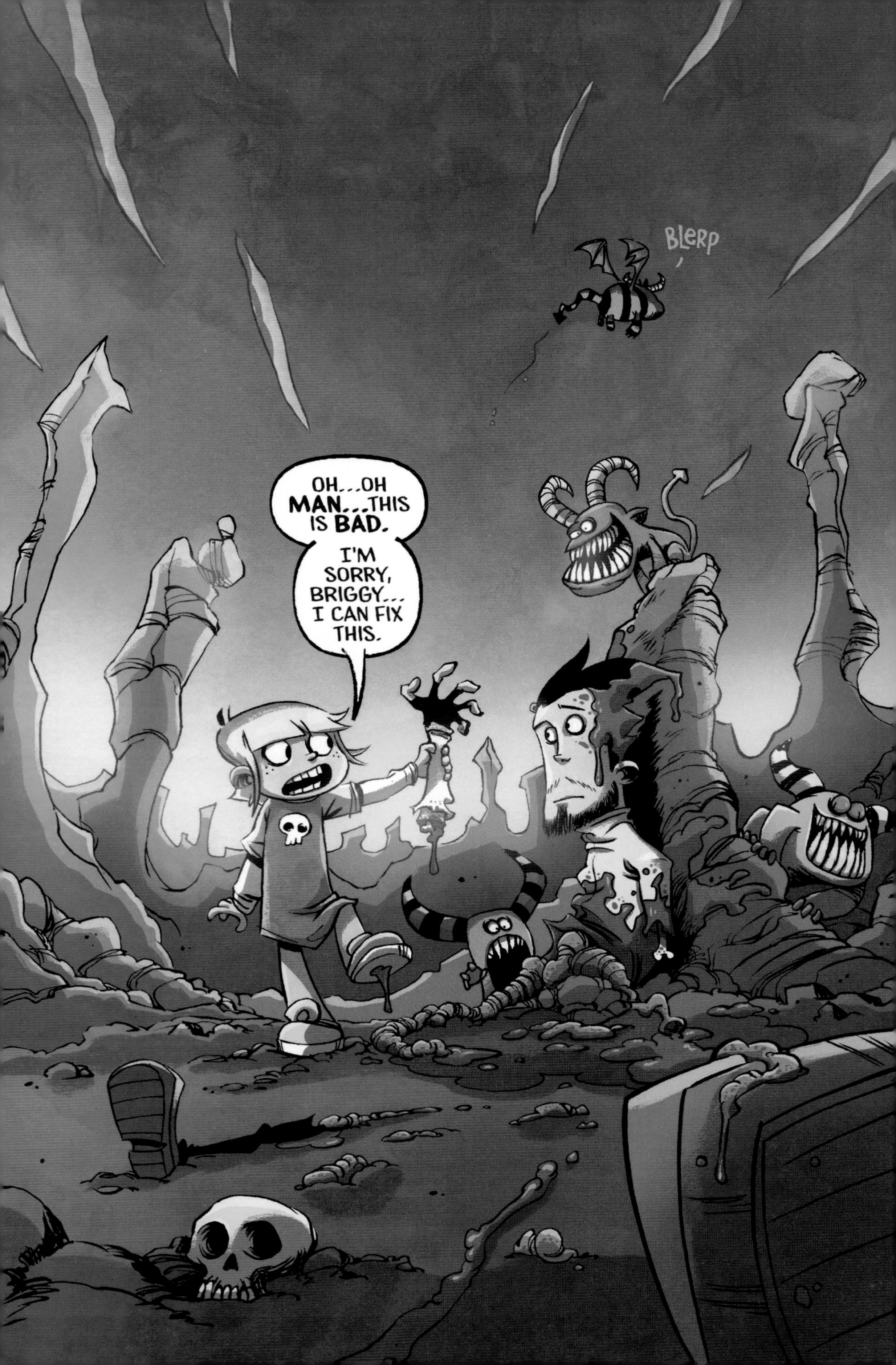
BLERP
OH...OH MAN...THIS IS BAD.
I'M SORRY, BRIGGY... I CAN FIX THIS.

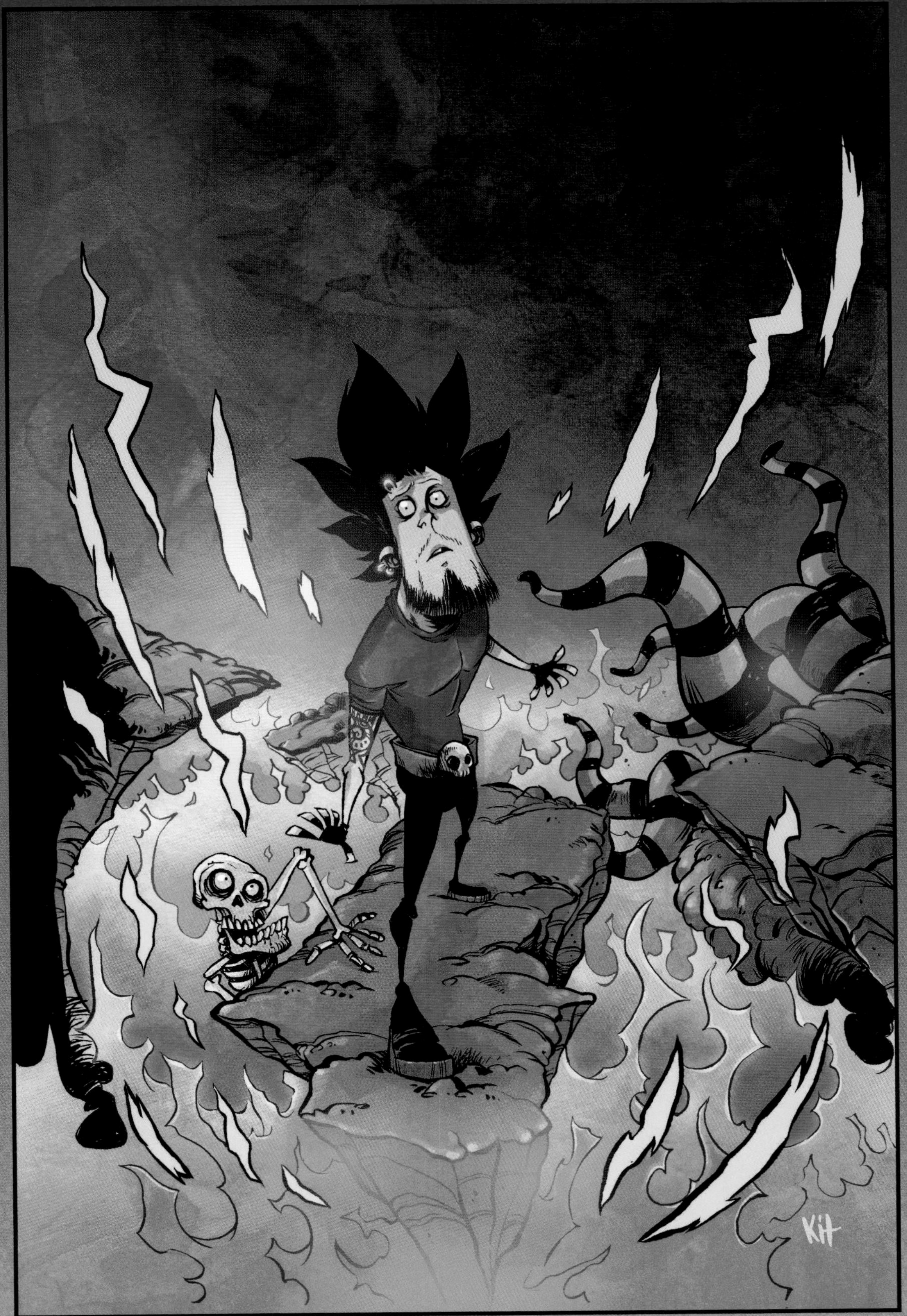
Kit

CHAPTER
THREE

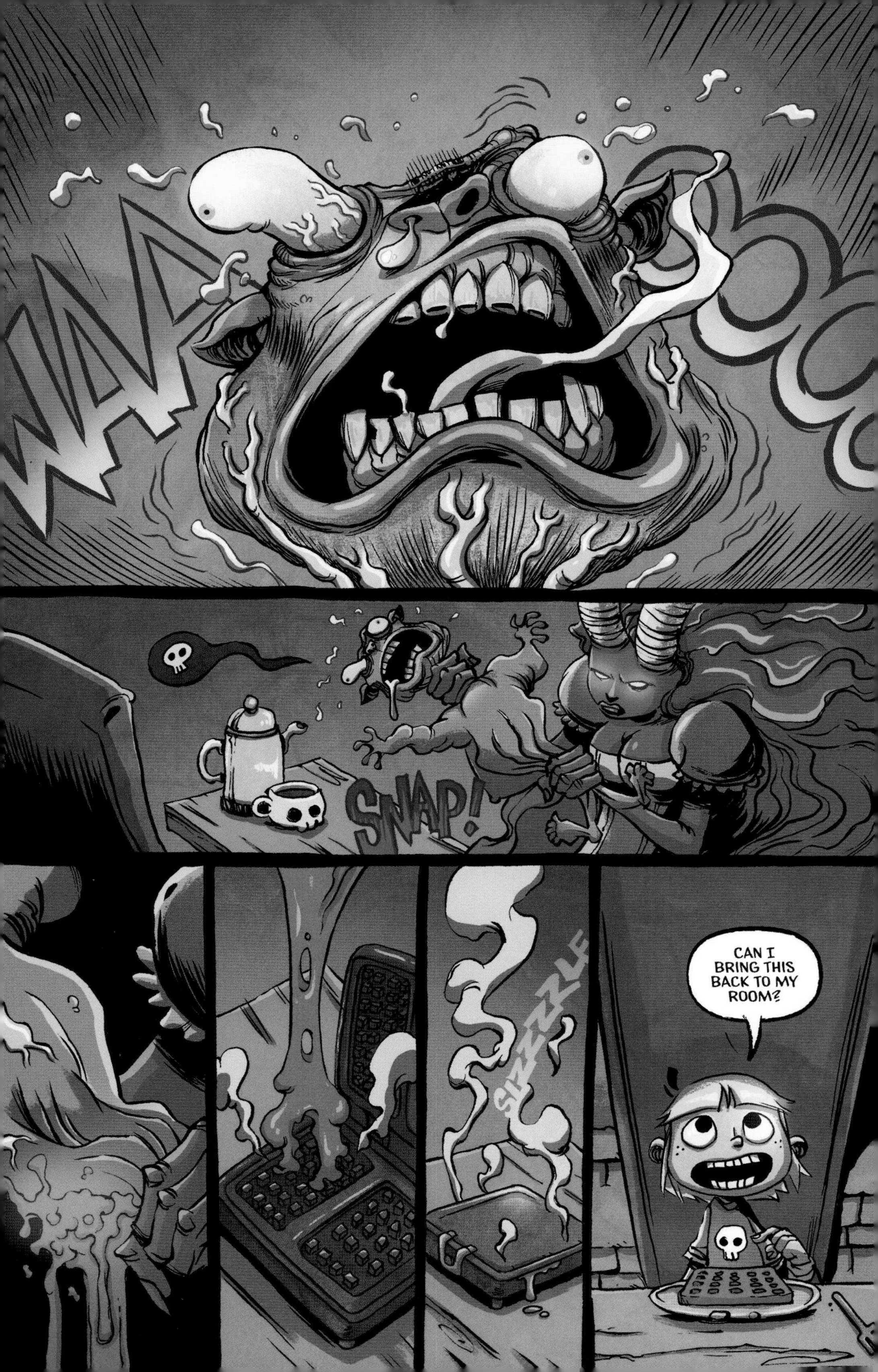
WAA
BOOO
SNAP!
SIZZZZLE
CAN I BRING THIS BACK TO MY ROOM?

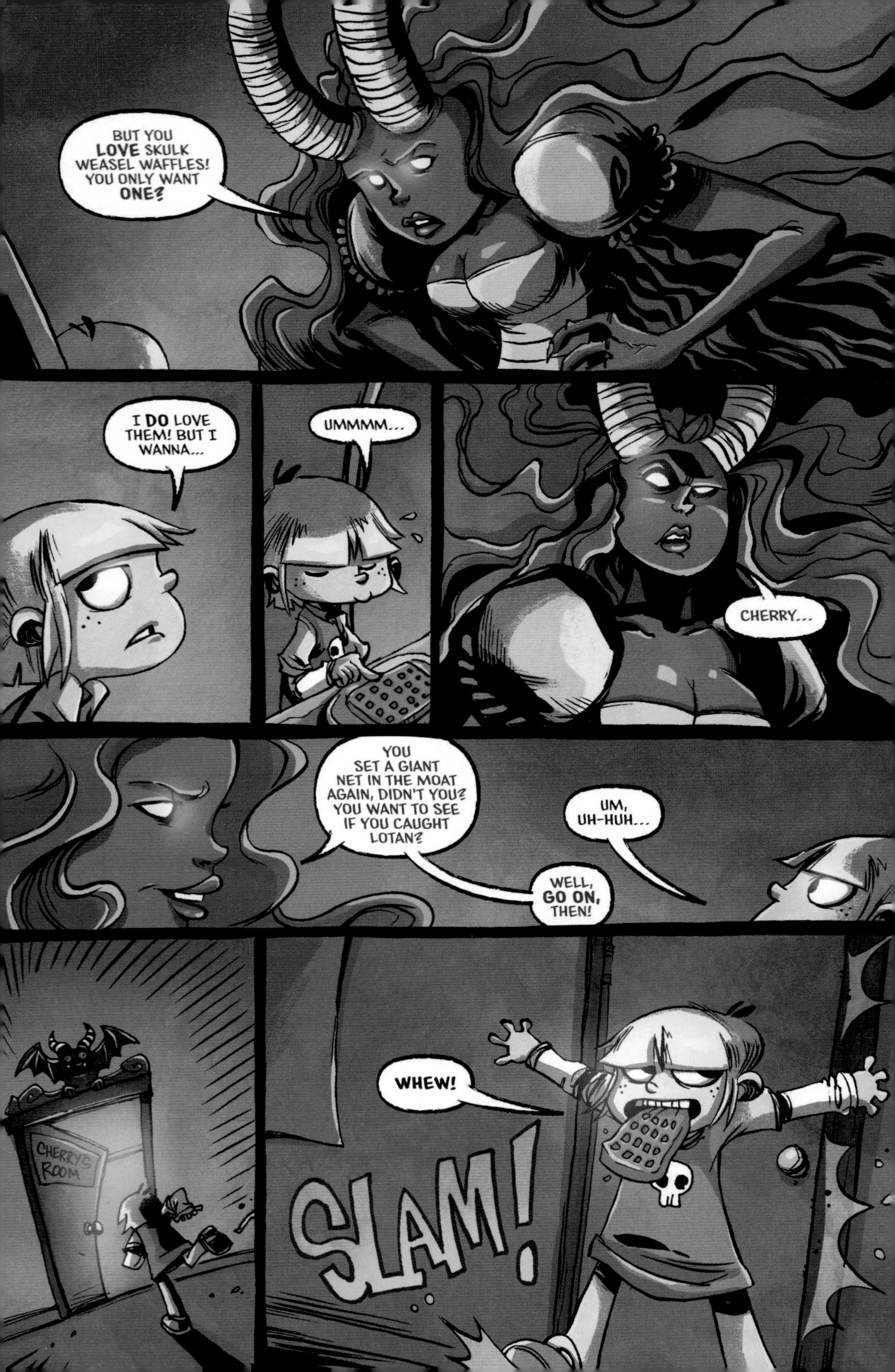
BUT YOU LOVE SKULK WEASEL WAFFLES! YOU ONLY WANT ONE?
I DO LOVE THEM! BUT I WANNA...
UMMMM...
CHERRY...
YOU SET A GIANT NET IN THE MOAT AGAIN, DIDN'T YOU? YOU WANT TO SEE IF YOU CAUGHT LOTAN?
UM, UH-HUH...
WELL, GO ON, THEN!
CHERRY'S ROOM
WHEW!
SLAM!

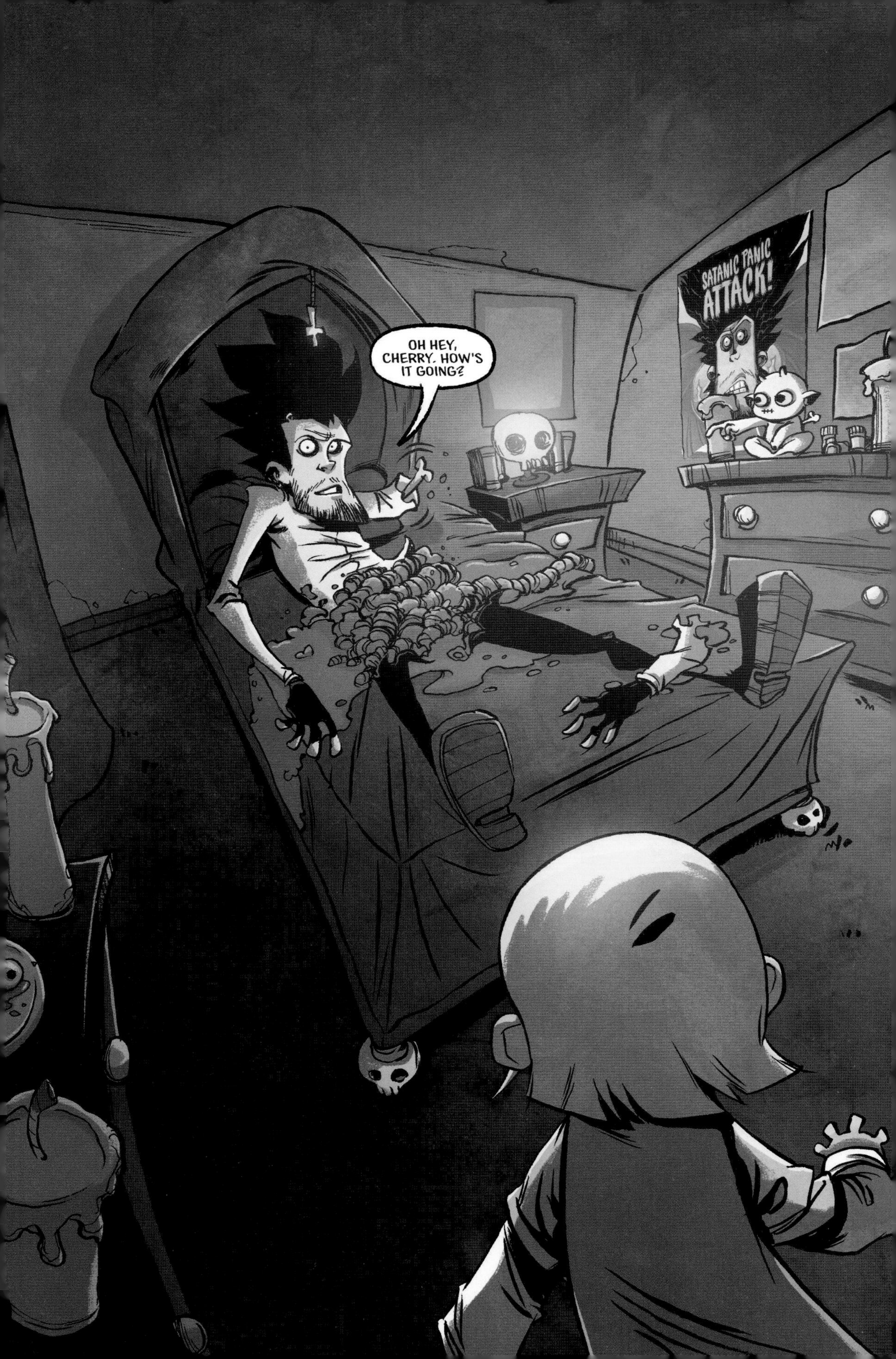
OH HEY, CHERRY. HOW'S IT GOING?
SATANIC PANIC ATTACK!

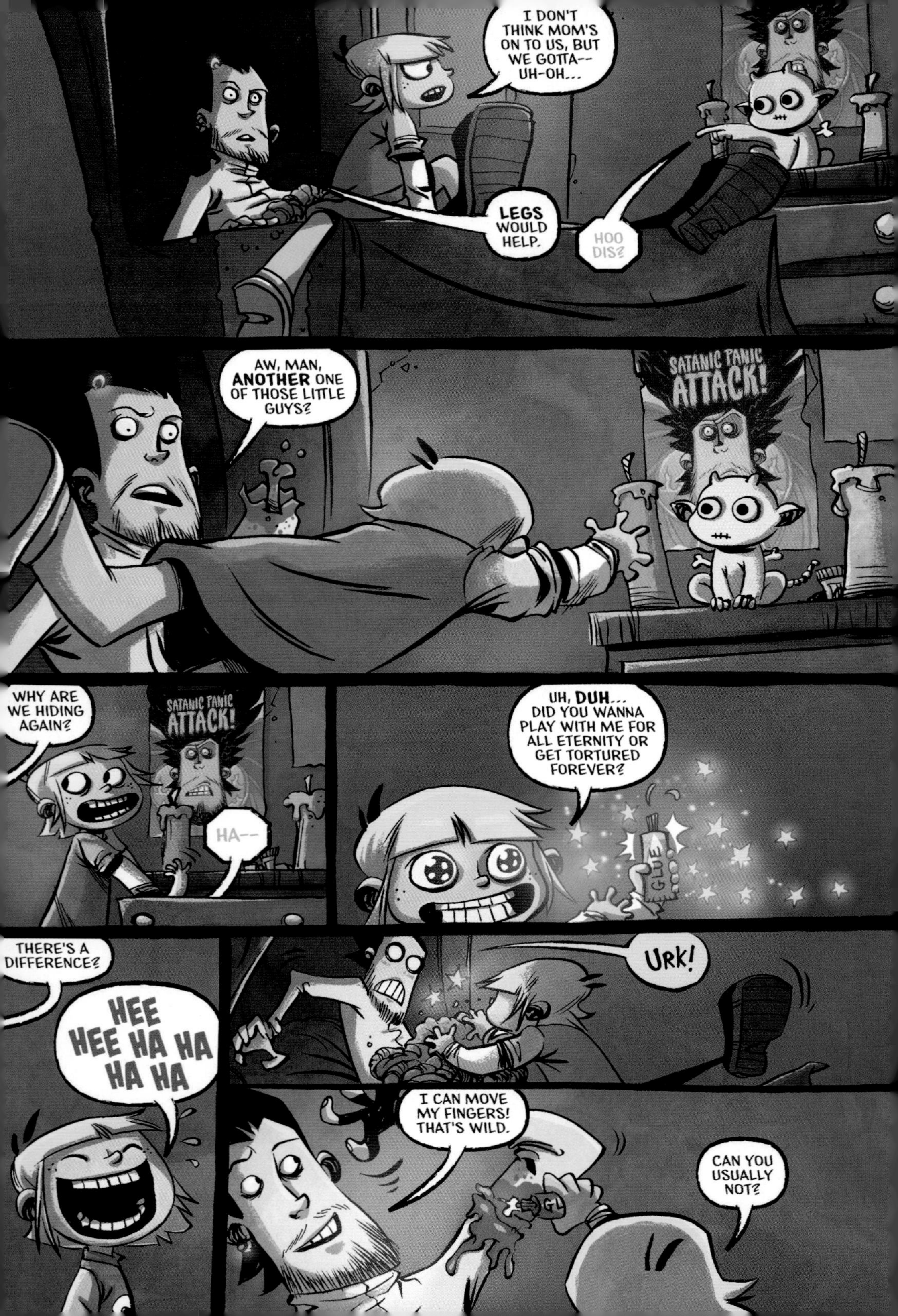
I DON'T THINK MOM'S ON TO US, BUT WE GOTTA-- UH-OH...
LEGS WOULD HELP.
HOO DIS?
AW, MAN, ANOTHER ONE OF THOSE LITTLE GUYS?
SATANIC PANIC ATTACK!
WHY ARE WE HIDING AGAIN?
SATANIC PANIC ATTACK!
HA--
UH, DUH... DID YOU WANNA PLAY WITH ME FOR ALL ETERNITY OR GET TORTURED FOREVER?
GLUE
THERE'S A DIFFERENCE?
HEE HEE HA HA HA HA
URK!
I CAN MOVE MY FINGERS! THAT'S WILD.
CAN YOU USUALLY NOT?

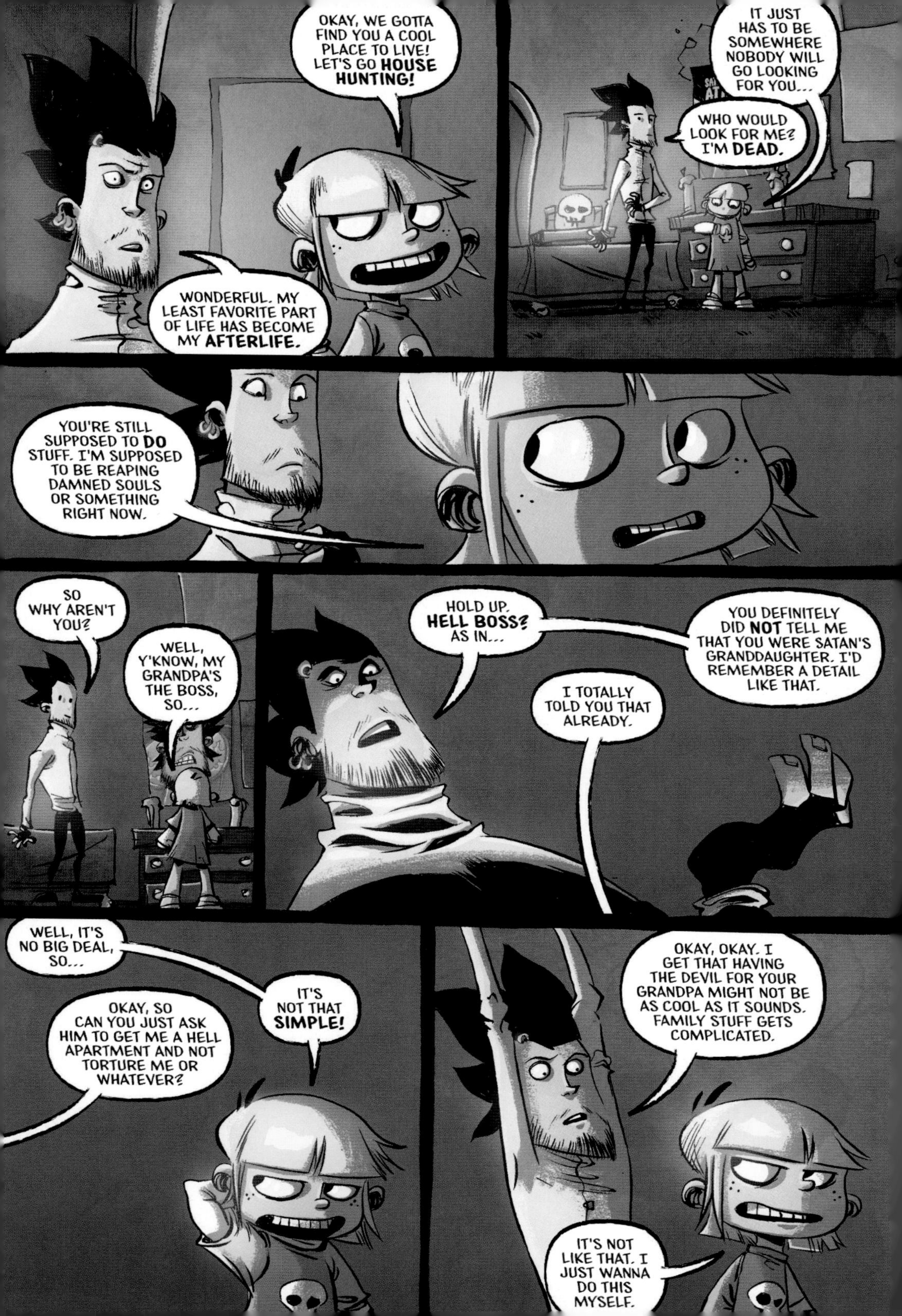

OKAY, WE GOTTA FIND YOU A COOL PLACE TO LIVE! LET'S GO HOUSE HUNTING!
WONDERFUL. MY LEAST FAVORITE PART OF LIFE HAS BECOME MY AFTERLIFE.
IT JUST HAS TO BE SOMEWHERE NOBODY WILL GO LOOKING FOR YOU...
WHO WOULD LOOK FOR ME? I'M DEAD.
YOU'RE STILL SUPPOSED TO DO STUFF. I'M SUPPOSED TO BE REAPING DAMNED SOULS OR SOMETHING RIGHT NOW.
SO WHY AREN'T YOU?
WELL, Y'KNOW, MY GRANDPA'S THE BOSS, SO...
HOLD UP. HELL BOSS? AS IN...
YOU DEFINITELY DID NOT TELL ME THAT YOU WERE SATAN'S GRANDDAUGHTER. I'D REMEMBER A DETAIL LIKE THAT.
I TOTALLY TOLD YOU THAT ALREADY.
WELL, IT'S NO BIG DEAL, SO...
OKAY, SO CAN YOU JUST ASK HIM TO GET ME A HELL APARTMENT AND NOT TORTURE ME OR WHATEVER?
IT'S NOT THAT SIMPLE!
OKAY, OKAY. I GET THAT HAVING THE DEVIL FOR YOUR GRANDPA MIGHT NOT BE AS COOL AS IT SOUNDS. FAMILY STUFF GETS COMPLICATED.
IT'S NOT LIKE THAT. I JUST WANNA DO THIS MYSELF.

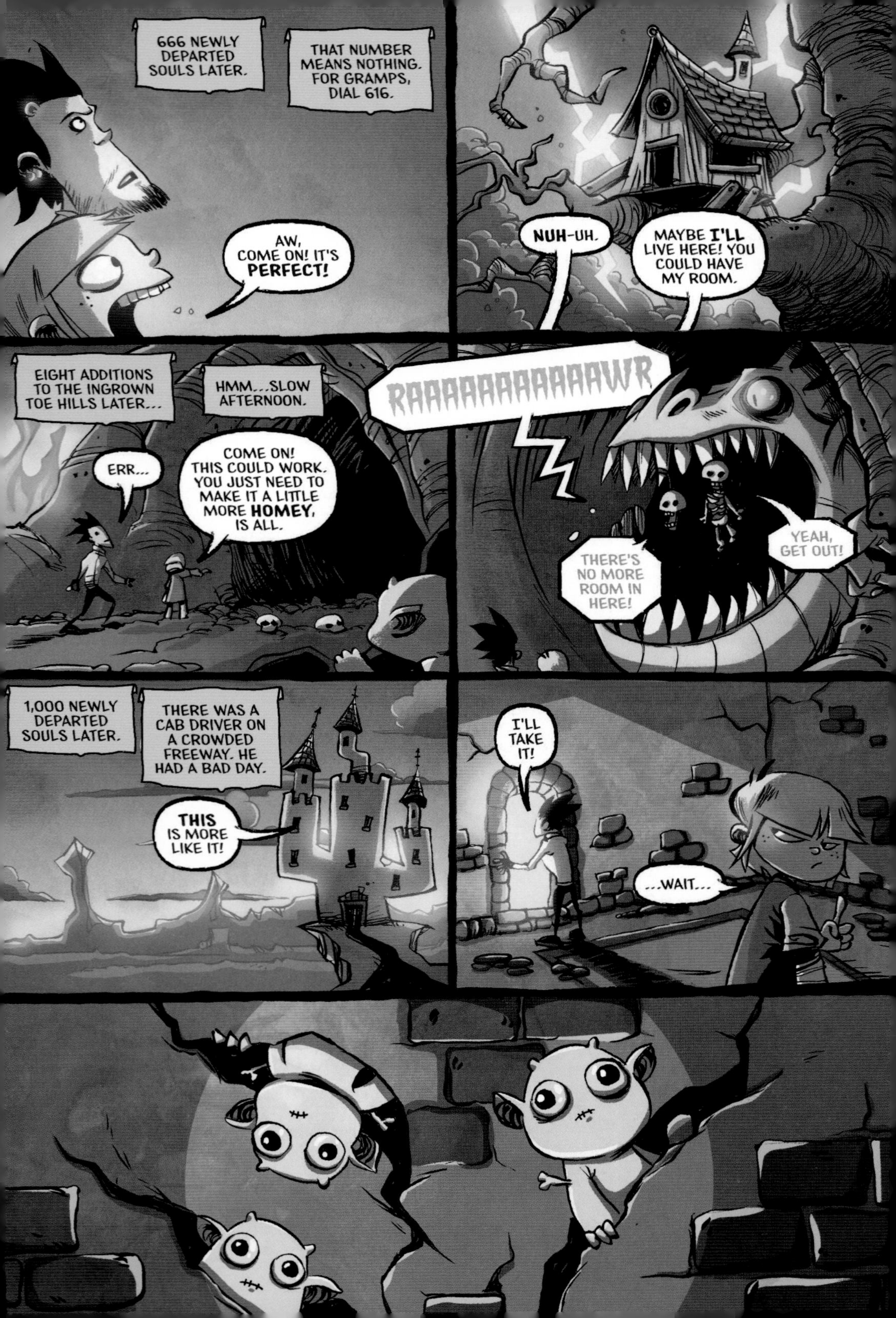

666 NEWLY DEPARTED SOULS LATER.
THAT NUMBER MEANS NOTHING. FOR GRAMPS, DIAL 616.
AW, COME ON! IT'S **PERFECT!**
MAYBE **I'LL** LIVE HERE! YOU COULD HAVE MY ROOM.
NUH-UH.
EIGHT ADDITIONS TO THE INGROWN TOE HILLS LATER...
HMM...SLOW AFTERNOON.
ERR...
COME ON! THIS COULD WORK. YOU JUST NEED TO MAKE IT A LITTLE MORE **HOMEY**, IS ALL.
RAAAAAAAAAAAWR
THERE'S NO MORE ROOM IN HERE!
YEAH, GET OUT!
1,000 NEWLY DEPARTED SOULS LATER.
THERE WAS A CAB DRIVER ON A CROWDED FREEWAY. HE HAD A BAD DAY.
THIS IS MORE LIKE IT!
I'LL TAKE IT!
...WAIT...

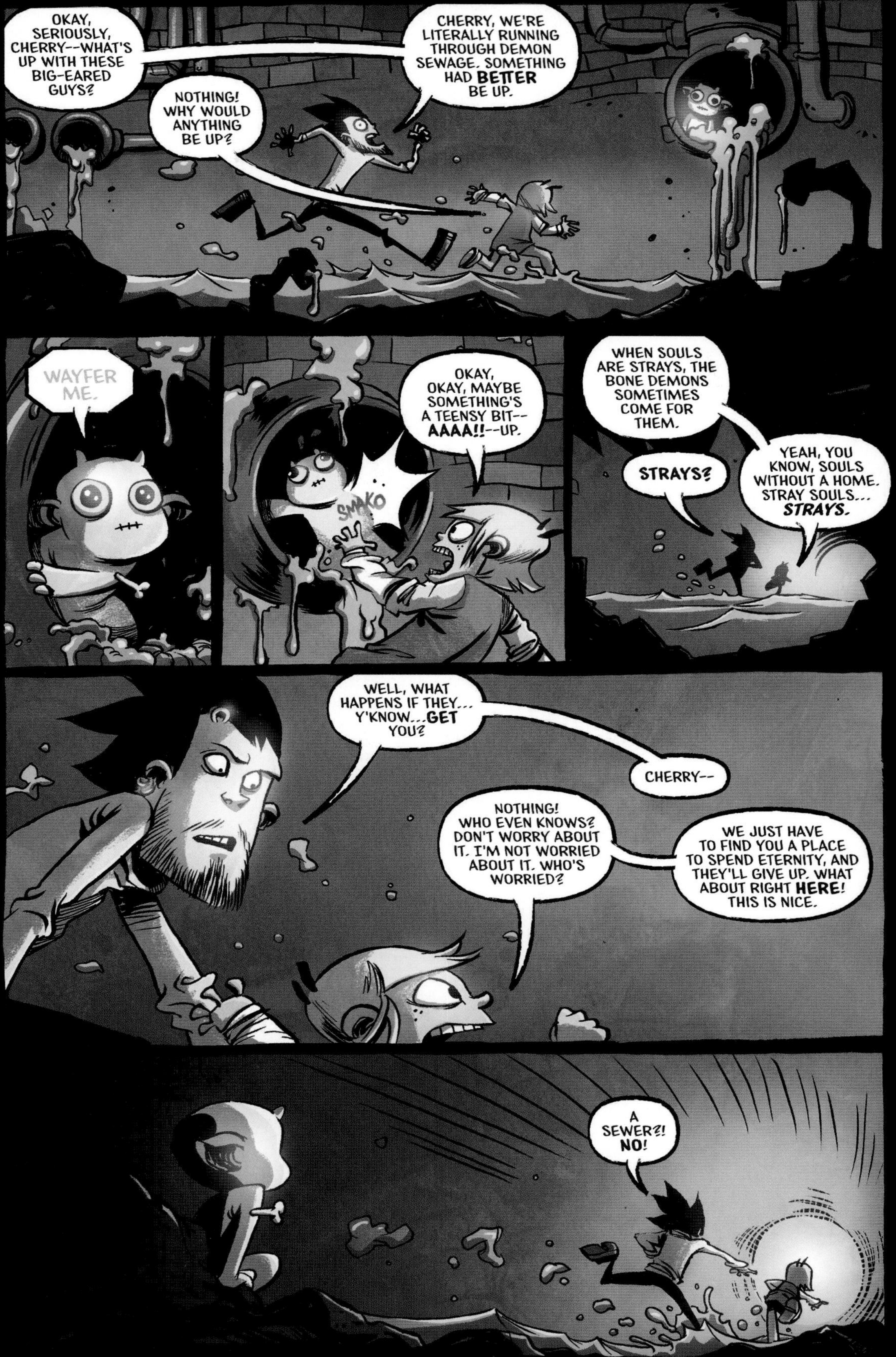
OKAY, SERIOUSLY, CHERRY--WHAT'S UP WITH THESE BIG-EARED GUYS?
NOTHING! WHY WOULD ANYTHING BE UP?
CHERRY, WE'RE LITERALLY RUNNING THROUGH DEMON SEWAGE. SOMETHING HAD BETTER BE UP.
WAYFER ME.
OKAY, OKAY, MAYBE SOMETHING'S A TEENSY BIT-- AAAA!!--UP.
SMAKO
WHEN SOULS ARE STRAYS, THE BONE DEMONS SOMETIMES COME FOR THEM.
STRAYS?
YEAH, YOU KNOW, SOULS WITHOUT A HOME. STRAY SOULS... STRAYS.
WELL, WHAT HAPPENS IF THEY... Y'KNOW...GET YOU?
CHERRY--
NOTHING! WHO EVEN KNOWS? DON'T WORRY ABOUT IT. I'M NOT WORRIED ABOUT IT. WHO'S WORRIED?
WE JUST HAVE TO FIND YOU A PLACE TO SPEND ETERNITY, AND THEY'LL GIVE UP. WHAT ABOUT RIGHT HERE! THIS IS NICE.
A SEWER?! NO!

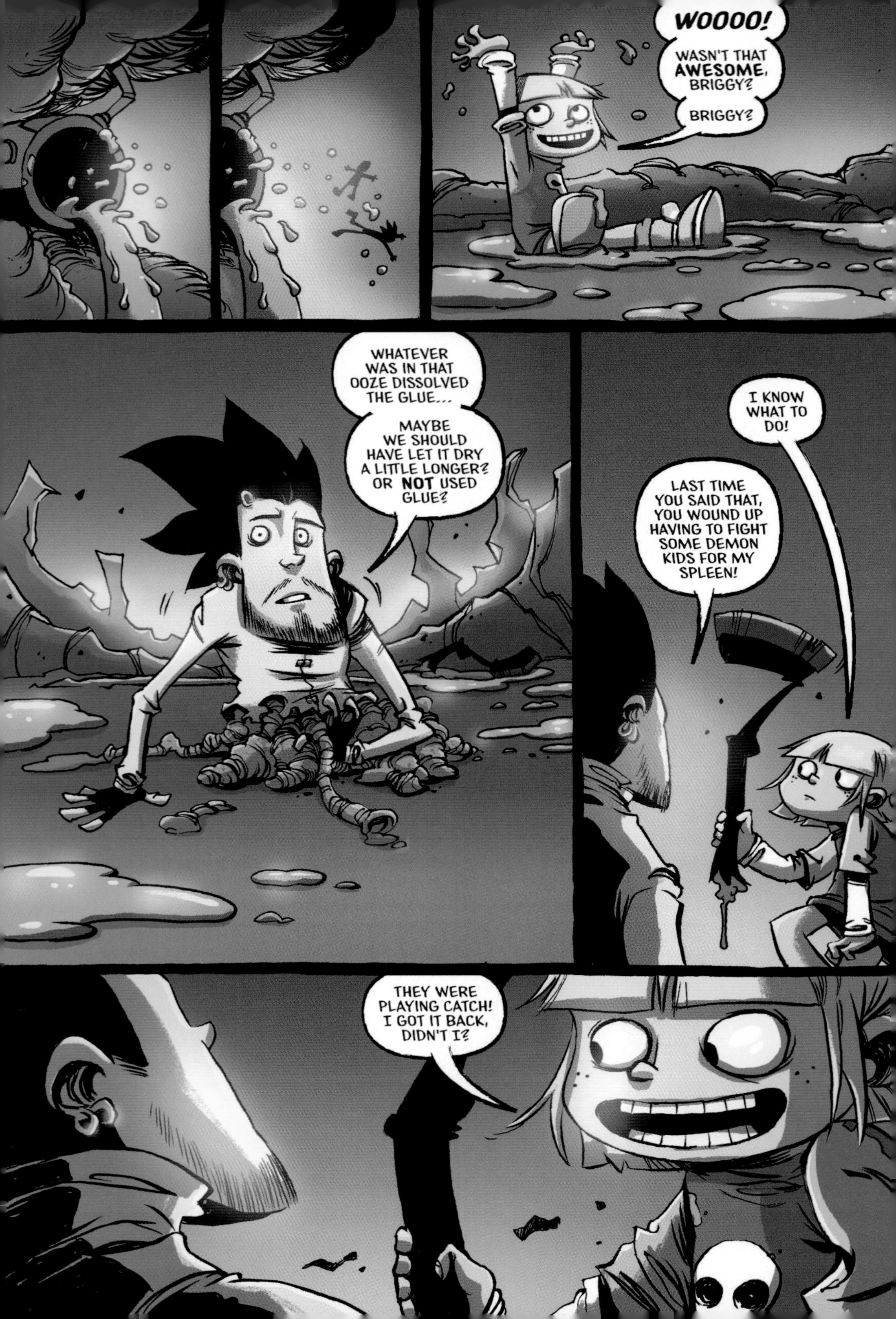

WOOOO!
WASN'T THAT AWESOME, BRIGGY?
BRIGGY?
WHATEVER WAS IN THAT OOZE DISSOLVED THE GLUE...
MAYBE WE SHOULD HAVE LET IT DRY A LITTLE LONGER? OR NOT USED GLUE?
I KNOW WHAT TO DO!
LAST TIME YOU SAID THAT, YOU WOUND UP HAVING TO FIGHT SOME DEMON KIDS FOR MY SPLEEN!
THEY WERE PLAYING CATCH! I GOT IT BACK, DIDN'T I?

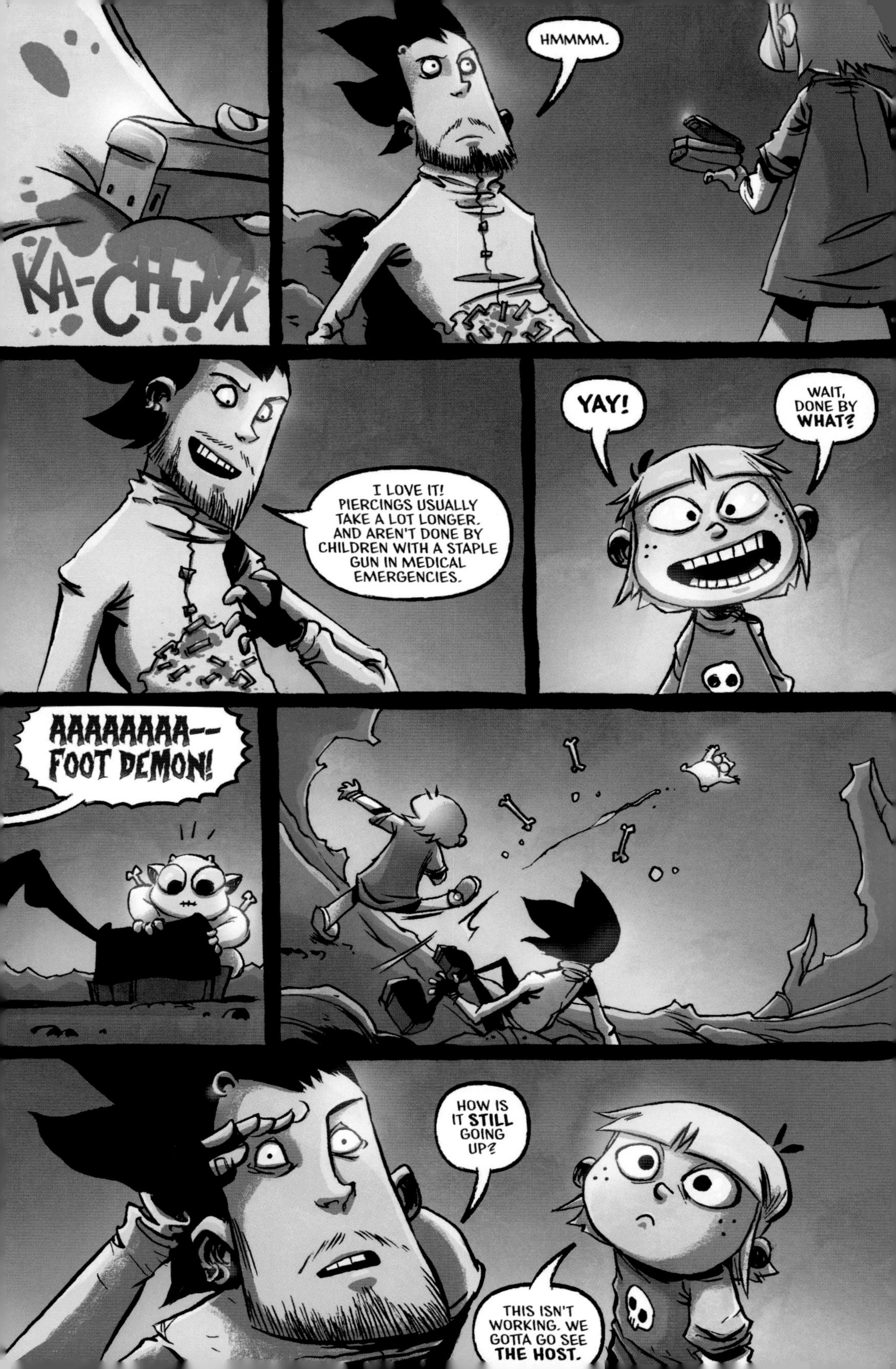
KA-CHUNK
HMMMM.
I LOVE IT! PIERCINGS USUALLY TAKE A LOT LONGER, AND AREN'T DONE BY CHILDREN WITH A STAPLE GUN IN MEDICAL EMERGENCIES.
YAY!
WAIT, DONE BY WHAT?
AAAAAAA--
FOOT DEMON!
HOW IS IT STILL GOING UP?
THIS ISN'T WORKING. WE GOTTA GO SEE THE HOST.

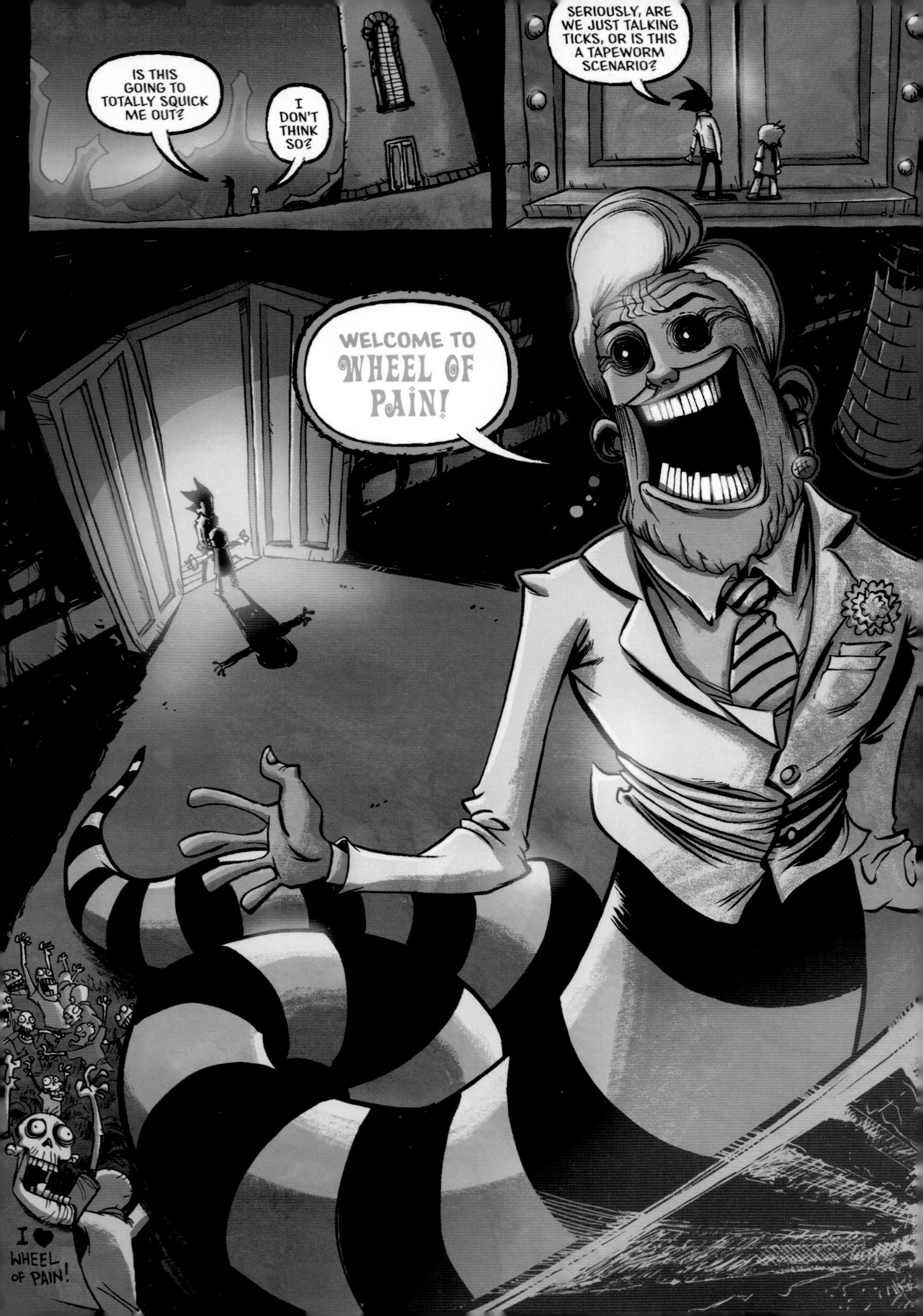
IS THIS GOING TO TOTALLY SQUICK ME OUT?
I DON'T THINK SO?
SERIOUSLY, ARE WE JUST TALKING TICKS, OR IS THIS A TAPEWORM SCENARIO?
WELCOME TO WHEEL OF PAIN!
I ♥ WHEEL OF PAIN!

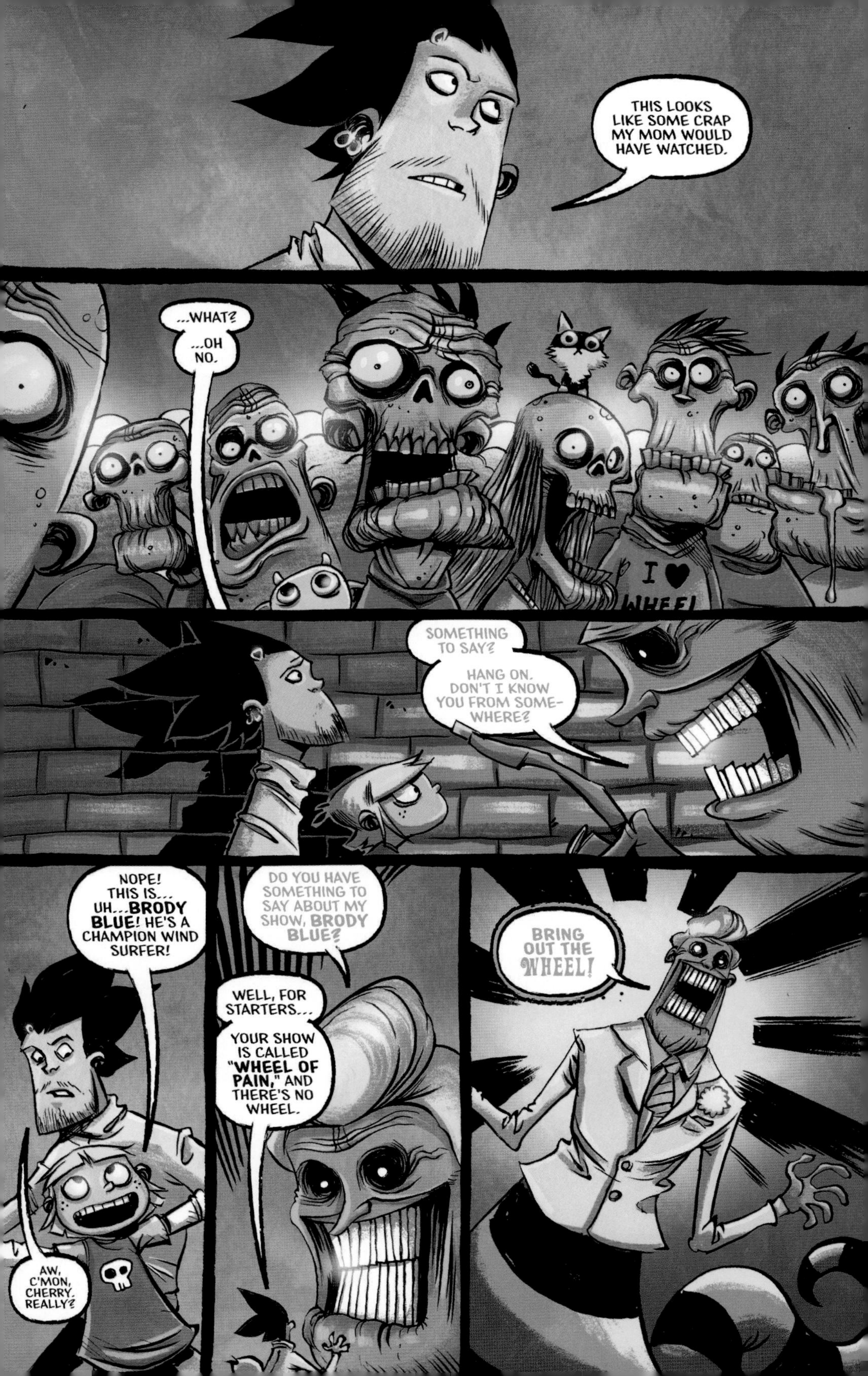
THIS LOOKS LIKE SOME CRAP MY MOM WOULD HAVE WATCHED.
...WHAT?
...OH NO.
I ♥ WHEEL
SOMETHING TO SAY?
HANG ON. DON'T I KNOW YOU FROM SOME-WHERE?
NOPE! THIS IS... UH...BRODY BLUE! HE'S A CHAMPION WIND SURFER!
AW, C'MON, CHERRY. REALLY?
DO YOU HAVE SOMETHING TO SAY ABOUT MY SHOW, BRODY BLUE?
WELL, FOR STARTERS...
YOUR SHOW IS CALLED "WHEEL OF PAIN," AND THERE'S NO WHEEL.
BRING OUT THE WHEEL!

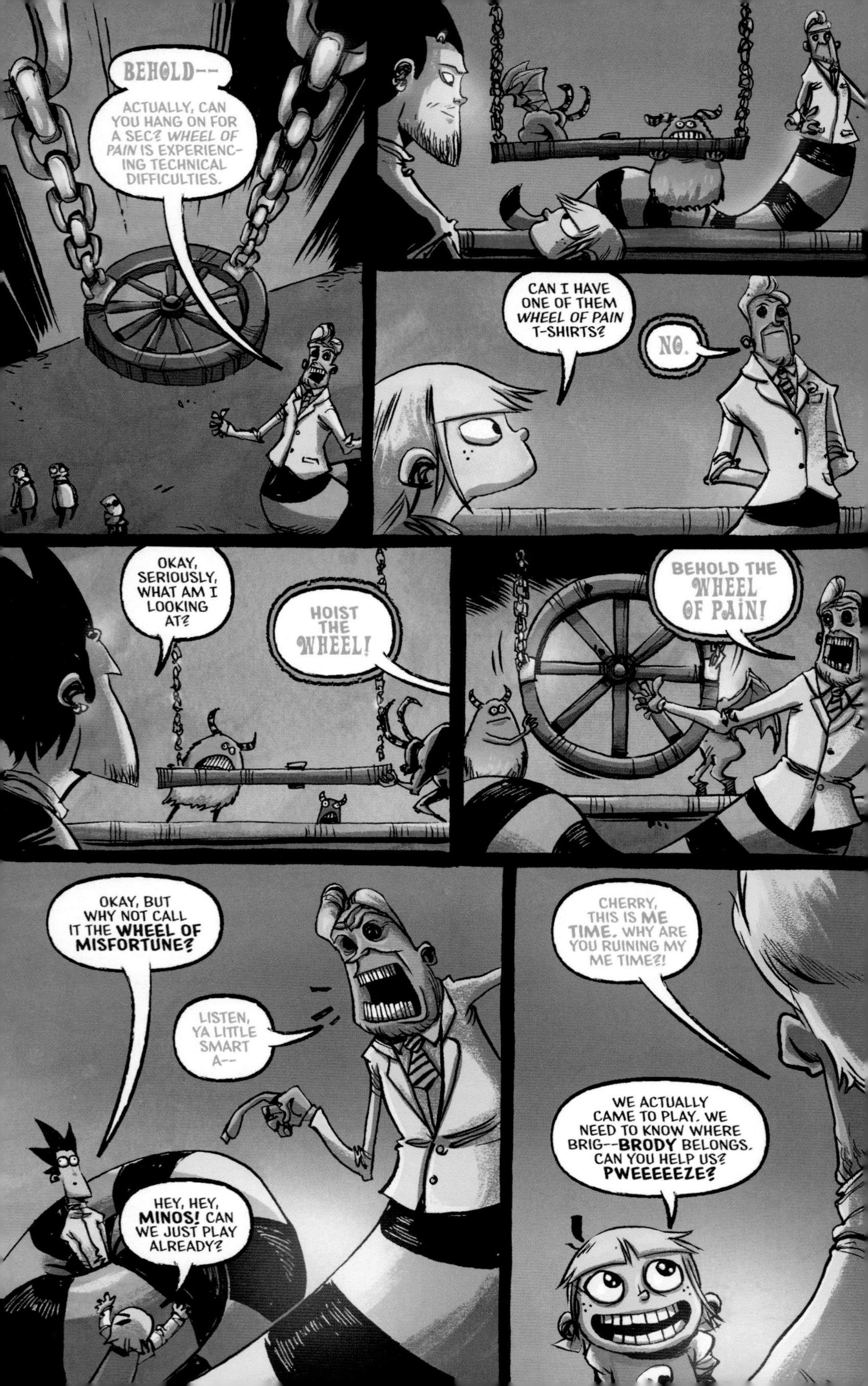
BEHOLD--
ACTUALLY, CAN YOU HANG ON FOR A SEC? WHEEL OF PAIN IS EXPERIENCING TECHNICAL DIFFICULTIES.
CAN I HAVE ONE OF THEM WHEEL OF PAIN T-SHIRTS?
NO.
OKAY, SERIOUSLY, WHAT AM I LOOKING AT?
HOIST THE WHEEL!
BEHOLD THE WHEEL OF PAIN!
OKAY, BUT WHY NOT CALL IT THE WHEEL OF MISFORTUNE?
LISTEN, YA LITTLE SMART A--
HEY, HEY, MINOS! CAN WE JUST PLAY ALREADY?
CHERRY, THIS IS ME TIME. WHY ARE YOU RUINING MY ME TIME?!
WE ACTUALLY CAME TO PLAY. WE NEED TO KNOW WHERE BRIG--BRODY BELONGS. CAN YOU HELP US? PWEEEEEZE?

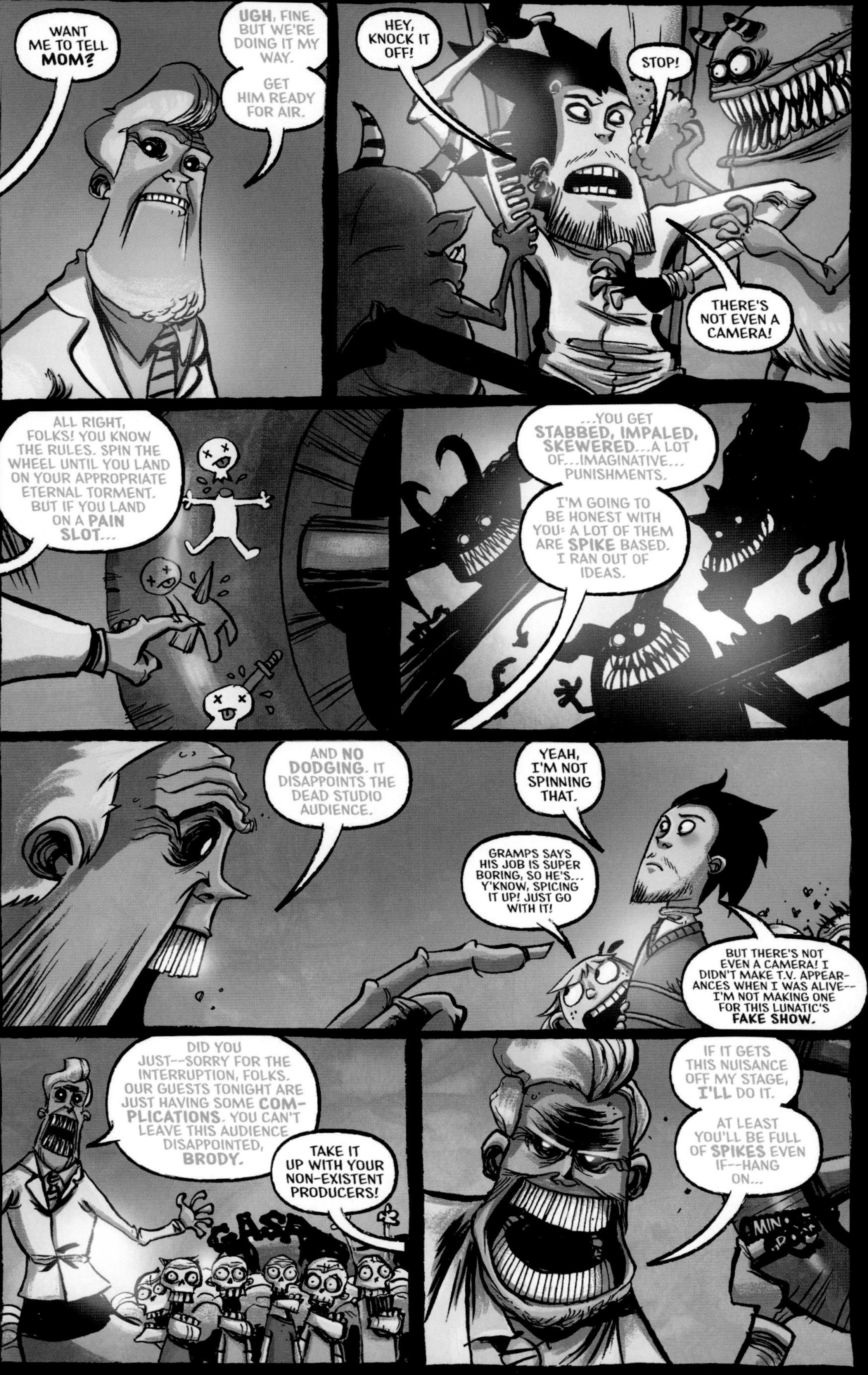
WANT ME TO TELL MOM?
UGH, FINE. BUT WE'RE DOING IT MY WAY.
GET HIM READY FOR AIR.
HEY, KNOCK IT OFF!
STOP!
THERE'S NOT EVEN A CAMERA!
ALL RIGHT, FOLKS! YOU KNOW THE RULES. SPIN THE WHEEL UNTIL YOU LAND ON YOUR APPROPRIATE ETERNAL TORMENT. BUT IF YOU LAND ON A PAIN SLOT...
...YOU GET STABBED, IMPALED, SKEWERED... A LOT OF... IMAGINATIVE... PUNISHMENTS.
I'M GOING TO BE HONEST WITH YOU: A LOT OF THEM ARE SPIKE BASED. I RAN OUT OF IDEAS.
AND NO DODGING. IT DISAPPOINTS THE DEAD STUDIO AUDIENCE.
YEAH, I'M NOT SPINNING THAT.
GRAMPS SAYS HIS JOB IS SUPER BORING, SO HE'S... Y'KNOW, SPICING IT UP! JUST GO WITH IT!
BUT THERE'S NOT EVEN A CAMERA! I DIDN'T MAKE T.V. APPEARANCES WHEN I WAS ALIVE--I'M NOT MAKING ONE FOR THIS LUNATIC'S FAKE SHOW.
DID YOU JUST--SORRY FOR THE INTERRUPTION, FOLKS. OUR GUESTS TONIGHT ARE JUST HAVING SOME COMPLICATIONS. YOU CAN'T LEAVE THIS AUDIENCE DISAPPOINTED, BRODY.
TAKE IT UP WITH YOUR NON-EXISTENT PRODUCERS!
GASP
IF IT GETS THIS NUISANCE OFF MY STAGE, I'LL DO IT.
AT LEAST YOU'LL BE FULL OF SPIKES EVEN IF--HANG ON...

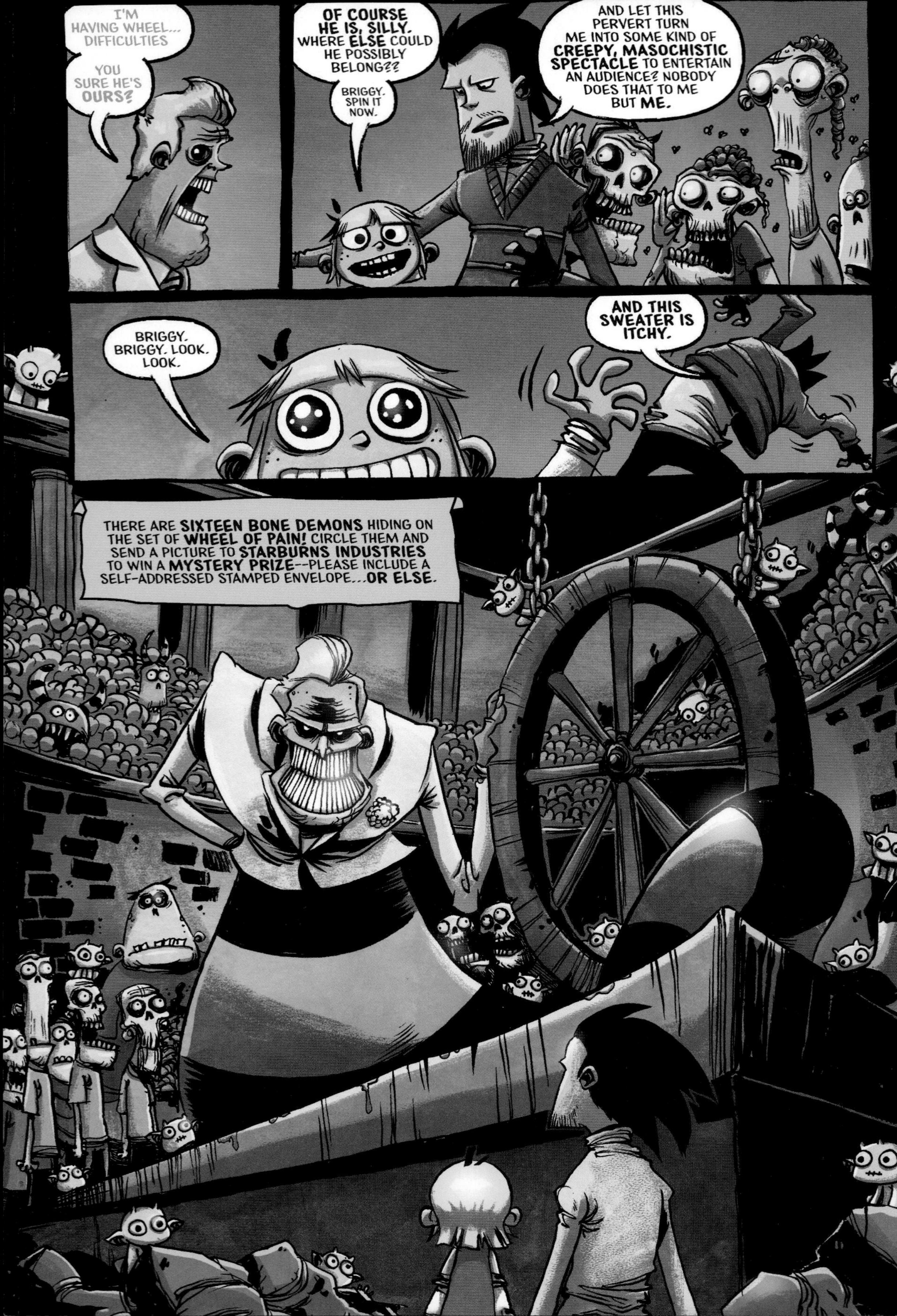

I'M HAVING WHEEL... DIFFICULTIES
YOU SURE HE'S OURS?
OF COURSE HE IS, SILLY. WHERE ELSE COULD HE POSSIBLY BELONG??
BRIGGY. SPIN IT NOW.
AND LET THIS PERVERT TURN ME INTO SOME KIND OF CREEPY, MASOCHISTIC SPECTACLE TO ENTERTAIN AN AUDIENCE? NOBODY DOES THAT TO ME BUT ME.
BRIGGY. BRIGGY. LOOK. LOOK.
AND THIS SWEATER IS ITCHY.
THERE ARE SIXTEEN BONE DEMONS HIDING ON THE SET OF WHEEL OF PAIN! CIRCLE THEM AND SEND A PICTURE TO STARBURNS INDUSTRIES TO WIN A MYSTERY PRIZE--PLEASE INCLUDE A SELF-ADDRESSED STAMPED ENVELOPE...OR ELSE.

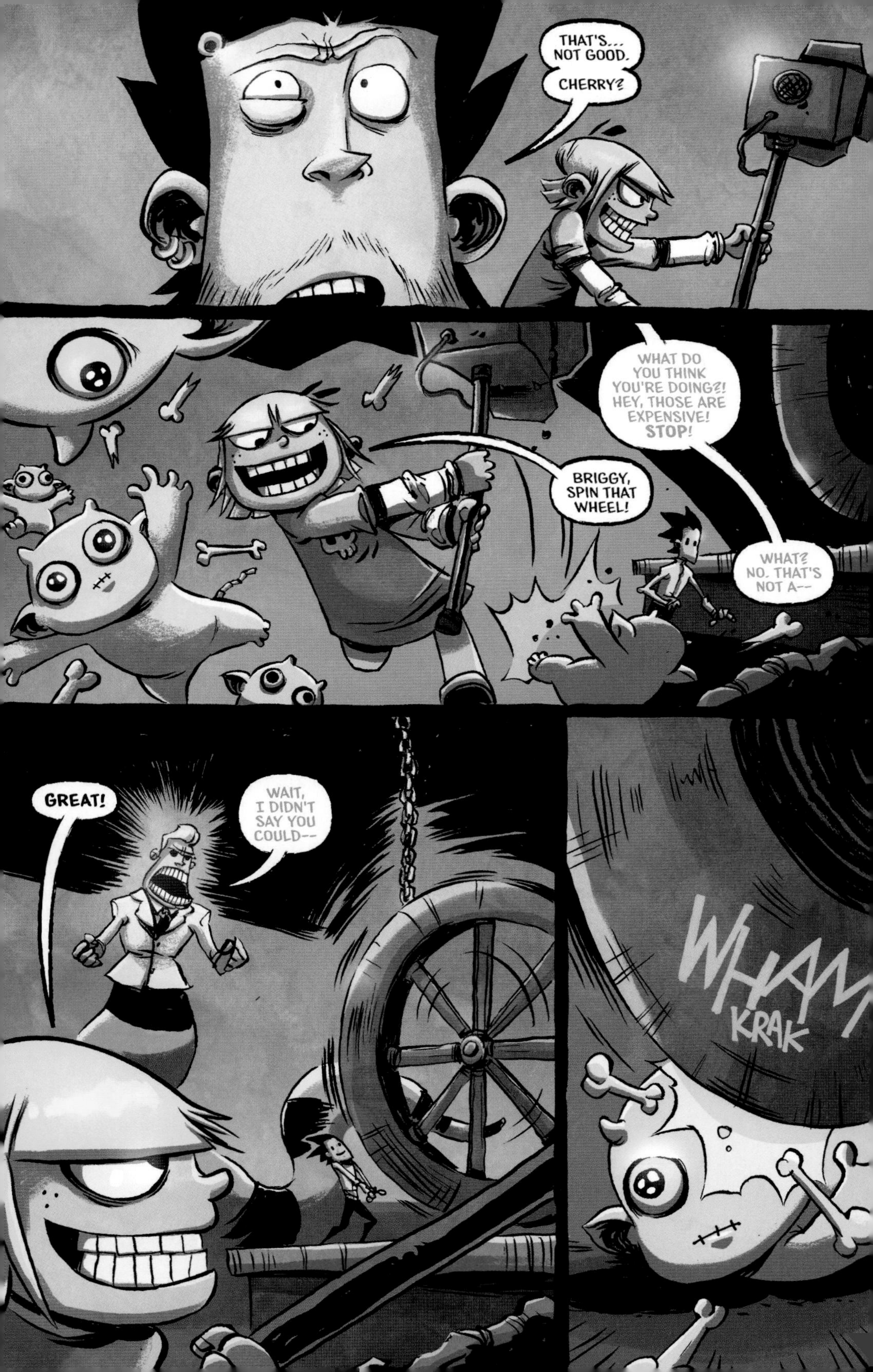
THAT'S... NOT GOOD.
CHERRY?
WHAT DO YOU THINK YOU'RE DOING?! HEY, THOSE ARE EXPENSIVE! STOP!
BRIGGY, SPIN THAT WHEEL!
WHAT? NO. THAT'S NOT A--
GREAT!
WAIT, I DIDN'T SAY YOU COULD--
WHAM
KRAK

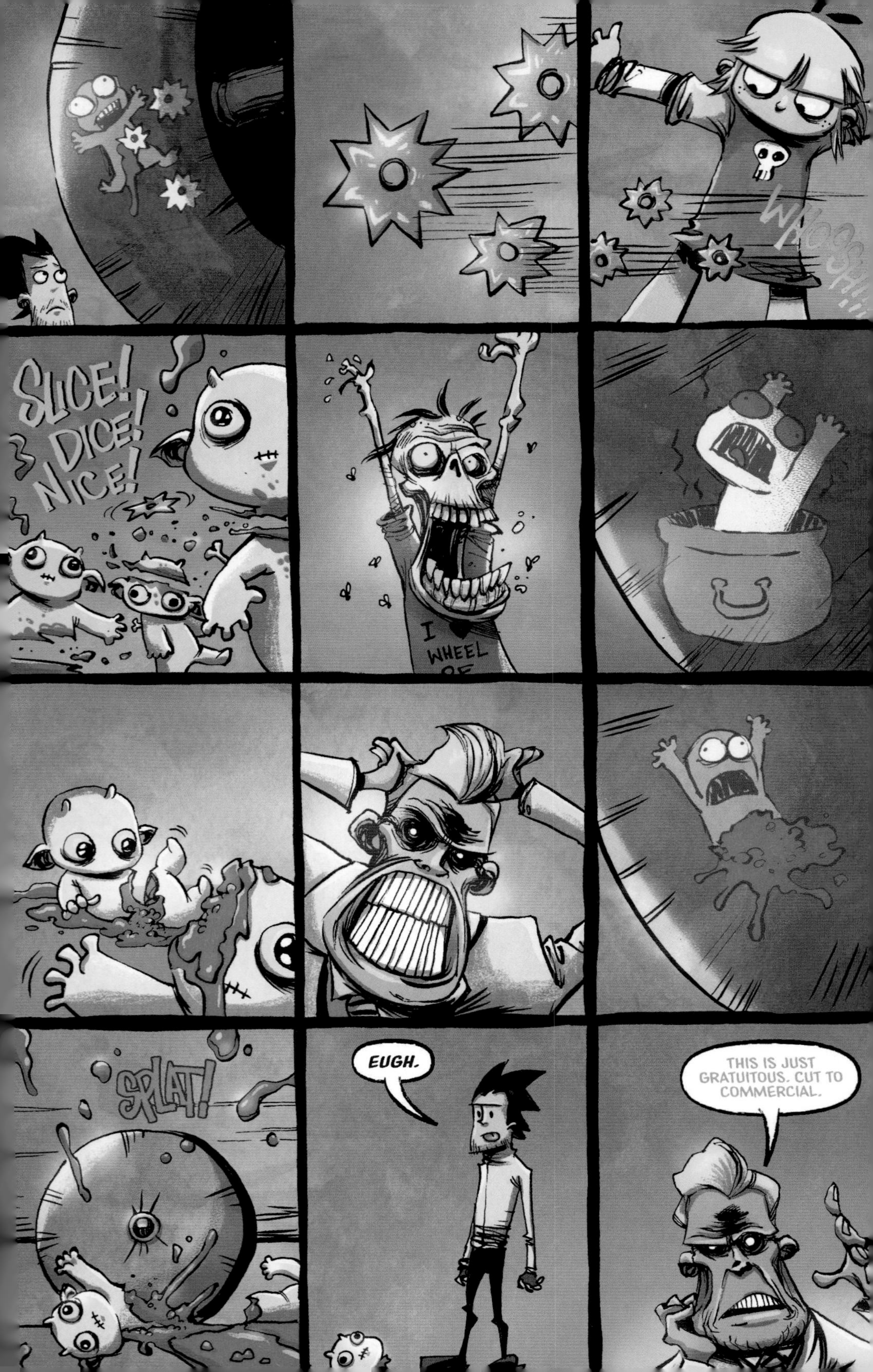
WHOOSH!!!
SLICE!
DICE!
NICE!
I WHEEL OF
SPLAT!
EUGH.
THIS IS JUST GRATUITOUS. CUT TO COMMERCIAL.

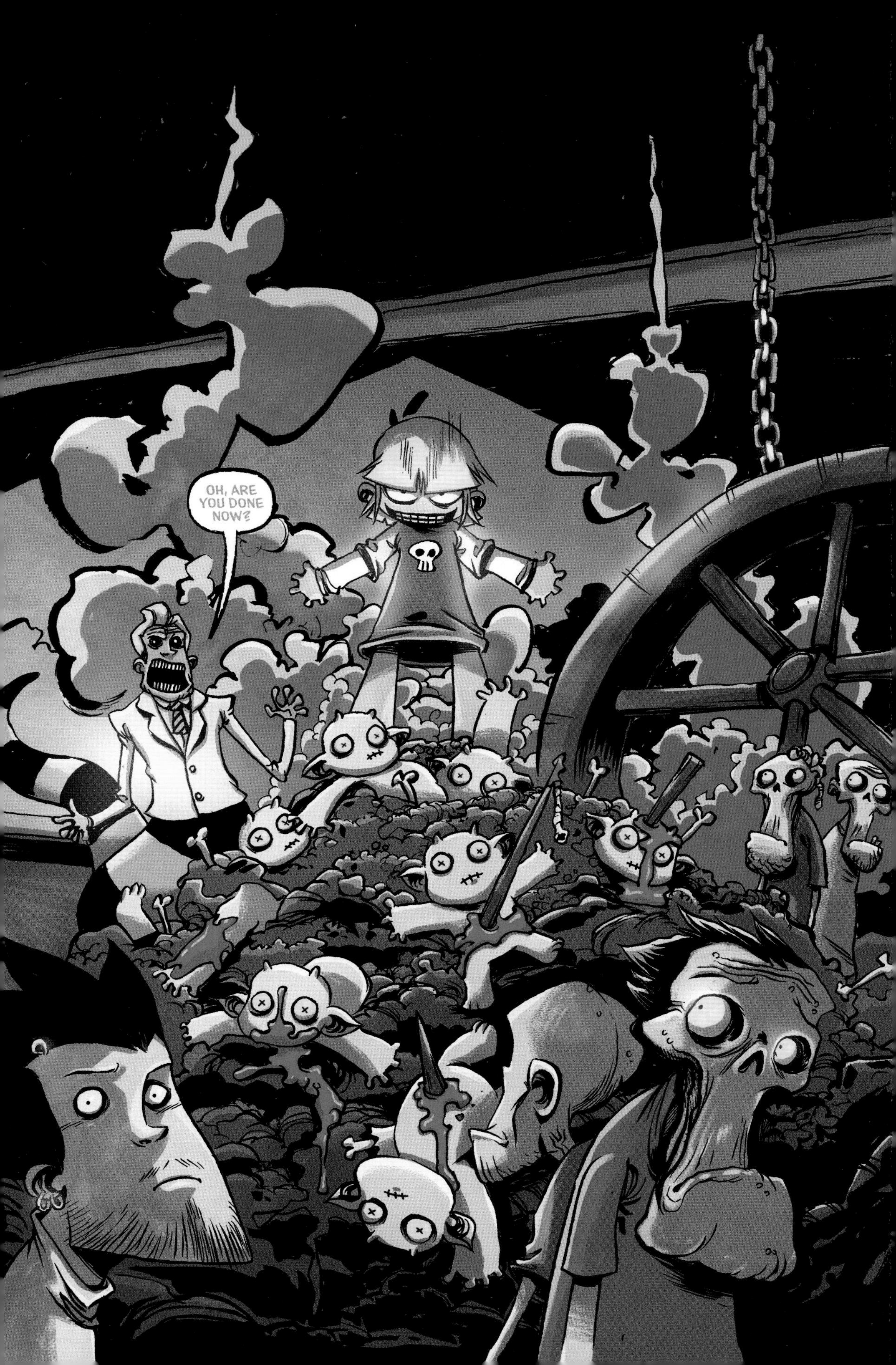
OH, ARE YOU DONE NOW?

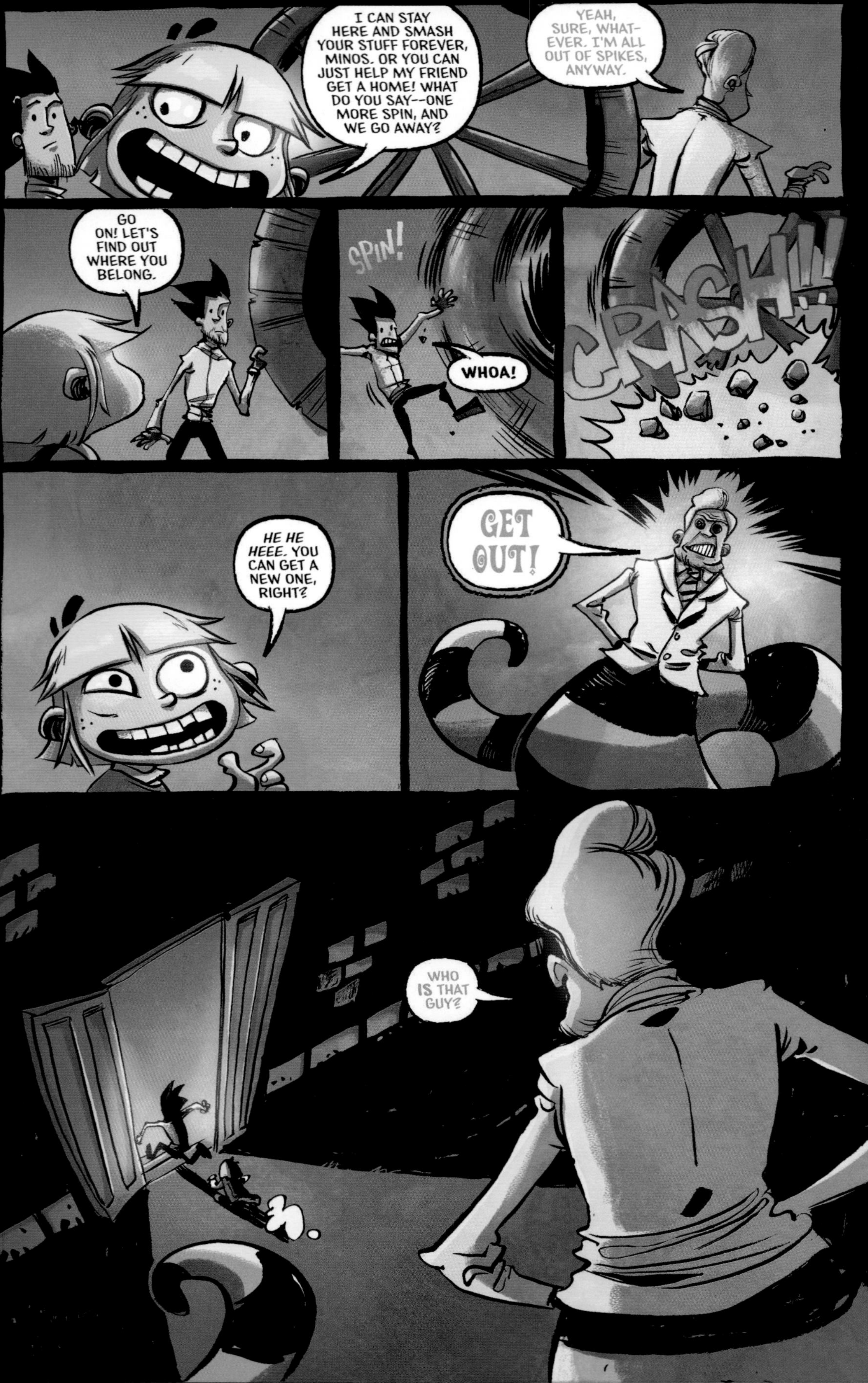
I CAN STAY HERE AND SMASH YOUR STUFF FOREVER, MINOS. OR YOU CAN JUST HELP MY FRIEND GET A HOME! WHAT DO YOU SAY--ONE MORE SPIN, AND WE GO AWAY?
YEAH, SURE, WHAT-EVER. I'M ALL OUT OF SPIKES, ANYWAY.
GO ON! LET'S FIND OUT WHERE YOU BELONG.
SPIN!
WHOA!
CRASH!!!
HE HE HEEE. YOU CAN GET A NEW ONE, RIGHT?
GET OUT!
WHO IS THAT GUY?

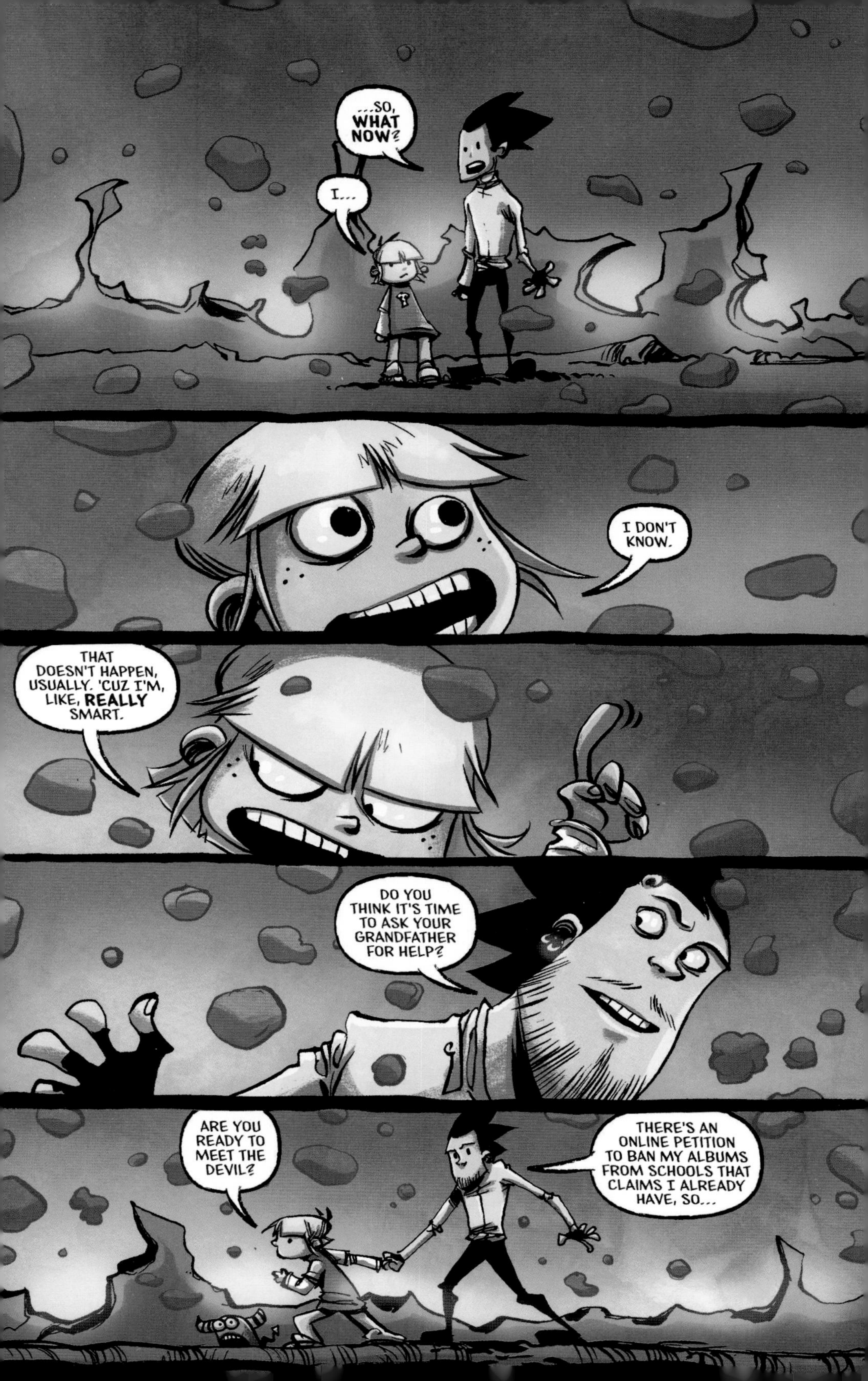
...SO, WHAT NOW?
I...
I DON'T KNOW.
THAT DOESN'T HAPPEN, USUALLY. 'CUZ I'M, LIKE, REALLY SMART.
DO YOU THINK IT'S TIME TO ASK YOUR GRANDFATHER FOR HELP?
ARE YOU READY TO MEET THE DEVIL?
THERE'S AN ONLINE PETITION TO BAN MY ALBUMS FROM SCHOOLS THAT CLAIMS I ALREADY HAVE, SO...

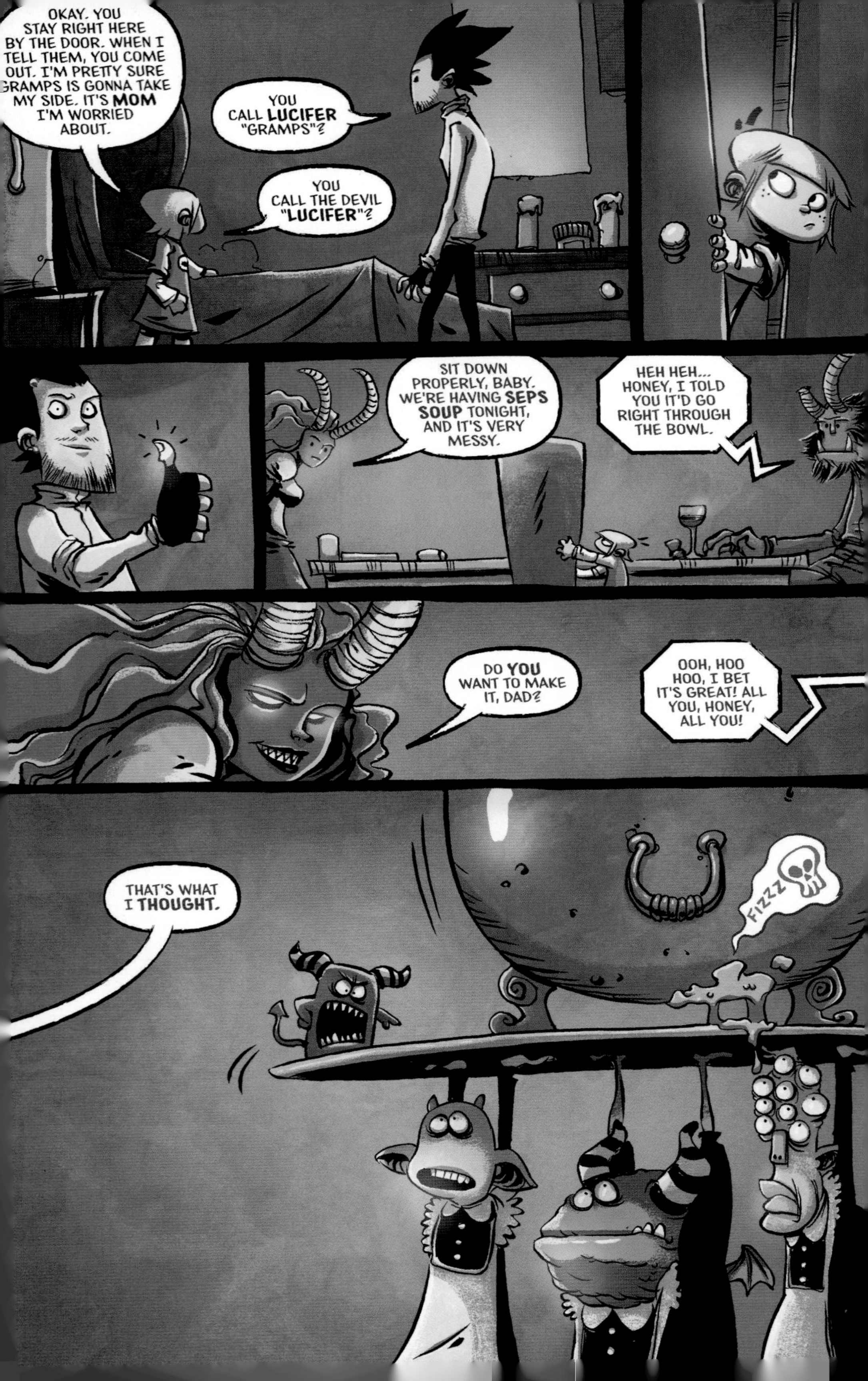
OKAY. YOU STAY RIGHT HERE BY THE DOOR. WHEN I TELL THEM, YOU COME OUT. I'M PRETTY SURE GRAMPS IS GONNA TAKE MY SIDE. IT'S **MOM** I'M WORRIED ABOUT.
YOU CALL **LUCIFER** "GRAMPS"?
YOU CALL THE DEVIL "**LUCIFER**"?
SIT DOWN PROPERLY, BABY. WE'RE HAVING **SEPS SOUP** TONIGHT, AND IT'S VERY MESSY.
HEH HEH... HONEY, I TOLD YOU IT'D GO RIGHT THROUGH THE BOWL.
DO **YOU** WANT TO MAKE IT, DAD?
OOH, HOO HOO, I BET IT'S GREAT! ALL YOU, HONEY, ALL YOU!
THAT'S WHAT I **THOUGHT**.
FIZZZ

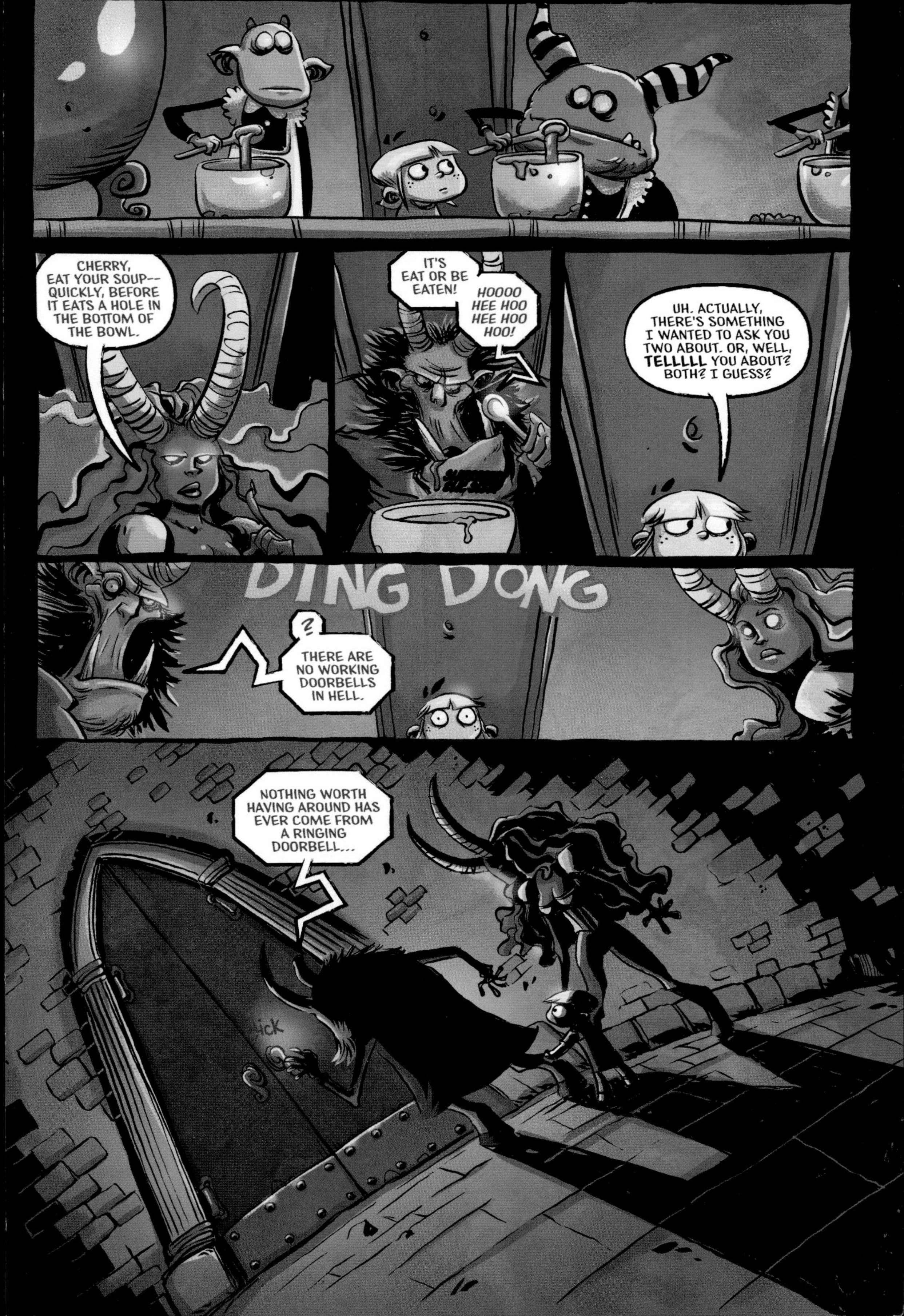
CHERRY, EAT YOUR SOUP-- QUICKLY, BEFORE IT EATS A HOLE IN THE BOTTOM OF THE BOWL.
IT'S EAT OR BE EATEN!
HOOOO HEE HOO HEE HOO HOO!
UH. ACTUALLY, THERE'S SOMETHING I WANTED TO ASK YOU TWO ABOUT. OR, WELL, TELLLLL YOU ABOUT? BOTH? I GUESS?
DING DONG
?
THERE ARE NO WORKING DOORBELLS IN HELL.
NOTHING WORTH HAVING AROUND HAS EVER COME FROM A RINGING DOORBELL...

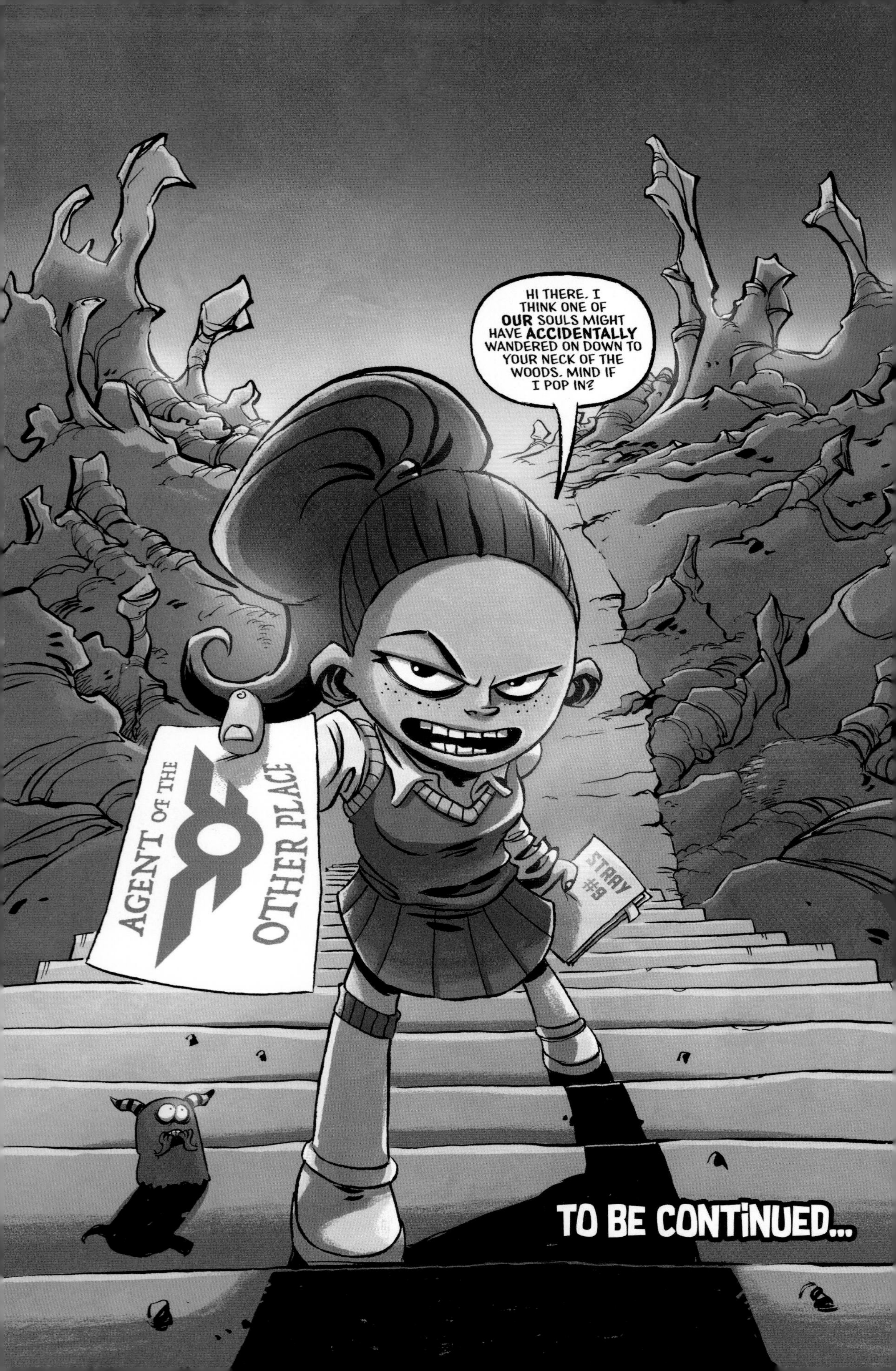
HI THERE. I THINK ONE OF OUR SOULS MIGHT HAVE ACCIDENTALLY WANDERED ON DOWN TO YOUR NECK OF THE WOODS. MIND IF I POP IN?
AGENT OF THE OTHER PLACE
STRAY #9
TO BE CONTINUED...

BONUS STORIES AND ART

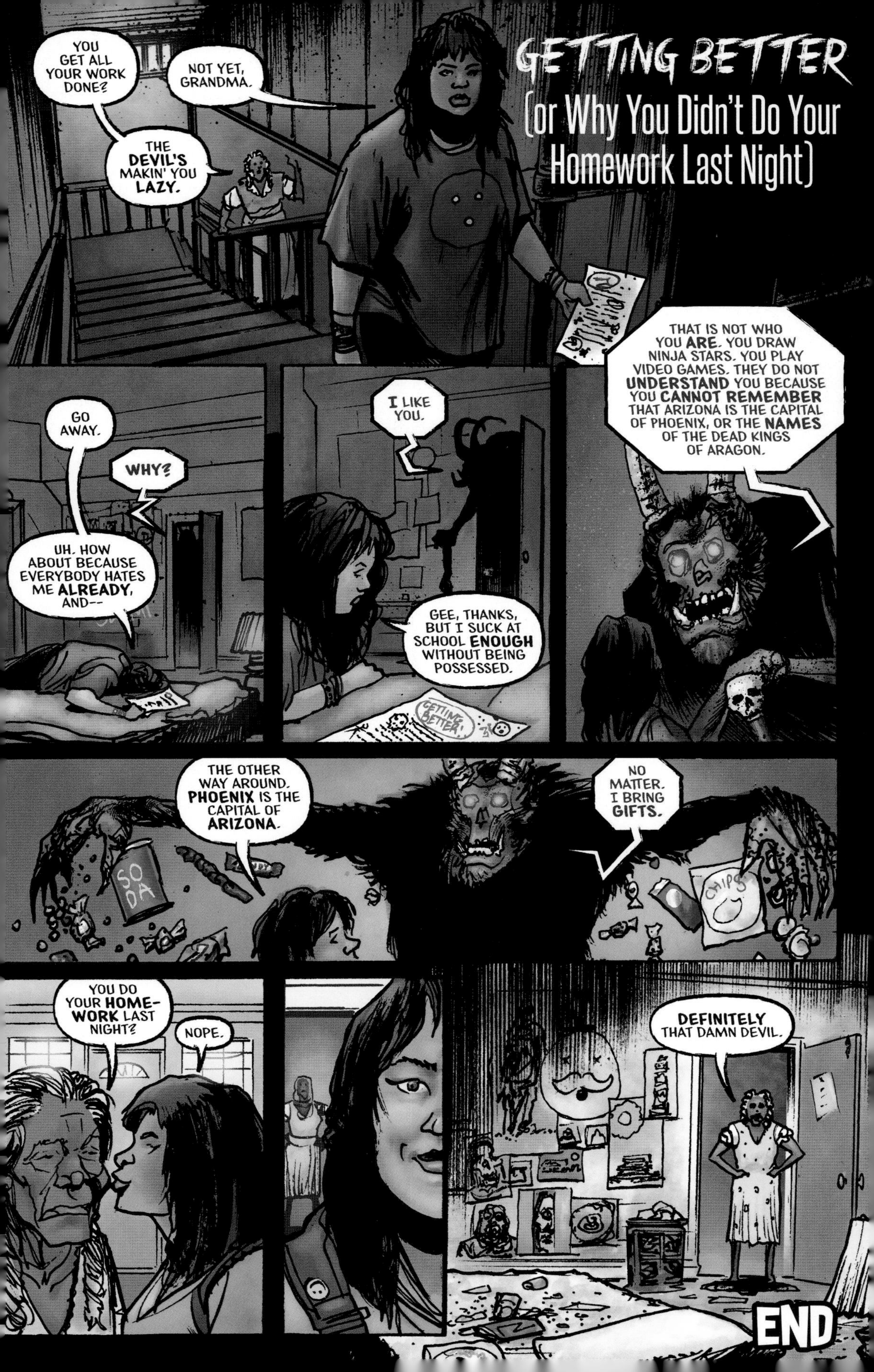

GETTING BETTER
(or Why You Didn't Do Your Homework Last Night)
YOU GET ALL YOUR WORK DONE?
NOT YET, GRANDMA.
THE DEVIL'S MAKIN' YOU LAZY.
GO AWAY.
WHY?
UH. HOW ABOUT BECAUSE EVERYBODY HATES ME ALREADY, AND--
I LIKE YOU.
GEE, THANKS, BUT I SUCK AT SCHOOL ENOUGH WITHOUT BEING POSSESSED.
GETTING BETTER!
THAT IS NOT WHO YOU ARE. YOU DRAW NINJA STARS. YOU PLAY VIDEO GAMES. THEY DO NOT UNDERSTAND YOU BECAUSE YOU CANNOT REMEMBER THAT ARIZONA IS THE CAPITAL OF PHOENIX, OR THE NAMES OF THE DEAD KINGS OF ARAGON.
THE OTHER WAY AROUND. PHOENIX IS THE CAPITAL OF ARIZONA.
NO MATTER. I BRING GIFTS.
SO DA
CHIPS
YOU DO YOUR HOME-WORK LAST NIGHT?
NOPE.
DEFINITELY THAT DAMN DEVIL.
END

THROUGHOUT MANY AN EVE AND THE RISE OF SUNS, MORTALS HAVE COMPETED IN A TEST OF STRENGTH, WILL, AND LOYALTY.

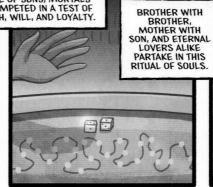

BROTHER WITH BROTHER, MOTHER WITH SON, AND ETERNAL LOVERS ALIKE PARTAKE IN THIS RITUAL OF SOULS.

THE RITUAL KNOWN AS...

GAME NIGHT!

DID YOU DRAW TWICE?!

I LANDED ON DOUBLE ROLL TWO TURNS AGO!

DOUBLE ROLL DOESN'T MEAN DOUBLE DRAW. I KNEW IT--YOU ARE CHEATING!

FINE, I DID DRAW TWICE!

YOU CROSSED THE LINE. I HATE THAT IT'S COME TO THIS.

BRING IT!

POW

HAPPY GAMING!

END

HOO HEE HAA

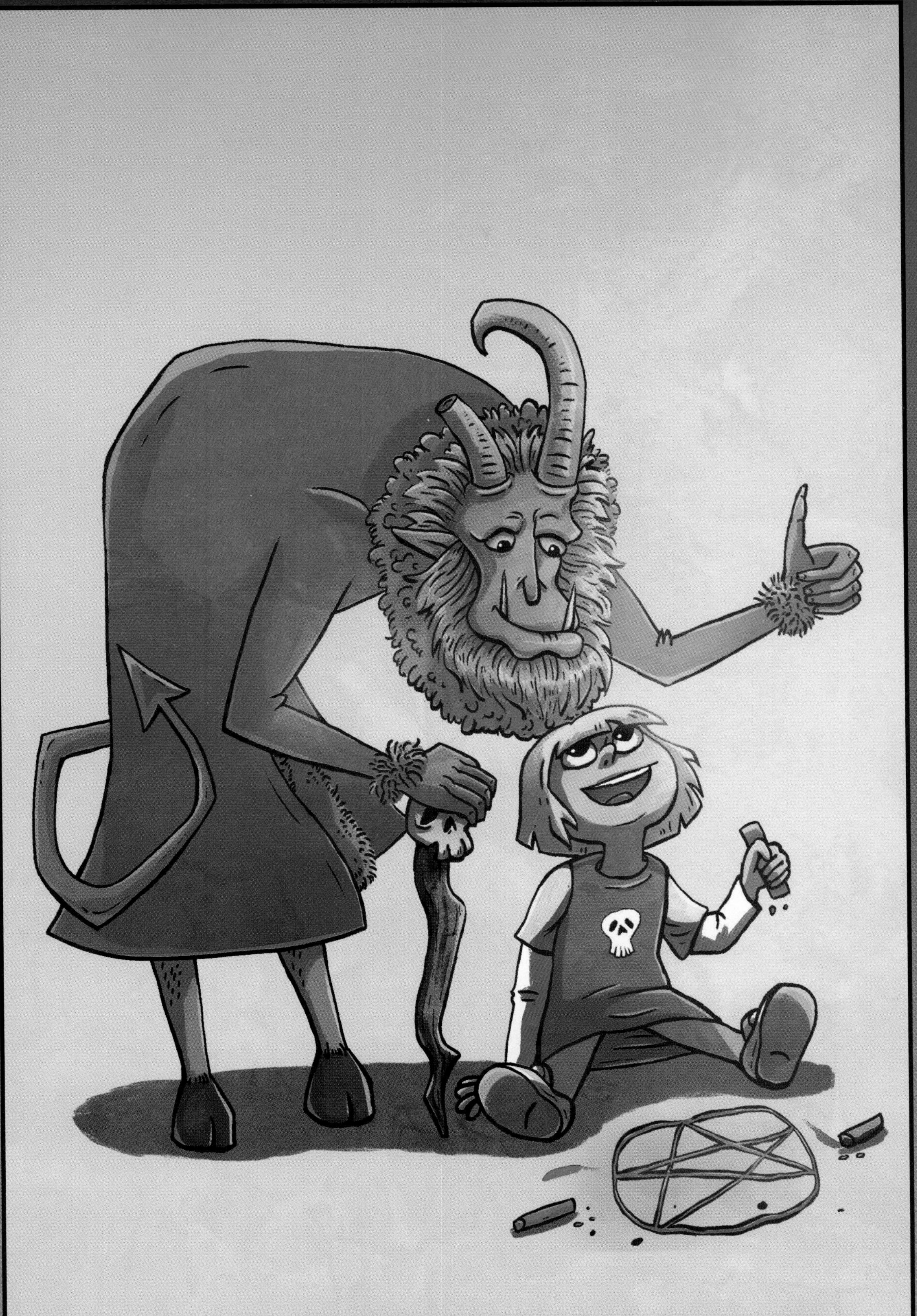

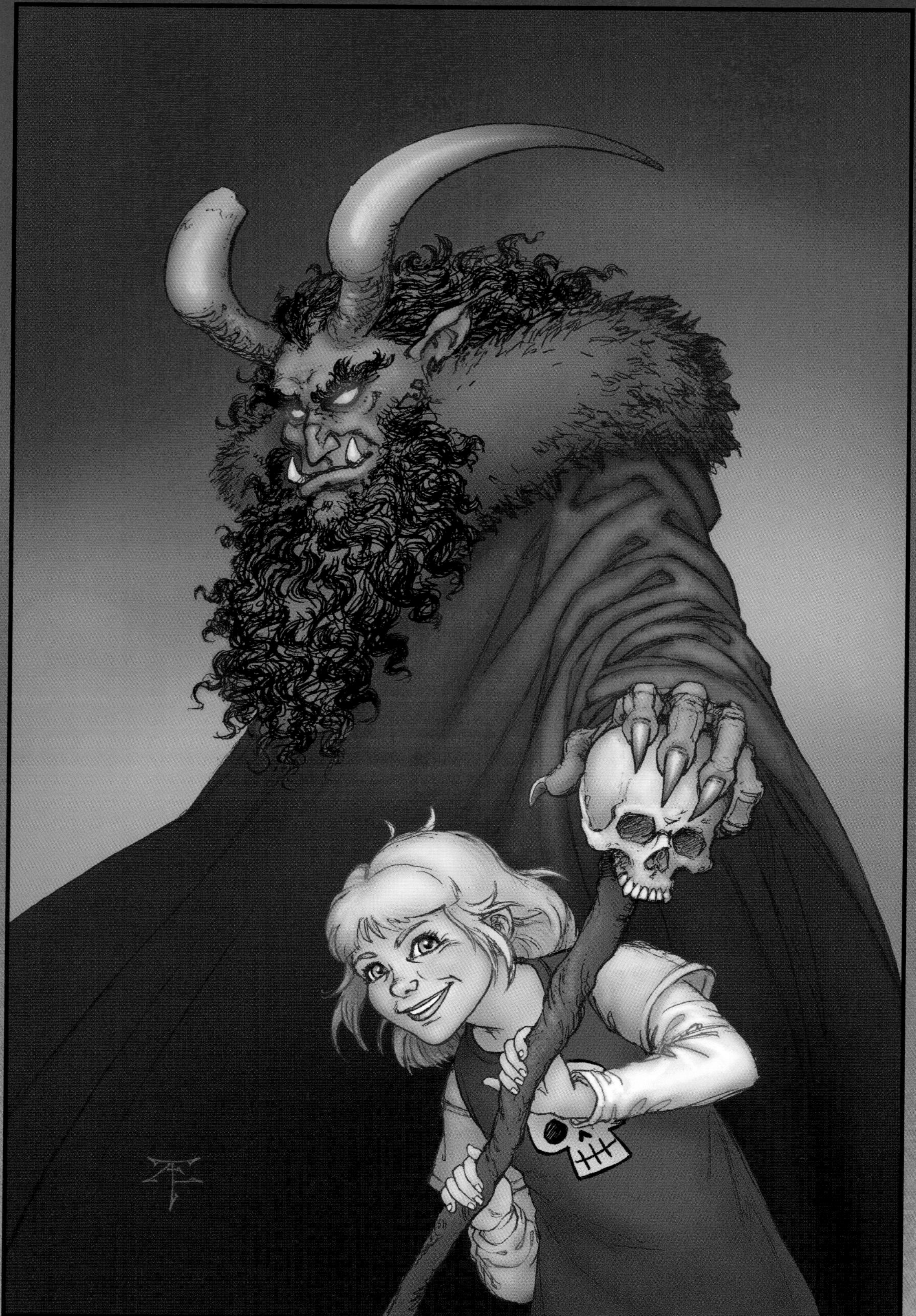

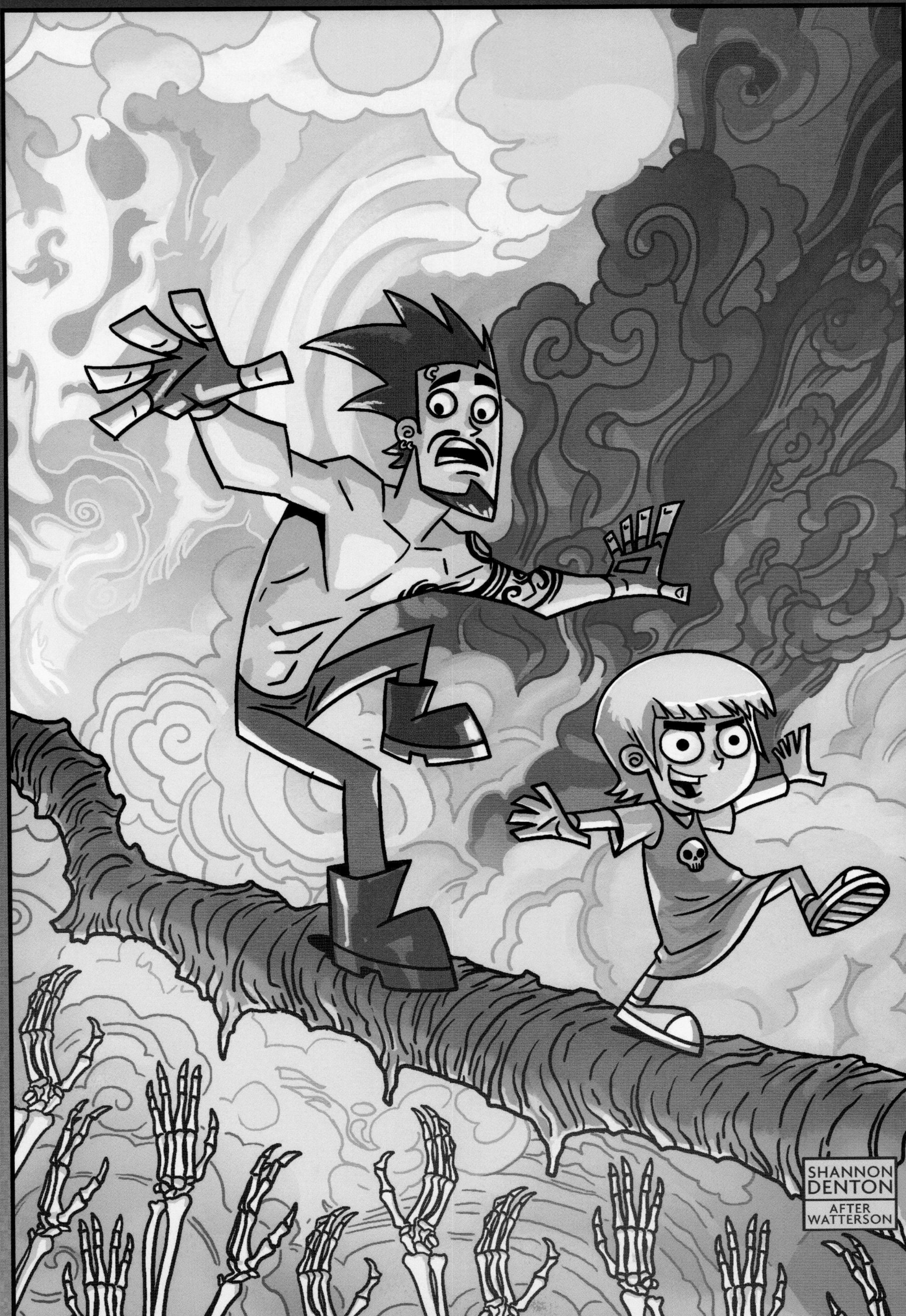
SHANNON DENTON
AFTER WATTERSON

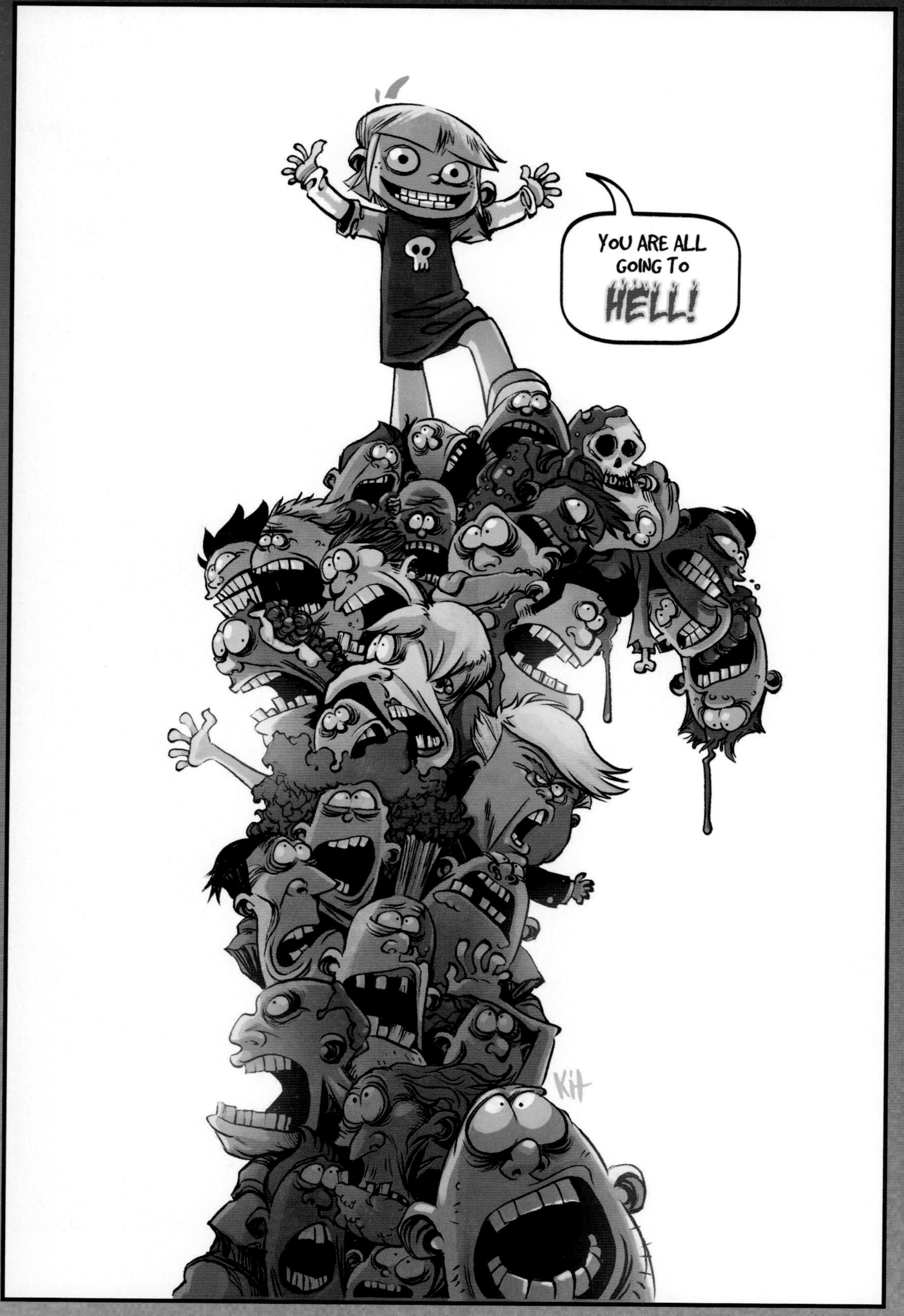
YOU ARE ALL GOING TO HELL!
Kit

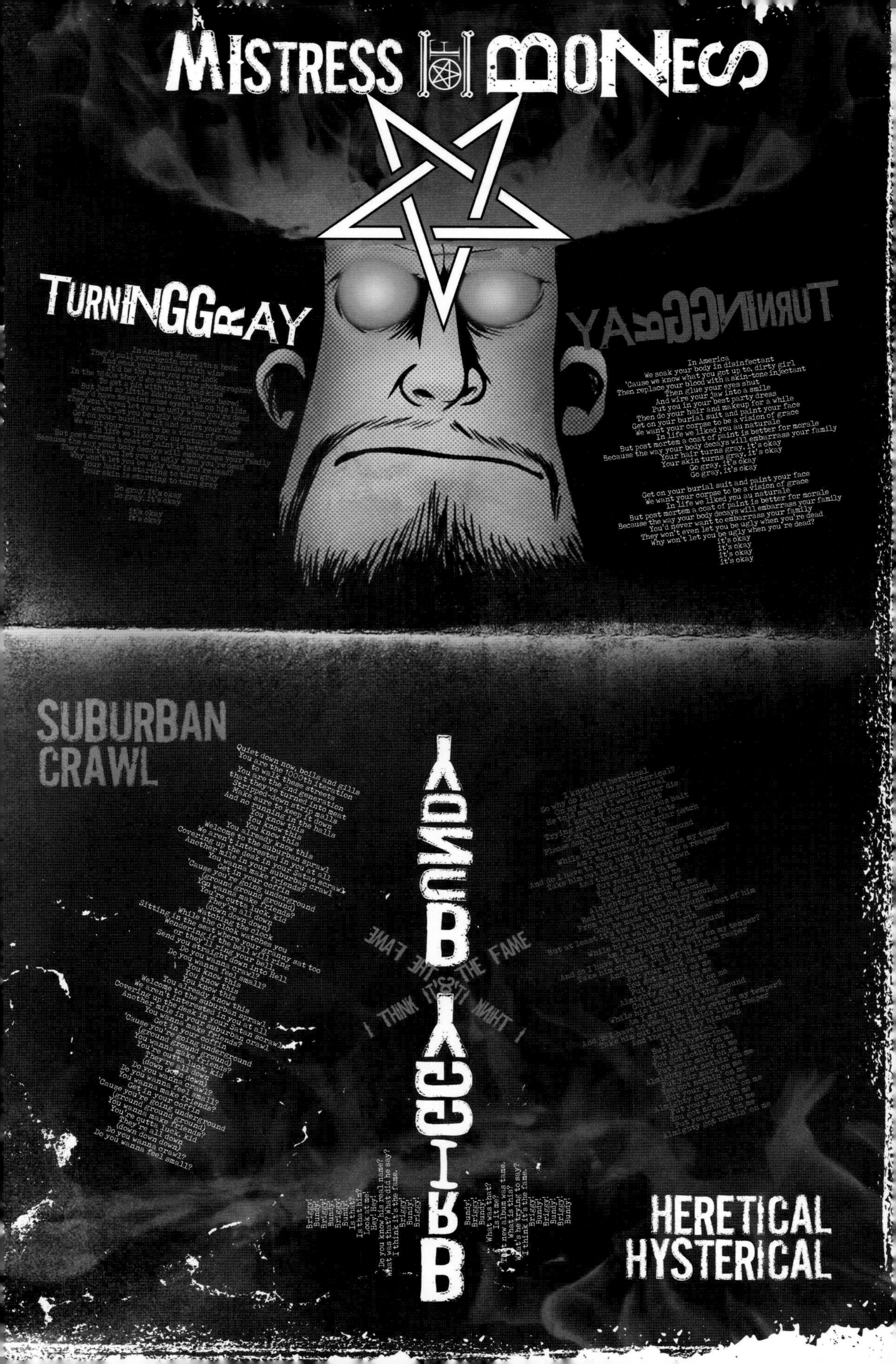

MISTRESS OF BONES
TURNING GRAY
In Ancient Egypt
They'd pull your brain out with a hook
And soak your insides with wine
It'd be the best you ever look
In the 1840s they'd go down to the photographer
To get a pic with their dead kids
But just so little Eddie didn't look bored
They'd have to paint some eyeballs on his lids
They won't even let you be ugly when you're dead
Why won't let you be ugly when you're dead?
Get on your burial suit and paint your face
We want your corpse to be a vision of grace
In life we liked you au naturale
But post mortem a coat of paint is better for morale
Because the way your body decays will embarrass your family
They won't even let you be ugly when you're dead
Why won't let you be ugly when you're dead?
Your hair is starting to turn gray
Your skin is starting to turn gray
Go gray, it's okay
Go gray, it's okay
it's okay
it's okay
In America
We soak your body in disinfectant
'Cause we know what you got up to, dirty girl
Then replace your blood with a skin-tone injectant
Then glue your eyes shut
And wire your jaw into a smile
Put you in your best party dress
Then do your hair and makeup for a while
Get on your burial suit and paint your face
We want your corpse to be a vision of grace
In life we liked you au naturale
But post mortem a coat of paint is better for morale
Because the way your body decays will embarrass your family
Your hair turns gray, it's okay
Your skin turns gray, it's okay
Go gray, it's okay
Go gray, it's okay
Get on your burial suit and paint your face
We want your corpse to be a vision of grace
In life we liked you au naturale
But post mortem a coat of paint is better for morale
Because the way your body decays will embarrass your family
You'd never want to embarrass your family
They won't even let you be ugly when you're dead
Why won't let you be ugly when you're dead?
it's okay
it's okay
it's okay
it's okay
SUBURBAN CRAWL
Quiet down now, boils and gills
You are the 1000th iteration
to walk these streets
You are the 2nd generation
that they've turned into meat
Stripped-down strip malls
Make sure to keep it down
And no running in the halls
You know this
You know this
You already know this
Welcome to the suburban sprawl
We aren't interested in you at all
Covering up the desk in your Satan scrawl
Another mile in your suburban crawl
You wanna make friends?
Get in your coffin
'Cause you're going underground
(ground ground ground)
You wanna make friends?
You're outta luck, kid
They're all down
(down down down)
Watching the clock
While the clock watches you
Sitting in the seat where your granny sat too
Wondering if the bell will ring
or they'll ring your bell,
Send you straight down into Hell
Do you wanna crawl?
Do you wanna feel small?
You know this
You know this
You already know this
Welcome to the suburban sprawl
We aren't interested in you at all
Covering up the desk in your Satan scrawl
Another mile in your suburban crawl
You wanna make friends?
Get in your coffin
'Cause you're going underground
(ground ground ground)
You wanna make friends?
You're outta luck, kid
They're all down
(down down down)
Do you wanna crawl?
Do you wanna feel small?
You wanna make friends?
Get in your coffin
'Cause you're going underground
(ground ground ground)
You wanna make friends?
You're outta luck, kid
They're all down
(down down down)
Do you wanna crawl?
Do you wanna feel small?
BRIGGY BUNDY
I THINK IT'S THE FAME
Briggy!
Bundy!
Briggy!
Bundy!
Briggy!
Bundy!
Is that?
Is that him?
Look at me!
Hey! Hey!
Do you know his real name?
What was that? What did he say?
I think it's the fame.
Briggy!
Bundy!
Briggy!
Bundy!
Briggy!
Bundy!
What was that?
Is it me?
That new album was tame.
What is this?
What's he trying to say?
I think it's the fame.
Briggy!
Bundy!
Briggy!
Bundy!
I know it's heretical
So why do I find it so hysterical?
On my omnipotent's arrival
He told me that I would never die
I kept my face straight
Trying not to take the obvious bait
Of my clearly superior fate
Please don't throw me in the briar patch
Cain walks the Earth
While his brother's in the ground
Am I my brother's keeper?
And do I have to keep him, if he gets on my temper?
Take him out into the fields like a reaper
And there I'll lay him down
Put your mark on me
You got nothin' on me
Put your mark on me
Almighty got nothin' on me
Red blood seeps into the ground
From the wound on his hairy mound
God, he made an awful sound
But at least it's the last thing I'll hear out of him
Cain walks the Earth
While his brother's in the ground
Am I my brother's keeper?
And do I have to keep him, if he gets on my temper?
Take him out into the fields like a reaper
And there I'll lay him down
Put your mark on me
You got nothin' on me
Put your mark on me
Almighty got nothin' on me
Put your mark on me
You got nothin' on me
Put your mark on me
Almighty got nothin' on me
HERETICAL HYSTERICAL

SKETCHBOOK

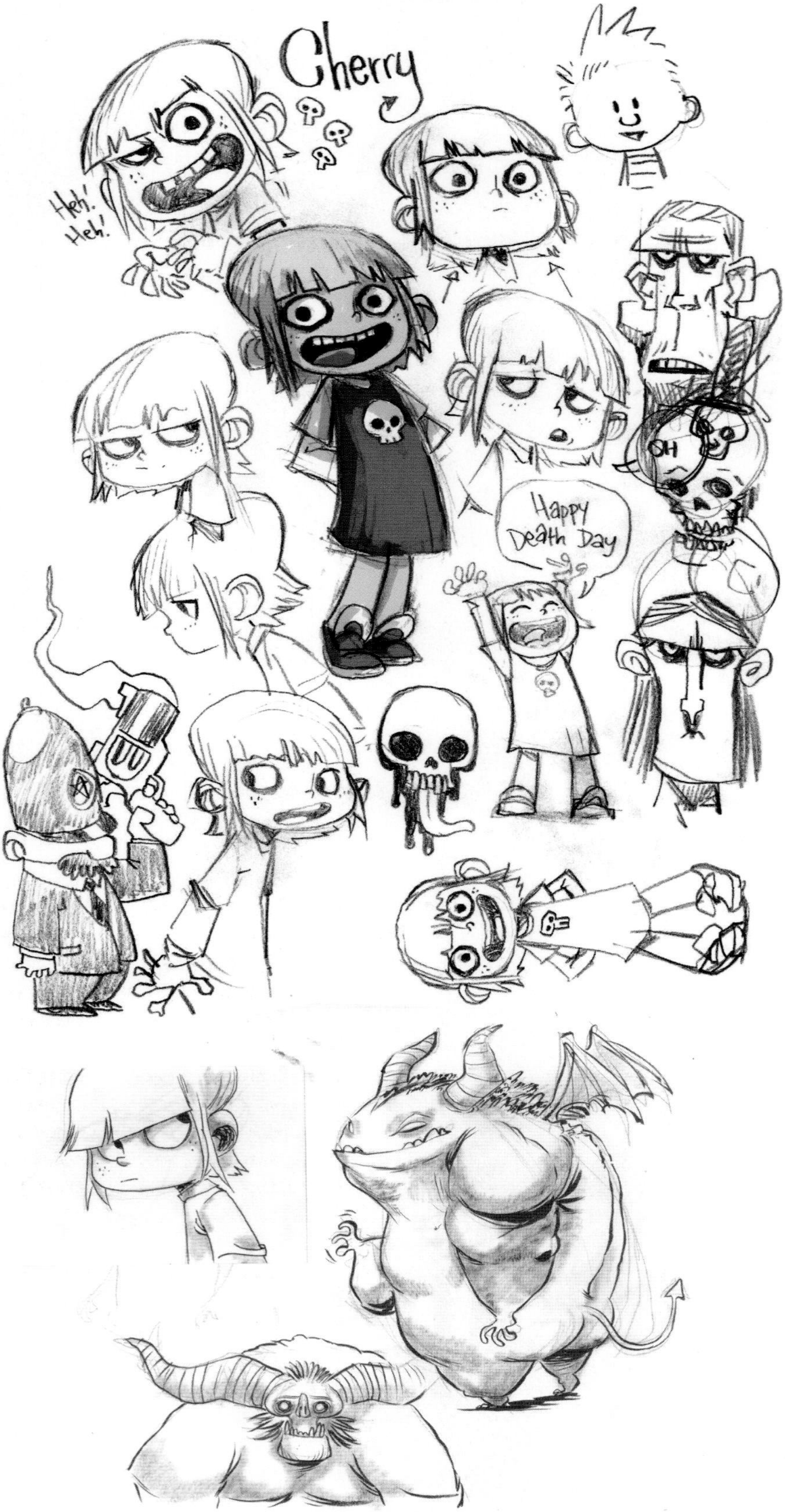
Cherry
Heh! Heh!
OH
Happy Death Day

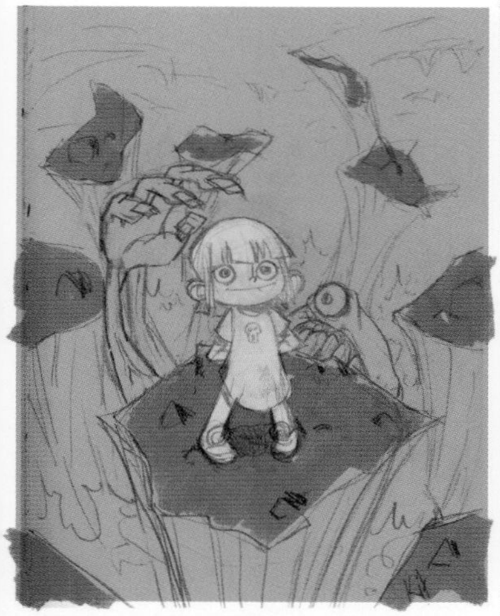

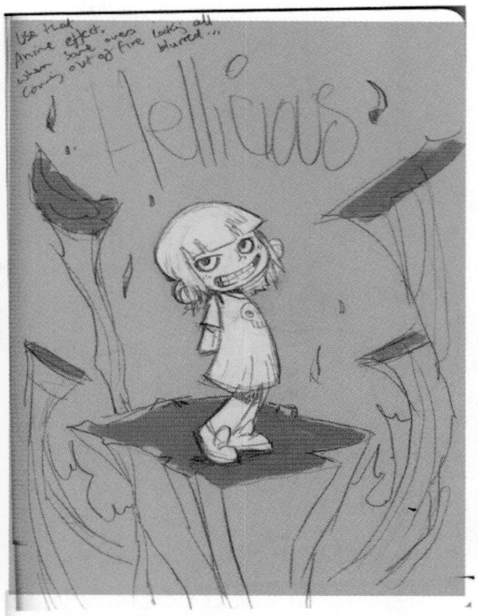
Use that Anime effect. when some ones looking all coming out of fire blurred...
Hellicious

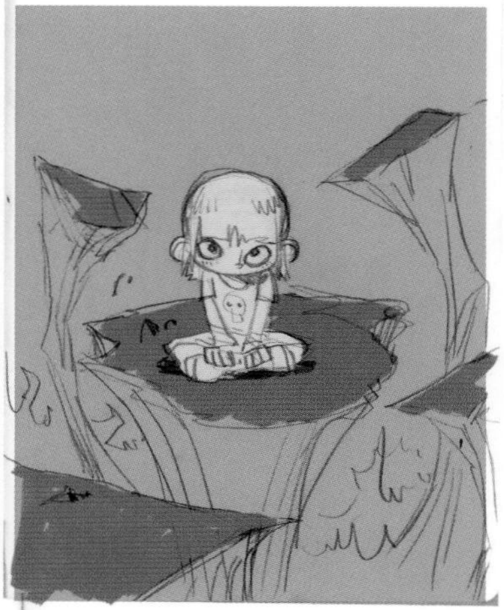

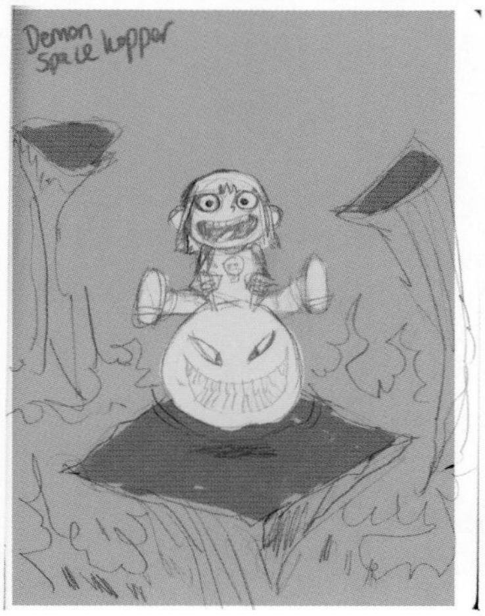
Demon space hopper

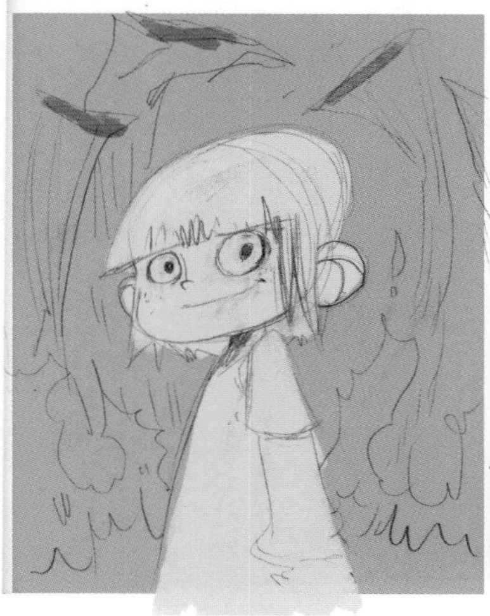

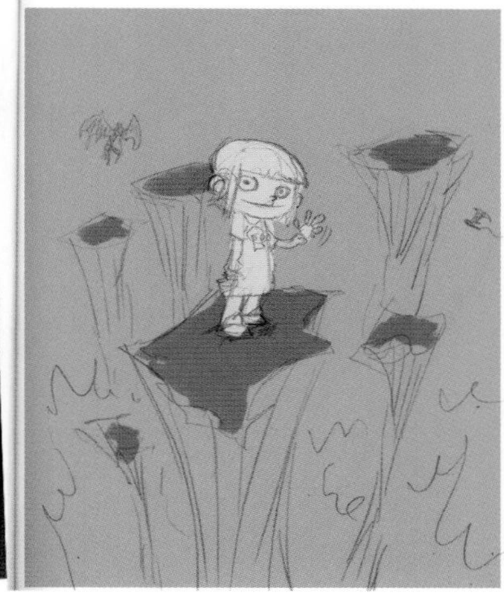

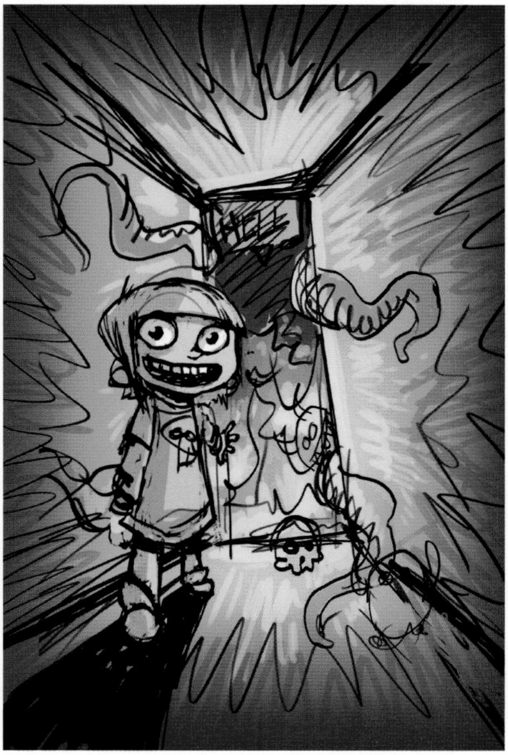
HELL

OPPOSITE PAGE: Playing with different attitudes for Cherry. Compared to her appearance in the pages created for the pitch (reprinted following this section), Cherry evolved into a much “cuter” character, a sort of Calvin-style design, mixed with the energy of a crazy/sweet—yet maniacal—demon.

THIS PAGE: Kit never stops drawing and produces several cover ideas per issue, sometimes giving the team a choice between multiple completed images. Even the unused ones are good enough that they often become pinups, promotional art, or part of the book designs.

This collection of “welcome to Hell” images resulted in one of issue #2’s covers.

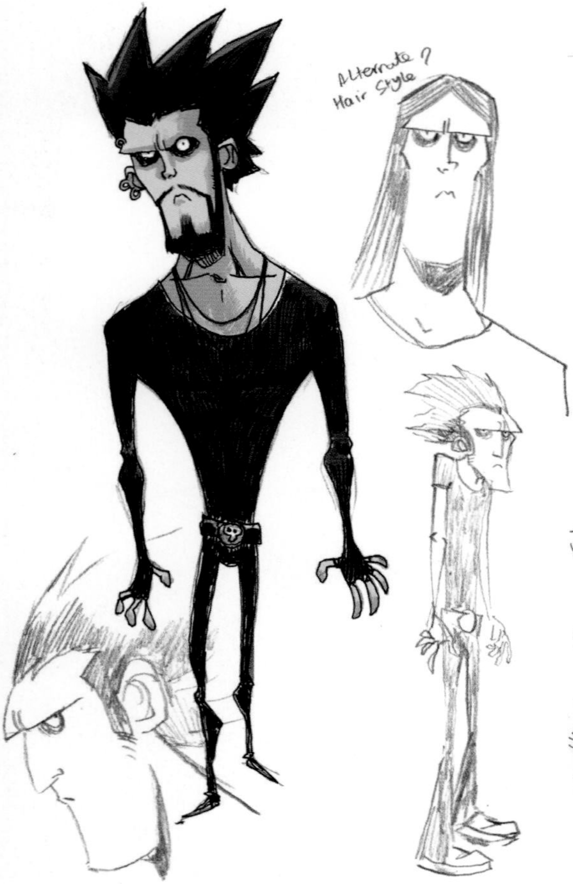
Alternate ?
Hair Style

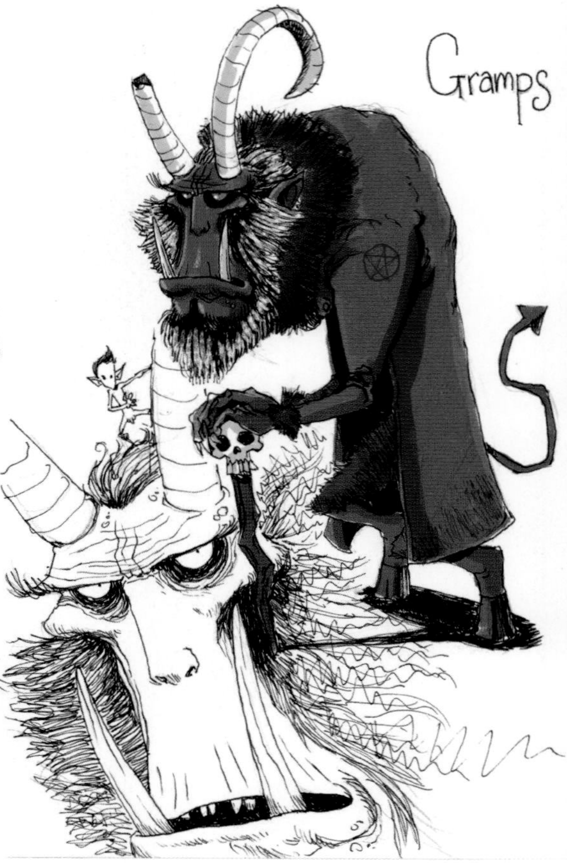
Gramps

CLOCKWISE FROM LEFT: The Hobbes to Cherry's Calvin, Briggy is loosely based on Marilyn Manson, but also incorporates elements from other death-metal artists.

Gramps is inspired by the Krampus and various William Blake illustrations.

Minos draws from a few old-school gameshow hosts, but ended up reminiscent of new-school gameshow host Donald Trump.

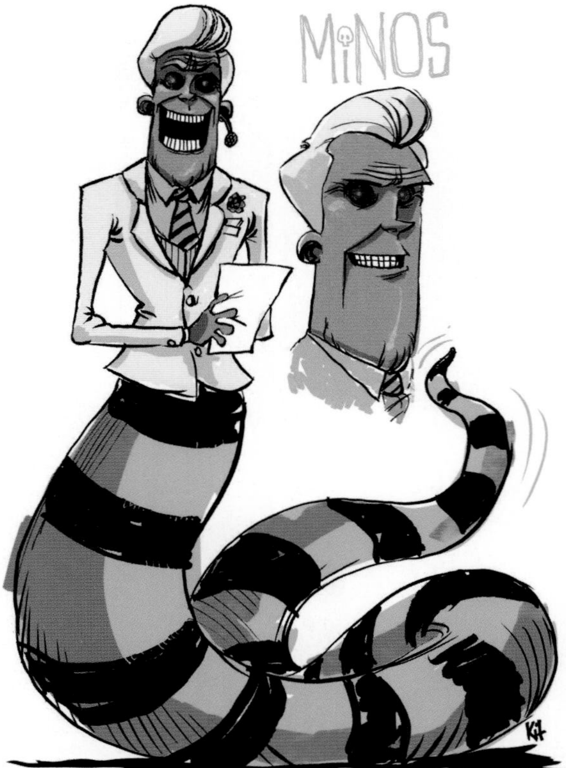
MiNOS

PITCH PAGES

An earlier version of Hellicious's cover and early pages by Kit Wallis, created for the pitch. At this stage, a lankier Cherry had less cartoony proportions and less manic body language, while Sin was slightly less menacing. Mickey is pretty much Mickey, though, because Mickey is a boss.

Cherry and co. continued to evolve, and once the series was approved, the sequence was reconceived. These originals remain a compelling look into Kit's process in developing the characters and setting.

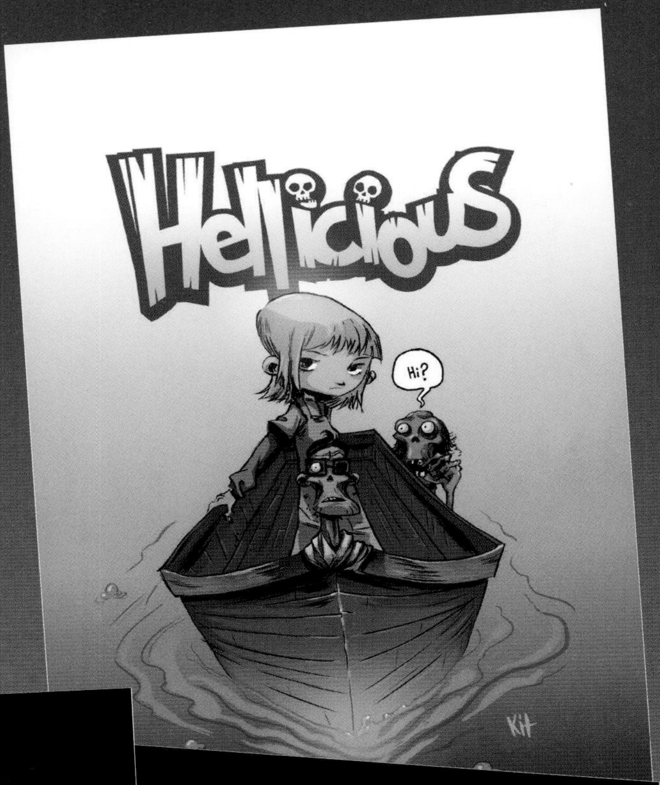
Hellicious
Hi?
Kit

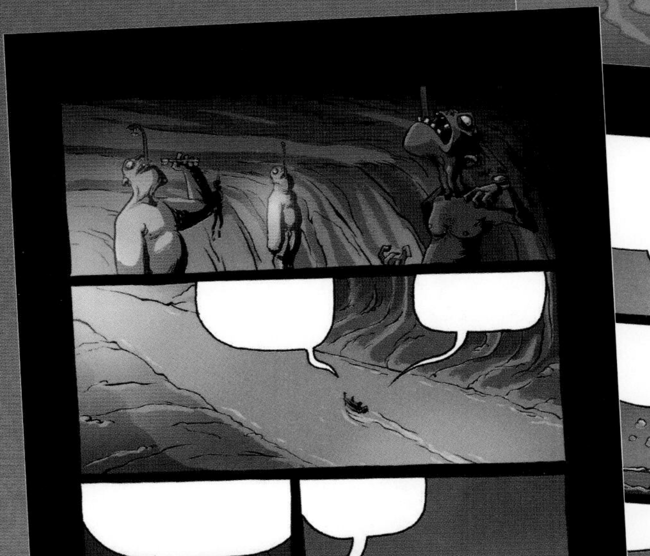

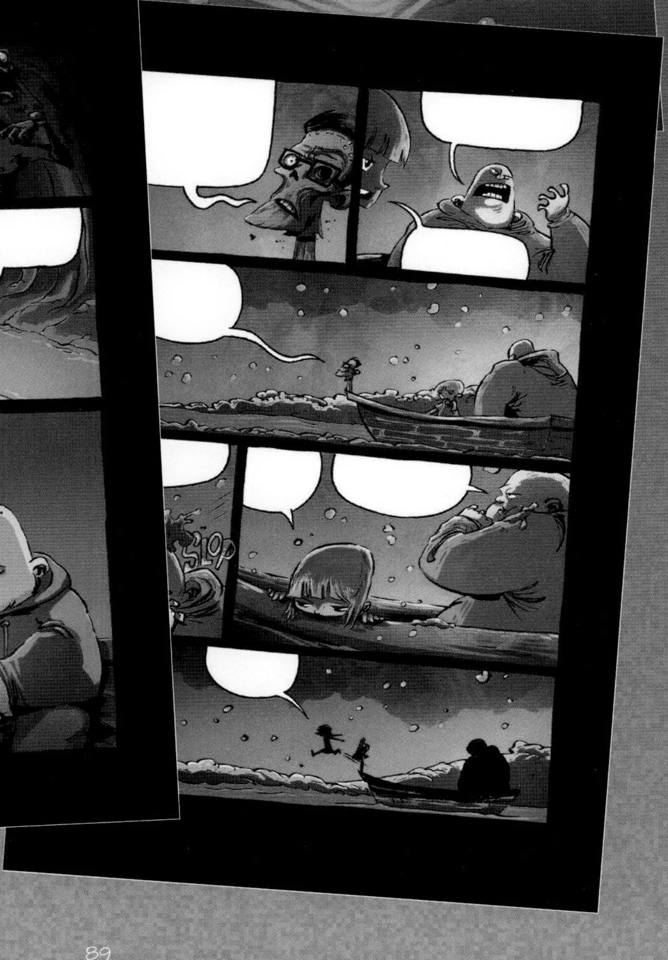
SLOP

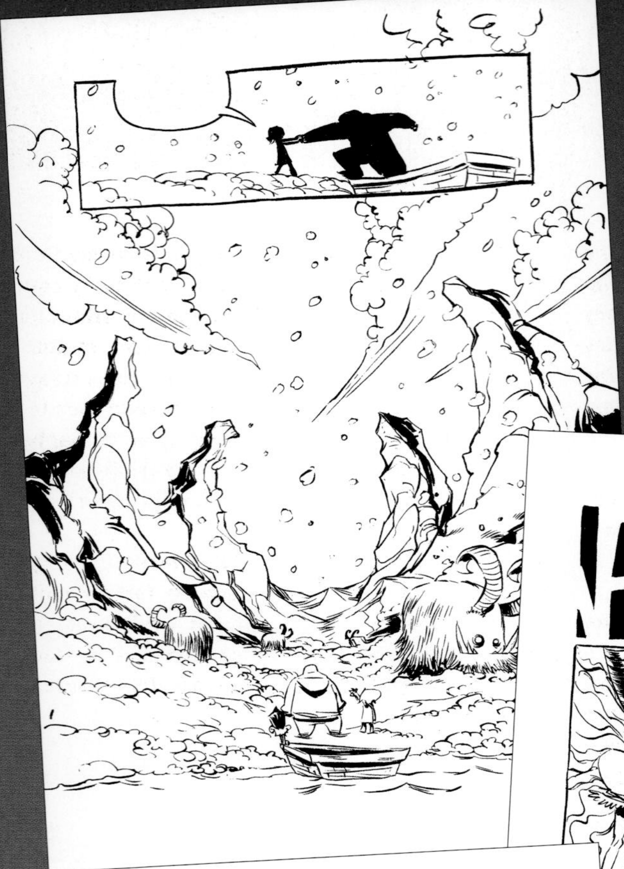

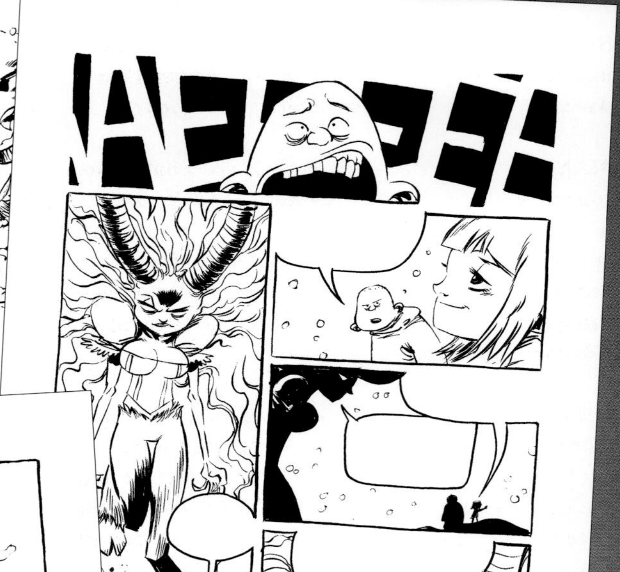

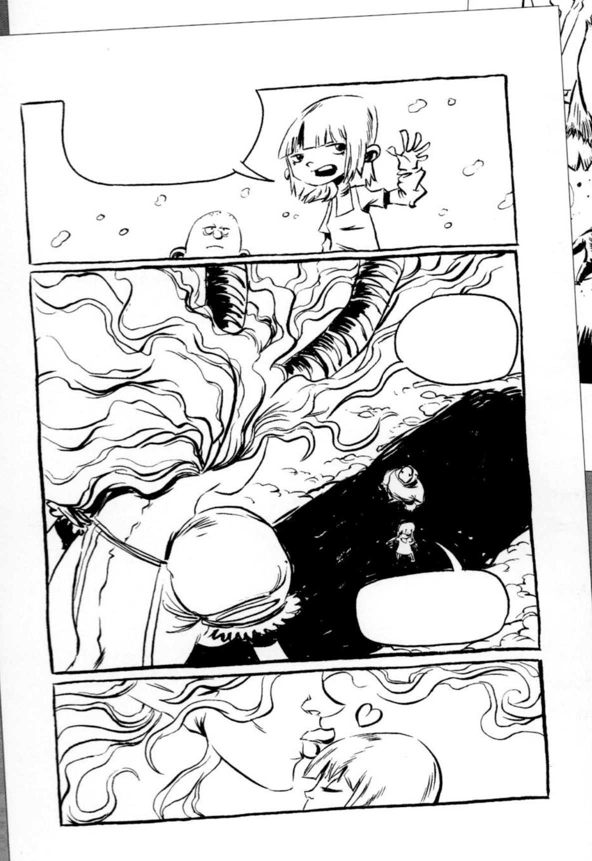

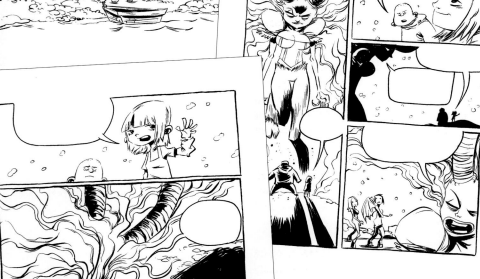

AN INTERVIEW WITH *HELLICIOUS* WRITERS ALAN C. MEDINA AND MINA ELWELL

BY ALAN C. MEDINA AND MINA ELWELL

Okay, we are interviewing each other, because the interviewer budget went to paying for all those fancy staples that're holding your comic together. They told us we could have one staple and an interviewer or multiple staples, and we said screw it—spring for the extras. Flip over that comic. Run your fingers along the spine. Admire those staples.

How about first, since you know people are wondering, how do we justify having two of us? And then if we can't, one of us just walks into the woods?

ALAN C. MEDINA: Basically, I ask Rocco what works, you ask your fish, and we take the credit. Really, it's a team effort. It's fun, though. I think it's definitely special. What I don't see, or you may not see in a scene, but the other does tends to come out eventually, and our own, individual styles come together like some symbiotic sci-fi monster.

MINA ELWELL: Yeah, we definitely have different skills and bring different things to the story. Any worthwhile emotional character building or fun pop-culture references I credit you with. I spend my time obsessing about plot structure and writing really gross *Paradise Lost* jokes.

So, because obviously I wasn't there and don't remember, how do we know each other and why do we work together? Without the part about Lyanne and the spittle bugs—I don't wanna get sued.

ACM: It's our mission from the home planet, right? We're aliens here to take comics—and eventually the world—over. No, we wish it was that cool. The real reasons are we're good friends, young writers, and share similar creative interests, so here we are!

Tell them about Rocco. He's cooler than us. Also kind of our muse.

ACM: Rocco is a 28-pound terror of French Bulldog. He's the star, creator, and main writer of his own TV show; I'm just a recurring side character.

ME: He's also the inspiration for Cerberus.

Let's tell them about our non-Rocco influences. That's something a real interviewer would ask.

ACM: I get a lot of my influences from my family. There's enough crazy in there to last me a career. Family is one of my favorite themes to write about, and *Hellicious* lets me explore that from a multitude of angles. My first book, *Elasticator*, was about a pissed-off kid who gets superpowers and tries to be a hero, but ends up being saved by an actual hero, his mother. Getting to write about a family and their dealings running Hell is a legit dream come true.

ME: I'm obsessed with Patricia Piccinini, and pretty much whenever I do research for my writing I find myself checking out her sculptures, even when it doesn't really make sense. I'm reading *Yummy Fur* right now. I fall asleep watching *Arrested Development* every night.

FAQ

ARE YOU TWO MARRIED?
ACM: No, a writing partnership is way too fun to be marriage.
ME: We're actually siblings. Common mistake.

DO YOU HAVE HOBBIES?
ACM: I like to watch professional badasses beat each other up in tights, or partake in some video game goodness.
ME: Does showering count as a hobby?

DO YOU ALSO DRAW?
ACM: I like to think Earth-33 (not ours, I think?) Alan does. But me, this A.C.? He doesn't draw.
ME: Constant monster doodles, and I'm kinda into scratchboard. You didn't mean well, right?

WHAT GENRE DO YOU CALL YOURSELF?
ACM: I don't have a set genre so much as I like to take my weirdness and spread it throughout all established genres.
ME: I kinda like bizarro and absurdism, but clearly this is a revenge-tragedy.

ARE YOU OKAY?
ACM: Are any of us okay? Is okay a good thing? None of those questions are as deep as you think they are; I just needed word count covered.
ME: I'm pretty okay.

AN INTERVIEW WITH *HELLICIOUS* ARTISTS KIT WALLIS AND JIO BUTLER

BY MINA ELWELL

Okay, folks, it's Mina again. We thought we were going to have room in the budget for an interviewer and staples this month, but we didn't account for how much it would cost to fly in the antennas for my theremin, or the amount of rubber bands that Trevor has apparently been using. Long story—actually longer than you needed—I'm still doing the interviews.

Today, the people you actually want to hear from, the ones who make the comic look like something cool and not a confusing jumble of jokes Alan and I thought of, KIT WALLIS & JIO BUTLER!

So, starting with Kit, the question on everyone's mind: Do you ever catch yourself sort of making the face you're drawing a little bit?

KIT WALLIS: All the time. It's an integral part of my creative process :) I take photos of my face doing some weird poses occasionally. It helps sometimes, I think.

Jio, we haven't actually met face to face, so there's a very real possibility that you're Kit's imaginary friend. Please put to rest these wild rumors I've just made up.

JIO BUTLER: Kit clearly has a crazy imagination to make the world of *Hellicious* come to life. It wouldn't be surprising if he made up such an awesome imaginary friend too. However, it's not true; I'm actually a sentient hologram.

For the kids at home who only make books on their own, can you explain how you two work together to make the comic?

KW: I basically send Jio my inked pages, and, if I want something specific, I will brief her on it. But, for the most part, she just works her magic on the line art.

JB: Communication is really important—we talk about each page to make sure we are both, well . . . on the same page. Kit makes up the high-resolution line art and sends it over to me to color, and I just go to town on it in Photoshop. We then make a food offering to the Comic Book God to ensure it has safe passage in order to get printed.

Kit, are the farting demon chef from issue #1 and the demon terrified of the Agent at the end of this issue related, or part of a similar demon species? That's not a good interview question—I just want to know.

KW: Ha! I'm not entirely sure, myself. It's more about the mood I'm in. I'd probably have a little fart if the devil burst into the room.

Do either you have a favorite character to work on? I hope it's not NAME OF CHARACTER WHO NEVER APPEARS AGAIN

KW: For me, I love drawing Cherry! I love her character.

JB: I love Mickey. Not only is his color scheme really nice, but he's also a great character. I bet he gets to see all sorts of different people in various states of death!

Jio, even though we mostly see you doing colors on Hellicious, you are also an artist who does standalone work. (That was called "exposition," kids, and I said it for you.) Tell us about your other work!

JB: My other work is mostly an ongoing journey. I'm still trying to find my own personal corner of the art world to settle in. Comics are a big part of me, and I hope to publish my own one day.

Kit, you design amazing, creepy, lovable creatures for Hellicious. What is the secret formula for the perfect combination of disturbing and adorable?

KW: When I was a child, my parents (both artists) would buy the best children's books for me, lots of Maurice Sendak, Judith Kerr, Arthur Rackham, and Brian Froud, to name a few. I guess those sorts of artists inspired me a lot. I've always been fascinated by grotesquely loveable creatures. Weird, I know.

Finally, who would you choose for your Hell best friend? Fictional, living, and dead answers accepted.

KW: That's a good one! Probably someone like Picasso. He liked to drink, right?!

JB: The psychologist Carl Jung. He'd learn a lot in Hell; I think he'd find it fascinating.

ABOUT THE AUTHORS

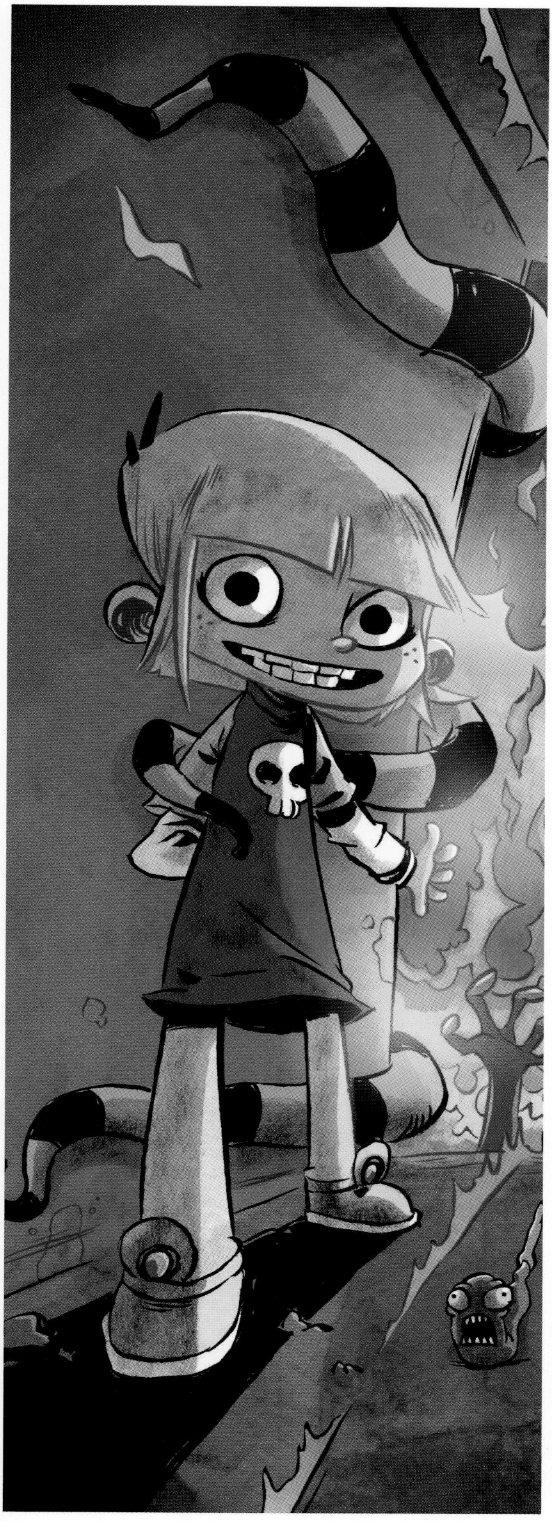

ALAN C. MEDINA is a 24-year-old who refers to himself as a high long hair. Along with *Hellicious*, Alan has cocreated *Elasticator*, *Welcome to Paradise*, and *Monarchs*. When not writing, Alan can also be found watching wrestling and playing video games with his French Bulldog, Rocco.

MINA ELWELL is a 22-year-old who had to use a calculator to determine her age for this bio. Before working on *Hellicious*, she was the cocreator of Lovecraftian horror comic *InferNoct*, along with artist Eli Powell. Mina currently lives in the East Village with an unusually large red betta fish, works in television, and takes freelance writing jobs in the time she should be taking a nap.

KIT WALLIS is an artist for video games and comics, having started drawing comics at the age of eight and first being published at eighteen. He is the creator of *Monster Club* and cocreator, with Derek Watson, of *Wonderland: Children of the Future Age*. Kit has worked with various publishers, including Antarctic Press, Scout Comics, ComX, and Oni press. *Hellicious* is his first professional comic work in a while.

MICAH MYERS is a comic book letterer. He has worked on books for Image and Dark Horse (technically only one book each, but it counts) and lots of comics for other companies, including SBI Press, Action Lab, and Aspen. He has also lettered tons of crowdfunded, self-published, and pitch comics. When not lettering, Micah crowdfunded his own comic, *The Disasters*. Oh, he also has a lovely wife and two kids.

JIO BUTLER is an artist from Oxfordshire who likes painting, reading, and annoying people with her musical instruments. She currently lives in Kent with her partner and two pet rats. *Hellicious* is her first large comic project, yet she hopes to take on more in the future.

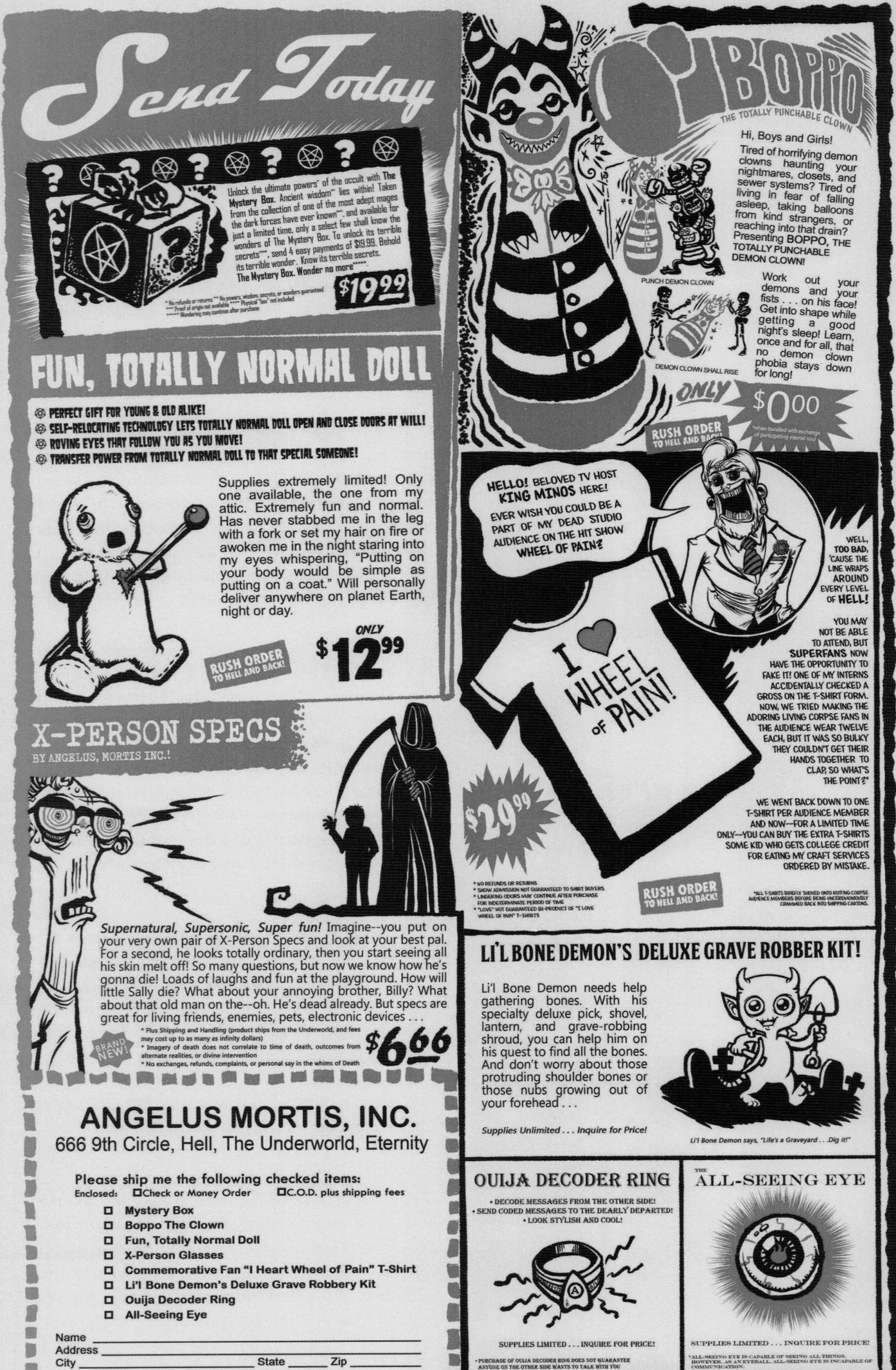

Send Today
Unlock the ultimate powers* of the occult with The Mystery Box. Ancient wisdom** lies within! Taken from the collection of one of the most adept mages the dark forces have ever known***, and available for just a limited time, only a select few shall know the wonders of The Mystery Box. To unlock its terrible secrets****, send 4 easy payments of $19.99. Behold its terrible wonder. Know its terrible secrets. The Mystery Box. Wonder no more*****.
$19.99
* No refunds or returns ** No powers, wisdom, secrets, or wonders guaranteed *** Proof of origin not available **** Physical "box" not included ***** Wondering may continue after purchase
FUN, TOTALLY NORMAL DOLL
PERFECT GIFT FOR YOUNG & OLD ALIKE!
SELF-RELOCATING TECHNOLOGY LETS TOTALLY NORMAL DOLL OPEN AND CLOSE DOORS AT WILL!
ROVING EYES THAT FOLLOW YOU AS YOU MOVE!
TRANSFER POWER FROM TOTALLY NORMAL DOLL TO THAT SPECIAL SOMEONE!
Supplies extremely limited! Only one available, the one from my attic. Extremely fun and normal. Has never stabbed me in the leg with a fork or set my hair on fire or awoken me in the night staring into my eyes whispering, "Putting on your body would be simple as putting on a coat." Will personally deliver anywhere on planet Earth, night or day.
RUSH ORDER TO HELL AND BACK!
ONLY $12.99
X-PERSON SPECS
BY ANGELUS, MORTIS INC.!
Supernatural, Supersonic, Super fun! Imagine--you put on your very own pair of X-Person Specs and look at your best pal. For a second, he looks totally ordinary, then you start seeing all his skin melt off! So many questions, but now we know how he's gonna die! Loads of laughs and fun at the playground. How will little Sally die? What about your annoying brother, Billy? What about that old man on the--oh. He's dead already. But specs are great for living friends, enemies, pets, electronic devices . . .
BRAND NEW!
* Plus Shipping and Handling (product ships from the Underworld, and fees may cost up to as many as infinity dollars)
* Imagery of death does not correlate to time of death, outcomes from alternate realities, or divine intervention
* No exchanges, refunds, complaints, or personal say in the whims of Death
$6.66
BOPPO
THE TOTALLY PUNCHABLE CLOWN
Hi, Boys and Girls!
Tired of horrifying demon clowns haunting your nightmares, closets, and sewer systems? Tired of living in fear of falling asleep, taking balloons from kind strangers, or reaching into that drain? Presenting BOPPO, THE TOTALLY PUNCHABLE DEMON CLOWN!
PUNCH DEMON CLOWN
Work out your demons and your fists . . . on his face! Get into shape while getting a good night's sleep! Learn, once and for all, that no demon clown phobia stays down for long!
DEMON CLOWN SHALL RISE
ONLY $0.00
*when bundled with exchange of participating eternal soul
RUSH ORDER TO HELL AND BACK!
HELLO! BELOVED TV HOST KING MINOS HERE!
EVER WISH YOU COULD BE A PART OF MY DEAD STUDIO AUDIENCE ON THE HIT SHOW WHEEL OF PAIN?
WELL, TOO BAD, 'CAUSE THE LINE WRAPS AROUND EVERY LEVEL OF HELL!
YOU MAY NOT BE ABLE TO ATTEND, BUT SUPERFANS NOW HAVE THE OPPORTUNITY TO FAKE IT! ONE OF MY INTERNS ACCIDENTALLY CHECKED A GROSS ON THE T-SHIRT FORM. NOW, WE TRIED MAKING THE ADORING LIVING CORPSE FANS IN THE AUDIENCE WEAR TWELVE EACH, BUT IT WAS SO BULKY THEY COULDN'T GET THEIR HANDS TOGETHER TO CLAP, SO WHAT'S THE POINT?*
WE WENT BACK DOWN TO ONE T-SHIRT PER AUDIENCE MEMBER AND NOW--FOR A LIMITED TIME ONLY--YOU CAN BUY THE EXTRA T-SHIRTS SOME KID WHO GETS COLLEGE CREDIT FOR EATING MY CRAFT SERVICES ORDERED BY MISTAKE.
I ♥ WHEEL of PAIN!
$29.99
* NO REFUNDS OR RETURNS
* SHOW ADMISSION NOT GUARANTEED TO SHIRT BUYERS
* LINGERING ODORS MAY CONTINUE AFTER PURCHASE FOR INDETERMINATE PERIOD OF TIME
* "LOVE" NOT GUARANTEED BI-PRODUCT OF "I LOVE WHEEL OF PAIN" T-SHIRTS
RUSH ORDER TO HELL AND BACK!
*ALL T-SHIRTS BRIEFLY SHOVED ONTO ROTTING CORPSE AUDIENCE MEMBERS BEFORE BEING UNCEREMONIOUSLY CRAMMED BACK INTO SHIPPING CARTONS.
LI'L BONE DEMON'S DELUXE GRAVE ROBBER KIT!
Li'l Bone Demon needs help gathering bones. With his specialty deluxe pick, shovel, lantern, and grave-robbing shroud, you can help him on his quest to find all the bones. And don't worry about those protruding shoulder bones or those nubs growing out of your forehead . . .
Supplies Unlimited . . . Inquire for Price!
Li'l Bone Demon says, "Life's a Graveyard . . . Dig it!"
ANGELUS MORTIS, INC.
666 9th Circle, Hell, The Underworld, Eternity
Please ship me the following checked items:
Enclosed: ☐Check or Money Order ☐C.O.D. plus shipping fees
☐ Mystery Box
☐ Boppo The Clown
☐ Fun, Totally Normal Doll
☐ X-Person Glasses
☐ Commemorative Fan "I Heart Wheel of Pain" T-Shirt
☐ Li'l Bone Demon's Deluxe Grave Robbery Kit
☐ Ouija Decoder Ring
☐ All-Seeing Eye
Name
Address
City State Zip
OUIJA DECODER RING
• DECODE MESSAGES FROM THE OTHER SIDE!
• SEND CODED MESSAGES TO THE DEARLY DEPARTED!
• LOOK STYLISH AND COOL!
SUPPLIES LIMITED . . . INQUIRE FOR PRICE!
• PURCHASE OF OUIJA DECODER RING DOES NOT GUARANTEE ANYONE ON THE OTHER SIDE WANTS TO TALK WITH YOU
THE ALL-SEEING EYE
SUPPLIES LIMITED . . . INQUIRE FOR PRICE!
*ALL-SEEING EYE IS CAPABLE OF SEEING ALL THINGS. HOWEVER, AS AN EYEBALL, ALL-SEEING EYE IS INCAPABLE OF COMMUNICATION.

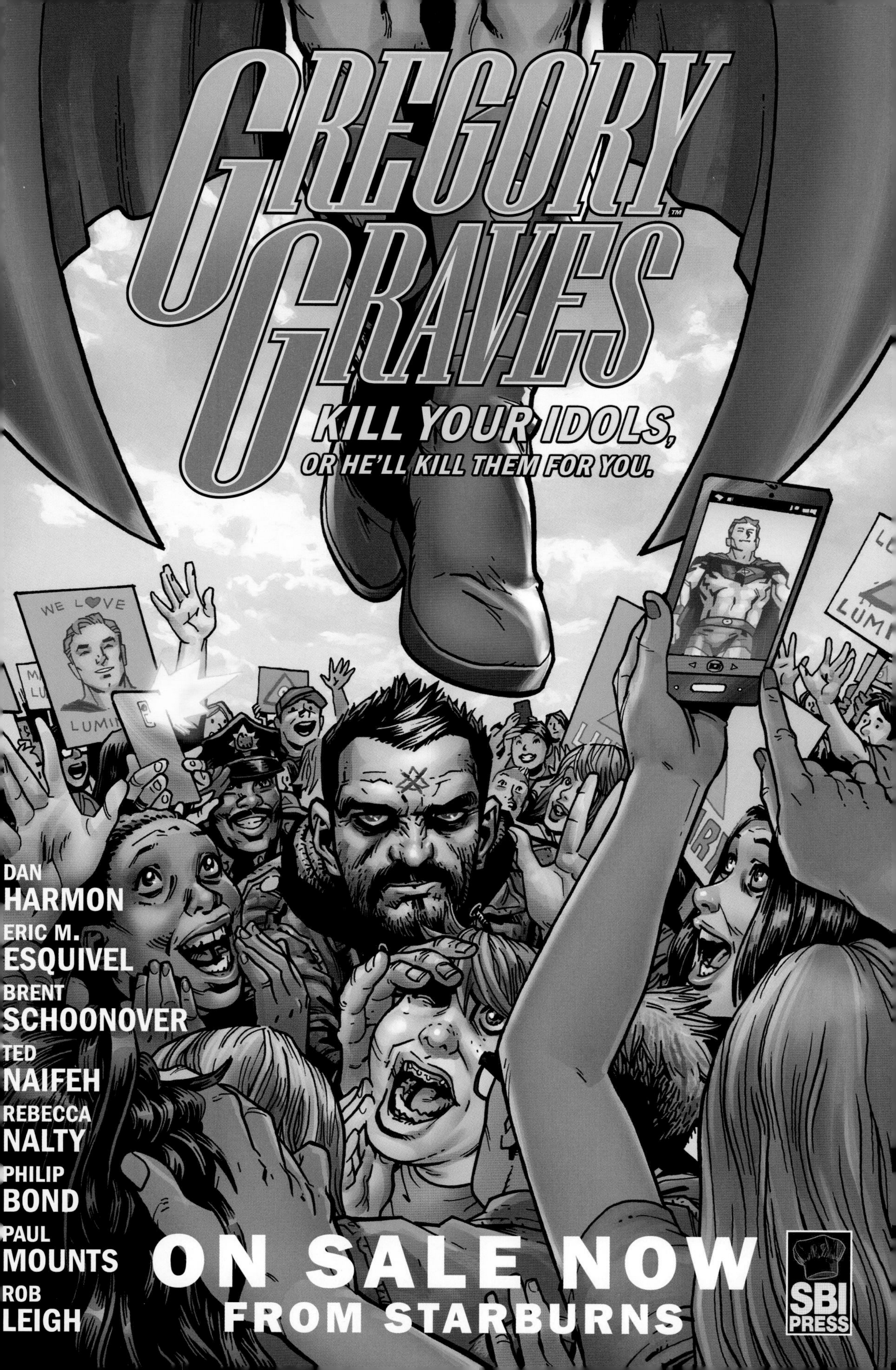
GREGORY GRAVES™
KILL YOUR IDOLS,
OR HE'LL KILL THEM FOR YOU.
WE LOVE
DAN HARMON
ERIC M. ESQUIVEL
BRENT SCHOONOVER
TED NAIFEH
REBECCA NALTY
PHILIP BOND
PAUL MOUNTS
ROB LEIGH
ON SALE NOW
FROM STARBURNS
SBI PRESS

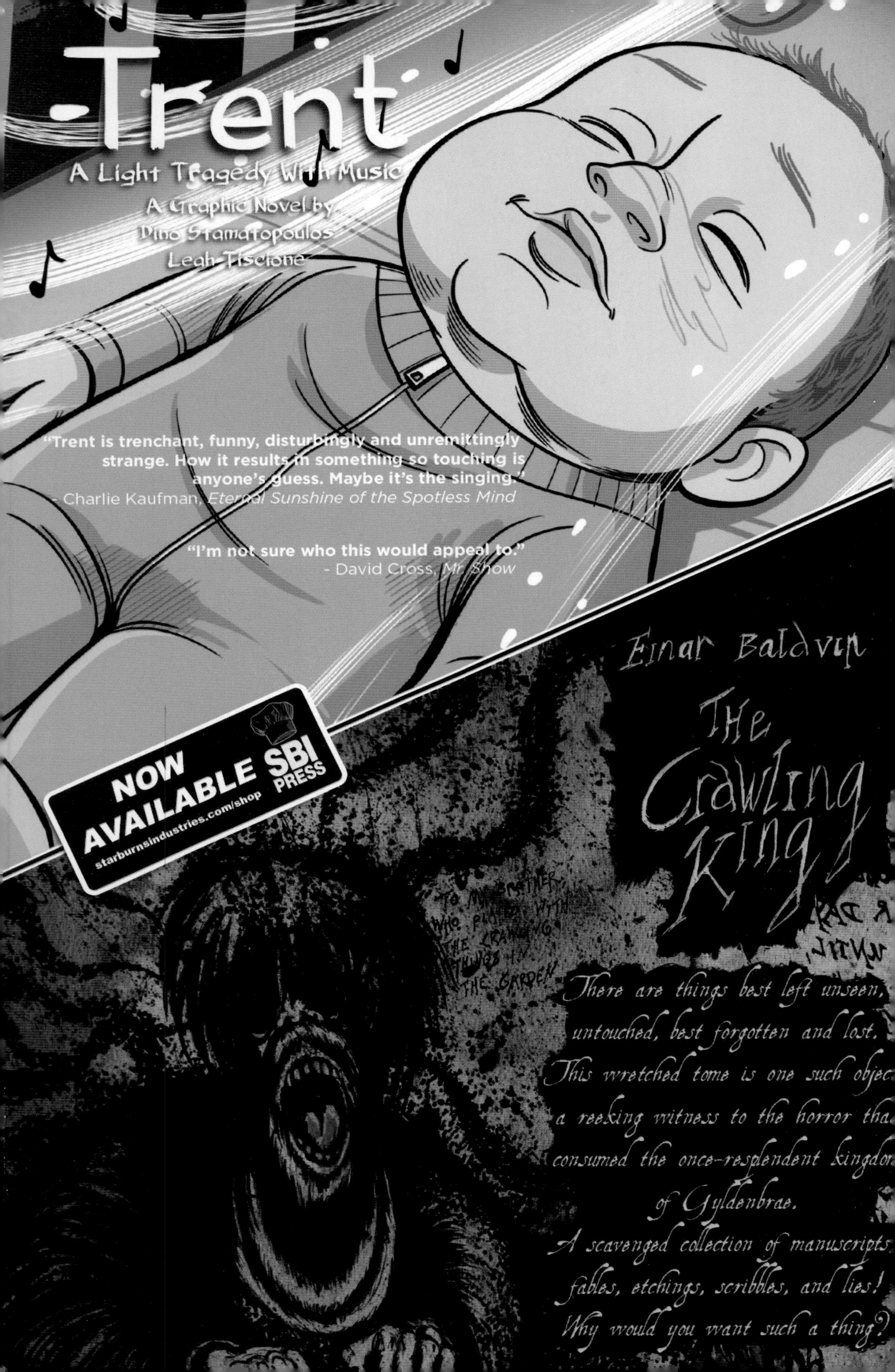

Trent
A Light Tragedy With Music
A Graphic Novel by
Dino Stamatopoulos
Leah Tiscione
"Trent is trenchant, funny, disturbingly and unremittingly strange. How it results in something so touching is anyone's guess. Maybe it's the singing."
- Charlie Kaufman, *Eternal Sunshine of the Spotless Mind*
"I'm not sure who this would appeal to."
- David Cross, *Mr. Show*
NOW AVAILABLE
SBI PRESS
starburnsindustries.com/shop
Einar Baldvin
The Crawling King
There are things best left unseen, untouched, best forgotten and lost.
This wretched tome is one such objec
a reeking witness to the horror tha
consumed the once-resplendent kingdor
of Gyldenbrae.
A scavenged collection of manuscripts
fables, etchings, scribbles, and lies!
Why would you want such a thing?